DATE			

Military expenditure in Third World countries

International Library of Economics

Editor: Richard Portes
Professor of Economics, Birkbeck College,
University of London

Military expenditure in Third World countries
The economic effects

Saadet Deger

Routledge & Kegan Paul
London, Boston and Henley

First published in 1986
by Routledge & Kegan Paul plc

14 Leicester Square, London WC2H 7PH, England

9 Park Street, Boston, Mass. 02108, USA and

Broadway House, Newtown Road,
Henley on Thames, Oxon RG9 1EN, England

Set in Times 10 on 12pt
by Columns of Reading
and printed in Great Britain
by T J Press (Padstow) Ltd
Padstow, Cornwall

Library of Congress Cataloging in Publication Data

Deger, Saadet, 1950
Military expenditure in Third World countries.
(International library of economics)
Bibliography: p.
Includes index.
1. Developing countries—Armed forces—Appropriations
and expenditures—Economic aspects. I. Title.
II. Series.
HC59.72.D4D44 1986 330.9172'4 85-18337

British Library CIP data available

ISBN 0-7102-0304-7

To the memory of Ene and Ette

Contents

Tables

Figures

Preface

The level of military expenditure and its share in the national product in Third World countries are high and still rising. This is of great concern to all. The issues are complex and need to be studied with care; yet the literature is scant. This monograph is an attempt to analyse the economic effects of defence spending in less developed countries, within the broad framework of development economics. Though it is principally addressed to economists and political scientists, it is fairly accessible to a wide readership.

This book is a product of research conducted at Birkbeck College, University of London, over the last few years. The intellectual stimulus provided by the intense academic environment of Birkbeck, particularly the work done by Ron Smith on military expenditure in OECD countries and Britain, has been a great source of help and inspiration in conducting the analysis reported here.

I have many intellectual debts to acknowledge. First and foremost to Ron Smith and Somnath Sen, who have read the whole book in manuscript form; their continuous suggestions, advice, help, and often telling criticisms, have contributed a great deal to my whole research programme; so much so that I presume all remaining errors are theirs.

I am grateful to Richard Portes for his constant encouragement and academic advice. I am thankful to Robin Marris for his help in providing facilities while I was writing this book. My colleagues read some of the material presented here at various stages, and I would specially thank Ben Fine, Yehuda Kotowitz, Dan Smith, Dennis Snower and Richard Portes for their perceptive comments. Discussions with V. Balasubramanyam, particularly the incisive questions he asked, helped me considerably to clarify certain points. I am also thankful to Nigel

Foster for drawing Figures 1.1 and 1.2.

I have had the good fortune to talk with a number of eminent economists on military expenditure in less developed countries, and possibly because of the controversial nature of the subject they have expressed a great deal of interest, as well as providing me with some valuable insights. I would particularly like to thank in this respect Sukhamoy Chakravarty, Michael Intriligator, P.N. Mathur, Prasanta Pattanaik, Amartya Sen and Robert West.

Herbert Wulf read my chapter on arms production and passed valuable comments which, in addition to being most helpful, was also encouraging, coming as it did from a leading expert in the field.

Many of the issues analysed here were discussed in papers presented at the SSRC Development Economics Study Group, London; the World Congress of Social Economics, Jerusalem; the European Meeting of the Econometric Society, Amsterdam; and the Development Studies Association Annual Conferences at Oxford, Dublin, Brighton and Bradford. I am thankful to seminar participants for ideas and comments.

I am deeply grateful to the Economic and Social Science Research Council for their financial support; this book is a product of a research grant awarded to Ron Smith and myself during 1982-83. The ESRC is also financing my current work, on the international aspects of military expenditure, under their Post-doctoral Fellowship Scheme. My very recent research, as a Fellow, is reflected in Chapters 6 and 7. However, the arguments presented here are my own and do not represent the views of the ESRC. I am also grateful to Elizabeth Fidlon of Routledge & Kegan Paul for her patience and perseverance in the face of my inability to keep to deadlines. My thanks also go to Elaine Donaldson for her excellent copy editing of the book.

I have drawn somewhat on my publications in various journals. But much of the analysis presented here is new, as is a lot of the information.

There is a long and respectable history of the analysis of militarism in the wider context of development studies. But economists *per se* have tended to fight shy of the subject, either thinking of the military-expenditure/economic-development nexus as a simple guns and butter trade-off or thinking that it has little analytical concern for our discipline, and is best left to allied social sciences. The attitude is changing, but there is still little literature on the application of the tools of economics – both theoretical and statistical – in the analysis of the economic effects of defence spending in developing countries. A major purpose of this book is to provide such an economic framework. We do not claim that the political, social and cultural factors that generate defence-related activities are unimportant; they are vital. However, much has been written on them and it is probably time to redress the balance. We will be able to get a more comprehensive view of these issues, at the end of the day, if we concentrate on the economic aspects at this stage of our understanding.

My main hope is that the work will raise some discussion on the economic merits and demerits of military spending in developing countries, so that these can be used in conjunction with security and strategic advantages of the defence sectors, to provide a proper cost-benefit analysis of military expenditure. The subject is controversial, and rightly so. I can do no better than quote Arthur Lewis, the Nobel Prize-winning economist who, delivering the Presidential Address to the American Economic Association on the subject of Development Economics itself, said, 'If conflict and dispute are indices of intellectual activity, our subject seems adequately contentious.' The same should be said about defence economics. The economic burden and benefits of military spending in the poor countries of the world need to be discussed vehemently but analytically. Military expenditure is too important an issue to be left to the military alone.

1 Introduction

1.1 Defence and the economy

In 1980, Third World countries taken together spent almost $54 thousand million on military expenditure. By 1983, the latest year for which figures are available, this had risen in *real terms* by 20 per cent. In 1975, developing countries imported over $6 thousand million worth of armaments; five years later the real value of weapons imports had risen by 70 per cent. It is estimated that about 800 million people worldwide live in absolute poverty and approximately half of these suffer from famine, hunger and malnutrition. Half the world's population of about 4,000 million people do not have access to safe drinking water and three-fourths of the less developed world have no sanitary facilities. After 1945, Third World wars (internal and external wars fought in less developed countries) have claimed over 16 million lives.

The numbers are mind-boggling; they can leave us frustrated or may become comparatively meaningless. But what is clear is that it is essential to study, analytically, the economic dimensions of military expenditure in less developed countries (LDCs) and carefully evaluate the costs and benefits involved. Defence spending goes far beyond the realm of economics: its main function is the provision of security, but it is also involved with the socio-political process. However, the economics of militarisation are crucial; not only because it affects us all directly, but also because evaluation of the effectiveness of security-related spending, relative to its direct and indirect opportunity costs, is not meaningful unless we have analysed the economic consequences of defence.

There have been two standard, but alternative, responses to the problem. The first claims that military spending is 'bad'; its elimination or reduction will lead to more resources being channelled towards socio-economic needs; thus disarmament will improve the economic conditions of LDCs. The argument is simplistic. There is no supposition that resources released from the military sector will *necessarily* be diverted towards channels which increase growth and create a more equitable distribution of the fruits of progress. On the other hand the military may transmit indirect benefits to the economy and society, which alternative forms of conspicuous consumption may not have. The second argument would have us believe that a true evaluation of military spending can only be done in a strategic sphere. Economic considerations are unimportant, what matters is security – the eternal vigilance theme! This again is inadequate. In so far as security can be costed, the economics of military expenditure become relevant. If defence projects, at both the micro and macro level, can be appraised and their costs/benefits formally evaluated, then the economics of defence become crucial. Defence spending has long since acquired a position almost akin to Caesar's wife – beyond question. But it is important and imperative, given the sums involved, to analyse critically the economic effects of defence expenditure. In this book, we concentrate on less developed countries and discuss these issues in a relatively formal way.

1.2 The nature of the problem

The relationship between defence expenditure and economic growth and development is a subject of considerable importance. The UN Committee for Development Planning exemplified the crucial importance of this issue by stating: 'The single and most massive [obstacle to development] is the world wide expenditure on national defence activity.'[1] The recent reports by the Brandt and Palme Commissions emphasise the trade-offs between military expenditure and world development. The total amounts of financial and physical resources spent all over the world in military and armaments expenditure are reaching staggering proportions. But nowhere is the contrast between defence and development more obvious than in Third World countries which are steadily increasing their military spending as well as striving for accelerated activity in defence-related areas. Increasing amounts of government budgets are being spent in defence sectors, military coups are a common phenomenon, and regional arms races between belligerent 'neighbours' are increasingly prevalent. On the other hand, in spite of massive efforts by both national and international agencies, economic growth in the less developed countries (LDCs) of the world tends to be low, poverty remains endemic and the vicious circle of underdevelopment difficult to break. Our purpose here is primarily concerned with studying, in a formal framework, the nature of military expenditure in LDCs and its effects on economic growth in particular and economic development in general.

A preliminary glimpse at the sums involved will show how important defence spending has become, as a principal component of LDCs' economic burden. The total Third World military expenditure increased from $4.065 billion per year (at 1970 prices and 1970 exchange rates) in 1955 to $26.299 billion per annum in 1975. In *real* terms this involves a sixfold increase in twenty years. Between 1970 and 1975, forty-six LDCs spent over 2.5 per cent of their GDP on the military. In 1955, all LDCs taken together were spending 3 per cent of total world military expenditure. In 1975 this ratio had increased to 12 per cent. More significantly, the growth rate of defence spending has been phenomenally high over these decades and still continues unabated. Between 1955 and 1975, military spending in LDCs increased at an average annual rate of 10 per cent compared with a world increase of only 2.7 per cent and a NATO increase of 1 per cent. Oil-importing poorer developing countries doubled their defence expenditure in real terms in the 1970s.[2] Given the not so impressive record of *economic* growth in the recent past for Third World countries, and the widespread poverty in these regions, it is imperative to analyse the interconnections between defence and development in a rigorous way.

Some comparative descriptive statistics will also help to put the subject in perspective and to indicate the size of the problem. Table 1.1 shows regional military expenditure of LDCs measured in constant 1980 prices and exchange rates (US $ million), for 1952 and 1983.

The Middle East multiplied its real military spending 56.4 times in these three decades while Africa (excluding Egypt) multiplied real defence expenditure 29.7 times. South Asia

Table 1.1 *Regional military expenditure of LDCs and DCs*

	(1) 1952	(2) 1983	(3) Ratio of cols 2 and 1
Middle East	886	50,000	56.4
South Asia	1,681	7,865	4.68
Far East excl. China	3,225	32,950	10.2
Africa excl. Egypt	475	14,100	29.7
Central America	375	2,825	7.5
South America	2,873	14,745	5.1
China	9,888	35,800	3.6
USSR	62,741	137,600	2.19
WTO	62,873	151,130	2.40
USA	148,652	186,544	1.25
NATO	219,986	307,171	1.39
OPEC	12,239*	48,745	3.98

Source: SIPRI; OPEC data is for 1972.

increased its outlay four-fold and so did South America, about five-fold. China increased military expenditure four-fold while Central America's rose seven-fold. In the light of these massive increases it is startling to note that the major powers did not raise their defence spending in such a phenomenal fashion. The United States and NATO remained stable while the Soviet Union and WTO (Warsaw Pact) doubled their strategic spending. Every single regional subgroup among the developing countries had a higher proportional growth rate of defence expenditure than the superpowers and their allies among the developed countries. Even noting that LDCs started from a very low base and their numbers have increased in the post-war period due to independence, the statistics are revealing.

In Figure 1.1 time series data of military expenditure from 1952 to 1983 is plotted for all LDCs (except China) and various regional groups. It is clear that the trend in the series is upward-rising and exponential. Similarily, Figure 1.2 shows defence for LDCs as contrasted with the major alliances, NATO and WTO. (OPEC is also included for comparison.) Note the continuous increase over time of LDC defence outlay, while for the alliances, even though an upward trend is discernible, there are cyclical fluctuations too. From the data it is clear that the magnitude of the defence problem is large and increasing.

In spite of the crucial importance of the effects of military expenditure on economic growth in LDCs, mainstream development economics has been relatively slow to explore this interesting area, particularly if we judge by published papers. Some important, and very recent, reports under the auspices of the UN have rectified this imbalance somewhat, and we shall be discussing them later. What is more worrying is the paucity of empirical and econometric work in the field (again the UN reports provide some exceptions). As Kaldor (1978) states: 'Most of the analyses . . . are necessarily speculative. Very little empirical work has been undertaken in the field.' There are two broad areas in which empirical evidence can be categorised. Firstly, the cross-sectional statistical analysis[3] takes a wide sample of LDCs and tries to examine the econometric correlationships between military spending and the rate of economic growth on the basis of common characteristics of underdevelopment. Secondly, there are a number of individual case studies of the role of the military in specific LDCs but, again as Kaldor (1978) points out, few of them are primarily concerned with economic development *per se* or with formally estimating the effects of defence on the economy. Rather the focus is on socio-political questions, and economic evidence seems mostly anecdotal. In the case of studies of particular countries, even the use of macrostatistical evidence on the burden of military spending has been the subject of some controversy. Without minimising the importance of studying the role of the military in its specific national setting, it must be said that the second approach, by its very nature, may be too narrow. Very few general conclusions can be derived which are applicable to a wide spectrum of underdeveloped nations. In our analysis the broad emphasis is on the former approach, where we try to analyse common characteristics. However, we also provide, where necessary, a great deal of evidence on individual countries. Even though the book will concentrate on a relatively accessible discussion of the subject and a broad survey of the issues involved, it should always be borne in mind that the results presented here are based on a large variety of econometric models which were tested to understand the simultaneous nature of the relationships involved.

Overall, therefore, we link macrostatistical analysis with case studies – country by country, regional and even sectoral.

As should be clear from the foregoing analysis, the purpose of this work is to analyse the economic effects of military expenditure on different variables such as growth, saving, investment, and human capital formation. This should give us relatively exact and quantifiable measures by which the role of the military in the process of economic development can be assessed. In this context it is necessary, at an early stage, to understand the twin concepts of development and militarisation; the next two sections contain some discussions on these issues. The fifth section gives a preliminary view of the economic effects of defence as well as a very brief literature survey. The final section of the chapter provides a rather detailed review of how the rest of the monograph is structured.

1.3 What is development economics?

In many ways the characteristics of underdevelopment, economic backwardness and poverty are obvious. It is often easy to identify countries as developing or underdeveloped simply by looking at them. What is not so easy or obvious is why countries remain backward or why some manage to break out of the apparent vicious circle of poverty, and maintain self-sustaining growth for long periods of time, until they acquire the characteristics of developed economies. Development economics tries to build a coherent framework of analysis as a subdiscipline of economics, to answer these questions and analyse related issues. Volumes have been written trying to precisely define the scope of the subject, but perhaps the simplest definition will suffice at this stage. The eminent development economist and Nobel Prize winner W. Arthur Lewis, in his presidential address to the distinguished American Economic Association on 'The State of Development Theory', started by saying: 'Development Economics deals with the structure and behaviour of economies where output per head is less than 1980 $2,000. Whether this dividing line is somewhat too high or too low is of no significance in this context.' Essentially, precision in definition is not an important issue; what matters is an identification of analytical theories and policy prescriptions that help us in understanding how underdevelopment can be overcome.

Traditional development economics as it burgeoned in the 1950s and 1960s was mainly concerned with the growth of overall output and the rise of *per capita* income. This was not surprising given the dismally low income of the majority of people in the poor countries of the world. The welfare of society, distribution of the social product and socio-cultural development were not considered unimportant, but without growth and rising income these would not be attainable. Not only among academics but also among policy-makers and politicians, the ideal of growth was considered crucial. The 1967 Declaration of the Association of South-East Asian Nations (ASEAN) is characteristic of this attitude: 'The aims and purposes of the Association shall be: to accelerate the economic growth, social progress and cultural development in the region through joint endeavours . . . to strengthen the foundation for a prosperous and peaceful community of South-Asian nations.'[4]

Growth of output and income was expected to precede and cause development in the broader sense of the term. It was realised that transition to a rich economy would not be easy; that a price would have to be paid; that there might be conflicts between the targets of growth and economic justice; and finally that the poor might get poorer even as the overall economy was getting richer. However, ultimately, there would be a 'trickle-down effect' and all sections of society and the economy would benefit. Economists are bad at predicting the time scale of the long run – when the millennium will arrive – but there was little doubt that it would come.

Many developing countries achieved high growth rates during the post-war period. Considerable structural changes were also achieved, thus vindicating the policy prescriptions of development economics. Yet the gains were unevenly spread, and large sections of the community failed to benefit from the high-growth strategy followed. It was slowly realised that growth *per se* would not do the trick; development is a much wider concept, and a wider set of measures needs to be taken if the position of the deprived is to be improved. Growth may be necessary for development, but it is definitely not sufficient. What is required is equitable growth, high *per capita* income but coupled with an egalitarian distribution of income, eradication of absolute poverty, and provision of basic needs. Fundamentally, the difference between this approach and the earlier one is one of degree and not of kind. The emphasis on growth alone looked at the total resource bundle that the economy can achieve as well as, probably, the average. The shift towards equity also considers the distribution, and what a wider range of individuals might be getting from the fruits of growth.

The reasons for giving the rate of growth of output its primary role is not difficult to understand. The high degree of poverty, low level of *per capita* income, lack of (or unutilisation of) resources, and desperate economic deprivation in both rural and urban areas can all be alleviated, in principle though often not in practice, if high economic growth is possible. Even concepts which have traditionally been divorced from growth-oriented economic policy have recently been related more and more often to their effects on economic growth. Rawlsian income distribution policies, with their emphasis on pulling up substantial parts of the population from below the poverty line, have been advocated not only from the point of view of social equity and justice, but also as a necessary prerequisite for increasing growth rates. It has been claimed that a well-fed, well-nourished, high-wage labour force will have substantial productivity effects and thus induce the economy to grow faster. The Basic Needs approach of the World Bank and the Food for Work campaign of LDC governments like India are essentially attempts to solve some of the fundamental problems of poverty (like starvation), but their effects can be measured (and justified) in terms of increasing growth rates. In general, growth can ultimately lead to development; but it may take a very long time.

The major focus of growth-oriented development economics has been the following: (a) capital accumulation and the concomitant increase in productivity; (b) industrialisation; (c) mobilisation of underemployed manpower in a labour-surplus economy; (d) planning and state intervention to actively promote developmental targets. In addition one can also have concepts of economic justice and equity, which have been important policy concerns of some, though not all, governments in developing countries. (See Sen, 1983.) The first three issues can also be linked to the theory of capital planning that confront any developing economy. There the three crucial concepts are: (1) choice of optimum rate of saving, (2) optimum use and allocation of investment, and finally (3) optimum choice of techniques. (See Chakravarty, 1969.) It is easy to identify the links. Increase in saving and resource mobilisation leads to investment and faster capital accumulation. The planners may decide that optimal allocation of investment may entail putting more funds into the industrial sector and consequent industrialisation. Use of surplus human resources may dictate the type of techniques to be adopted by the economy. The foregoing analysis can also be extended to the problems of the open economy. The supply of foreign resources (foreign aid and investment) is intimately connected with capital accumulation. Domestic industrialisation strategy (*vis-à-vis* the rest of the world), in the form of export promotion or import substitution, is obviously related to investment allocation and overall industrialisation. Finally, the appropriateness of international imported technology must be inter-related with domestic choice of techniques.

The ubiquitous role of the government in the form of explicit or implicit planning has been a major feature of developing countries. Understandably, early development economics literature also emphasised state intervention and relatively rigid forms of imperative planning. However, it has been increasingly realised that, outside of socialist countries, the market does play an important role. This does not mean that we should abandon all notions of planning and adopt a strict market-oriented orthodox neoclassical economic strategy. What it does imply is that incentive schemes are important and there must be a close interrelationship between government's planned actions and the working of the market mechanism.

Development economics has made important and independent contributions to our understanding of economic issues, in terms of theories of resource allocation in the short run as well as equitable growth in the long run. We have had major works on resource gaps, dual economies, disguised unemployment, structural inflation, appropriate technology, long-term changes in saving ratio/mobilisation of resources, and planning techniques. Both the proponents and the persistent critics[5] have enhanced our understanding of these subjects.[6]

In recent years, however, there has been mounting criticism

about the definition, scope, analytical methods, policy prescriptions – in short, the very foundations of development economics itself. In part this may be due to the discrepancy between the expectations that the subject generated in its earlier intoxicating years, and the results actually observed in Third World countries. Growth has occurred overall (though there are substantial inter-country differences), structural changes have taken place, and direct measures to alleviate poverty and provide a more equitable distribution of income have not been too unsuccessful. Yet the general balance sheet seems to give a pessimistic picture. When one looks at overall indices of economic development, moving away from a limited focus on growth of *per capita* income, one observes that the fruits of development and socio-economic progress are still elusive for a vast majority of people in the LDCs. Sivard (1983) gives telling figures which show quite clearly that in spite of over three decades of reasonable growth, many millions of people in developing countries still do not have the barest necessities of life. It is claimed that even by 1980, less than 10 per cent of children in developing countries were being immunised against the six commonest childhood diseases, and 5 million were killed by these annually. Out of a total Third World population of about 3,000 million in 1980, 450 million people suffered from hunger, malnutrition and starvation. Fifty-six per cent of the population of developing countries do not have access to safe drinking water. Faced with such figures, the growth orientation of development economics seems odd.

Yet the criticism of development theory may be misplaced. Growth is a means toward an end, that of socio-economic transformation. In the long run it is necessary for development, since in its absence it will be difficult to achieve the whole menu of characteristics that identify a developed country. A. Sen (1983) puts it succinctly:

> I believe the real limitations of traditional development economics arose not from the choice of means to the end of economic growth, but in the insufficient recognition that economic growth was no more than a means to some other objectives. The point is not the same as saying that growth does not matter. It may matter a great deal, but, if it does, this is because of some associated benefits that are realised in the process of economic growth.

In a sense, growth and corresponding increases in income must be viewed as one important way (though not the only one) of achieving a wider range of economic and social betterment, of increasing the capability of as wide a section of society as possible, and of improving the quality of life in general. Thus an analysis of growth must also be supplemented by noting the progress made in reducing infant mortality, and increasing life expectancy, literacy, education, health and nutrition. It is necessary to discuss not only physical capital formation but also human capital accumulation. As we shall see later, there may even be an intimate interconnection between them.

Amartya Sen has recently argued for a shift in emphasis from a study of growth of national income to an analysis of 'entitlements' of individuals and groups of people in developing countries, as well as the 'capabilities' that these entitlements can produce. I can do no better than quote him:

> Entitlement refers to the set of alternative commodity bundles that a person can command in a society using the totality of rights and opportunities that he or she faces.

Further:

> On the basis of this entitlement, a person can acquire some capabilities, i.e. the ability to do this or that (e.g. be well nourished), and fail to acquire some other capabilities. The process of economic development can be seen as a process of expanding the capabilities of people. Given the functional relation between entitlements of persons over goods and their capabilities, a useful – though derivative – characterisation of economic development is in terms of expansion of entitlements. (A. Sen, 1983)[7]

Entitlement in general consists of an individual's endowment vector (the goods and services he or she owns), and the possibilities of exchange open to him or her. Exchange can be of many types; it can be with 'nature', the use of technology, capital and production possibility to acquire more goods; it can be through the market, using relative prices to determine the amount of goods it is possible to get; it can be through nonmarket transactions, own consumption, social security, government expenditure on public goods; and finally one can include noneconomic entitlements, such as security, justice, status, freedom, human rights, which are difficult to quantify but nevertheless important for their own sakes as well as their effect on economic variables.

Within this framework, the emphasis of traditional development theory on growth, income and its egalitarian distribution can be linked to the endowment vector of society as a whole as well as of individual members in it. Income, of course, is a rather narrow way of characterising the much richer concept of an endowment vector, but it will suffice. Thus high growth, leading to a high *per capita* income, implies that society as a whole has more endowments. But this does not mean that the entitlements enjoyed by people are higher. Emphasising entitlements therefore leads us on to a broader and in a sense more worthwhile concept of development.

Table 1.2 gives comparative data, for 1980, on five countries regarding *per capita* income (the traditional focus and end-product of growth), as well as indices of a broad set of empirical criteria that may stand proxy for entitlements. Brazil and South Korea are examples of high-growth countries, while Nigeria is oil-rich and relatively prosperous within the African context. On the other hand Sri Lanka and Tanzania have low *per capita* income, and the latter has had major problems with the

Table 1.2 *Income and entitlements*

	Sri Lanka	South Korea	Brazil	Tanzania	Nigeria
1	279	1,388	2,002	264	1,035
2	42	22	38	20	16
3	85	94	76	70	34
4	343	608	250	482	1,251
5	40	34	77	103	135
6	66	65	63	52	48
7	2,251	2,926	2,513	2,028	2,337
8	22	79	63	39	28

Source: Sivard (1983).
Rows: (1) GNP *per capita* in US$; (2) % of women in total university enrolment; (3) Literacy rate %; (4) Population per hospital bed; (5) Infant mortality rate; (6) Life expectancy in years; (7) Calories *per capita*; (8) % of population with safe water.

International Monetary Fund in recent years regarding its domestic economic policies. Even a quick glance will show that these two countries, in spite of having very poor economies in the conventional sense, have done well in terms of entitlements to their citizens. Compare Tanzania and Nigeria, both major African countries. The former's Gross National Product (GNP) per head is a quarter of the latter's, yet it has a far better record in terms of health, mortality, sanitation, and possibly women's rights. Similar comments are applicable to Sri Lanka as compared to South Korea and Brazil. Sri Lanka has a national product per head of about one-fifth that of South Korea, yet it has a better record in terms of women going on to higher education, provision of hospital beds, and life expectancy. Its literacy rate, infant mortality rate and life expectancy are superior to Brazil's, yet the *per capita* income is about one-eighth. By conventional criteria Sri Lanka and Tanzania are less developed than South Korea, Nigeria and Brazil, but given the wider definition, we cannot be sure.

It should be noted that it is also possible to have conflicts between the two components of the concept of entitlement – endowment and exchange entitlements. Thus, increasing the endowment vector of society and enlarging the degree of entitlements may not be compatible. If, for example, infant mortality drops, birth rate rises, famines are eradicated, health care improved, safe water provided, public services made available, then population may increase. Higher growth of population may reduce the growth of *per capita* income and pull down endowments available to each member of society. Bauer gives an early exposition of this:

> Economic progress is usually measured by the growth of real income per head. This procedure implies various judgements which are generally covert and unrecognised. The increase in population in underdeveloped countries has been brought about by the fall in the death rate (especially, but not only, among children) and this implies a longer expectation of life. The position of those who have failed to die has certainly improved as has the situation of those whose children continue to live. Thus there is here an obvious and real psychic income. Its reality is clear from people's readiness to pay for the

> satisfaction of the postponement of death. Thus the usual way of drawing conclusions from income per head obscures important conceptual problems of the defined and measured income. (Bauer, 1965)

Summing up, therefore, we believe that growth is important, so also are related features such as high saving, rapid capital accumulation, industrialisation, choice of optimum techniques and short-term policies to improve allocative efficiency and achieve stabilisation. However, the concept of entitlements must also be considered and the developmental process should incorporate both equitable growth and enlarged entitlements.

1.4 Militarisation and militarism

The main focus of this book is not on militarism *per se*, but rather on the possible militarisation of society caused by higher defence spending as well as the effects of increased military expenditure on economic growth and development. However, it might be of some interest to analyse very briefly the nature of militarism in developing countries.

The definition of militarism is fraught with difficulties and controversy. Vagts (1937) gives the classic definition, where militarism implies 'a dominance of the military over the civilian, an undue preponderance of military demands, and emphasis on military considerations, spirit, ideals, and scales of value in the life of states'. (The quotation is taken from an excellent review written by Albrecht (1984) for the UNESCO Colloquium on Armament – Development – Human Rights – Disarmament.) The concept is qualitative, exceedingly broad in scope, and it is probably difficult to compare countries on this basis. More specific is the description provided by Thee (1977): 'under the term "militarism" I subsume such symptoms as a rush to armaments, the growing role of the military . . . in national and international affairs, the use of force as an instrument of prevalent and political power, and the increasing influence of the military in civilian affairs'.

Sivard (1983) claims that for a sample of 114 developing countries, 56 have some form of explicit or implicit military control. Militarism is identified by one or more of the following criteria: 'key political leadership by military officers; existence of a state of martial law; extra-judicial authority exercised by security forces; lack of central political control over large sections of the country where official or unofficial security forces rule; control by foreign military forces'. Clearly, these attributes are empirical, in that they can be verified for a particular society.

In a sense, militarism by its very nature is an abstract concept, and like other analytical concepts in political theory (such as, for example, legitimacy) difficult to pin down. Alternatively, if perchance it is strictly defined, it becomes controversial. For our purposes, it will be much more fruitful if we restrict ourselves to the much narrower, but also more quantifiable, concept of 'militarisation'. This is defined by Albrecht (1984) as 'the process of enlargement of the military establishment within a society'. Militarisation, then, is a dynamic phenomenon, which changes with time as the role of the military increases. Various forms of quantifiable indices can be derived to see whether or not militarisation is occurring. Some of these are political and strategic: the number of military coups and years of military rule, total armed forces or their size relative to the population or area of the country, the nature of wars fought, the number of times the military was used (and its intensity) to suppress civil disorder. Others are economic: the proportion of Gross Domestic Product (GDP) or government budget spent on the military, the value of foreign arms imports, the size of the domestic arms industry. Thus it is possible to quantify and compare – over time for a single country, as well as over a cross-section of countries during any given time period.

However, problems remain. Consider the relation between militarisation and one of the major economic indices to identify the concept, that of the *military burden – the share of defence expenditure in national output*. In 1980, considering regional groups of less developed countries, the Middle East, South Asia, the Far East, Africa, and Latin America, the military burden for each group was, respectively, 10.9, 2.9, 3.2, 3.2, and 1.2. By any conventional criterion, Latin America is highly militarised, yet it spent the lowest share of national product on the military. Again, India, considered by many to be an exemplary case of nonintervention by the military in the body politic and thus nonmilitarised, had a defence burden of 2.8 per cent in 1980. On the other end of the scale, militarised countries like Argentina, Brazil and Paraguay had military burdens of the order of 1.3 per cent, 0.6 per cent, and 1.6 per cent in the same year.

Therefore one should be very careful about the linkages between militarisation and military expenditure. The same holds true for military governments. It is not always true that military governments necessarily spend more on defence than do their civilian counterparts. Much has been made of the poor economic record of the recent military government in Argentina (1976-83), particularly its profligate external spending which has increased the country's external debt immensely. Yet the data does not indicate that the military government was very much more extravagant in its defence spending than the civilian Peronist government that preceded it during 1973-76. In constant US dollar prices Argentina spent the following annually, for defence, from 1973 to 1981: 2,642, 2,691, 3,419, 3,890, 3,979, 4,025, 3,980, 3,942, and 4,106 (all in US $ million, 1980 prices, 1980 exchange rates).[8] It is clear that, during military rule, the percentage increase in real defence spending was not significantly higher than before; more important, there were two years when (constant price) military spending actually *fell*.

As has been mentioned earlier, our main interest here is to study the economic effects of military expenditure *per se* rather than the wider concept of militarism and development. Thus we shall be focusing on the actual spending of governments and countries on defence budgets, and their *economic* consequences in the broadest sense of the term. However, militarisation does have implicit effects; early writers extolled the virtues of 'modernisation' emanating from the military; recently we have had reports of military suppression of labour unrest which tends to keep real wages low; on a broader front the military provides 'security' which fosters an environment in which production and exchange takes place more effectively; yet it is the military which provokes violence and suppresses human and economic rights without which no nation can grow in the long run. Therefore, we must always keep the concept of militarisation at the back of our minds. Emphasising the economic aspects is to provide another dimension of the kaleidoscope, not stressed before, that constitutes the military in less developed countries. It is admittedly partial, but it is hoped that it will provide us with more information and analysis at the end of the day to further our understanding of the whole complex process.

Even though our main interest is to study the *effects* of military expenditure, it may be interesting at this stage to discuss briefly the rather voluminous literature that tries to explain the *causes* of defence spending in LDCs, particularly as it pertains to the economic forces. Our discussion is cursory, partly because a much fuller discussion is beyond the scope of this book, but also because one major economic aspect will be treated in some detail in a later chapter.

Neoclassical economic theory would conceive of the government or the state it represents as a rational agent, maximising social welfare subject to the resource constraints of the government or society. Military expenditure, like any other form of macroeconomic expenditure, is based on the benefits it provides, as well as the costs it entails. Though the notion is simplistic, it has its virtues, since some form of cost-benefit analysis undoubtedly takes place. This book itself is an example of how the economic effectiveness *vis-à-vis* the price of defence may be judged. Similar analysis is possible for the purely strategic role.

In practice, however, domestic and international forces in the form of power relations, class structure, technological factors and bureaucratic influence, may upset the fine tuning of welfare maximisation. Military expenditure acquires its own momentum and is generated by its internal logic untrammelled by the calculus of marginal gains and losses. Less developed countries often provide examples of irrational military spending difficult to justify in terms of strategic gains. The acquisition of the latest vintage arms and technology by the Shah of Iran, irrespective of the absorptive capacity of the domestic armed forces, may be a classic example.

There has been some speculation and empirical testing of the role of economic variables in the determination of defence budgets. Some economists have found a positive correlation between military expenditure and economic growth in LDCs. This obviously raises the crucial question of causation – does high growth lead to high defence spending or vice versa? There are two important reasons why the former causation might be valid.

First, an economy with a high growth rate may be able to *afford* a high defence programme. Second, a higher national income might imply more tax revenue so that the defence sector, supplying a public good, may be able to bid increasing amounts from government budgets.

As we shall see later, the defence burden does not depend on growth of total or *per capita* product nor on saving and investment rates. Thus most economic variables do not 'explain' the military burden well. However, the 'public good' argument is a valid one. An increase in national income will relax some of the resource constraints that LDCs perennially face and this may lead to an increase in defence spending. It is safe to postulate that the *overall* framework within which military authorities work may be given by the level of national output, but the detailed variations come predominantly from strategic rather than economic considerations.

Given that military budgets in LDCs are relatively independent of economic causes, the question remains as to its important determinants. Military expenditure is primarily influenced by the need for 'security' and the perception of 'threat' that a country faces. As Barnaby (1978) states: 'Many societies seem to demand "security" as much as they demand social services like health and education. Because security is seen to be linked with military force, the psychological need to feel "secure" is normally (and politically, probably most conveniently) satisfied by military expenditure.' Further, 'military expenditure is high when countries feel directly threatened or when political leaders deliberately pursue aggressive policies likely to lead to war'.

The twin concepts of 'security' and 'threat' seem to be extremely important in the determination of military expenditure. However, from Richardson's seminal work (1960) it has also been recognised that 'inertia' may also have a crucial influence on defence spending. If past military spending or stocks of armaments have been relatively high, then it is difficult to increase the current rate of strategic expenditure. Thus the current increment of a nation's defence expenditure is negatively related to its own past value (due to 'inertia') and positively related to the opposition's value (due to 'threat' and 'security'). Though it has not often been fully realised in the literature, the concept of 'inertia' is even more crucial for LDCs. Given stringent resource constraints, they have to be extra careful about the defence spending/civilian expenditure (consumption and investment) mix. The higher the previous military expenditure or arms stock, the more difficult it becomes for a resource-poor country to call up more resources for current increases in defence outlays.

A large number of mathematical models have been constructed purporting to explain military expenditure, armament stockpiling and arms races in a theoretical framework. Following Richardson's contribution (1960), Brito (1972), Brito and Intriligator (1976), Simaan and Cruz (1975), Deger and Sen (1984a) and others have used various methods to explain action-reaction behaviour in arms races. These have to lead to formal analyses of military spending between *dyads* of belligerent nations. The basic concepts of security, threat and inertia have been used to derive differential equations which give the time path of strategic variables. Both behavioural and optimisation models have been used to explain the interactive pattern of defence activity among pairs of aggressive power blocs or countries. The use of dyad reaction functions is particularly appropriate for LDCs. Quite often we observe conflicts such as those between India and Pakistan, Iran and Iraq, Vietnam and Cambodia, Israel and the Arabs, Turkey and Greece, Somalia and Ethiopia, Tanzania and Uganda, and many others, where belligerent 'neighbours' get involved in high military budgets, start an arms race and even go to war with each other for relatively localised reasons. Thus a two-agent model is an appropriate method of analysing these situations.

It should be noted that almost all the mathematical analyses have generally been based on superpower considerations, East-West strategic relations and the arms race between countries like the US and the USSR or between alliances like NATO and WTO, even though they can be adapted to LDC behaviour. For example, Richardson left the quantification of variables involved in arms race modelling relatively vague by calling it 'arms might' of participating dyads; there has been some debate on whether flows of military expenditure or stocks of armaments should be used as the appropriate variable. In theory as well as in practice, arms race models of LDCs have many specific characteristics which cannot be all accommodated within the Richardson prototype. A richer variety of models are needed to encompass all the stylised facts that LDC regional conflicts present. Specifically, the operationalisation of the formal models in terms of quantifiable variables has special significance for underdeveloped countries.

Coupled with mathematical modelling, some empirical literature has grown up in recent years to estimate the theoretical propositions of the Richardson model.[9] However, these estimated equations from empirical and econometric studies have not given very satisfactory results. This is because the underlying theoretical models were constructed with *developed countries'* or superpowers' economies in mind. When those models were used for LDCs, since the structure of the countries was vastly different, it is not surprising that the results did not explain the conflicting situations. Thus both theoretical models and empirical estimation have to be worked out in the context of stylised facts which are *specific* to *developing countries*. We discuss some of these features now.

Military expenditures may be motivated by the needs of security within the country. This is particularly true of paramilitary forces which are often used to quell domestic disturbances. On a more general level, civil wars, as in Nigeria, can increase defence budgets. Further guerrilla wars or those of domestic surversion may contribute substantially to milex (*vide* countries like Burma, the Philippines or Thailand). However, it may be argued that such wars, as well as more widely defined internal conflicts, are such a widespread phenomenon in LDCs that any country is always a potential candidate for internal security problems. These may increase the average level of milex in developing countries, but may not adequately indicate cross-country differences.

Territorial disputes and competitive arms races between adjacent countries in the Third World are an obvious and major source of escalating military expenditure. Some of the disputes are embedded in the deep historical consciousness of the people concerned; others are a product of arbitrary colonial divisions of geographical areas, without a proper awareness of tribal, racial or national needs; some have been fuelled by genuine economic and occasionally hegemonic motives of acquiring more land or control over access routes; still others have been caused by dictatorial or fanatical leaders of strong countries. The current Iran-Iraq war, itself a cumulation of an arms race over the last decade, is a classic example of almost all those reasons. It has been variously ascribed to an ancient rivalry between Persians and Arabs, or Shia and Sunni Muslims intent on fratricide; to a struggle for control of the Persian Gulf; or to personal animosity between the Ayatollah Khomeini and President Saddam Hussein.

Even in Latin America, where by international standards territorial disputes are not that important, some increases in military expenditures have been caused by regional rivalry among neighbours. Peru and Chile have a long-standing conflict (apparently over land conquered during the War of the Pacific more than a hundred years ago!), and are among the highest spenders in Latin America in terms of the share of GDP devoted to the military. Other examples are easy to give: Venezuela and Colombia have disputes over territorial waters, supposedly with oil reserves; Honduras and El Salvador have fought a so-called 'soccer war'; Argentina and Chile have had difficulties in the past, though relations are better after the Falklands/Malvinas crisis. Even though South America has had less violent inter-state disputes relative to other developing regions, part of its arms expenditure must be attributable to competition over defence and the existence of perceived threats.

Other areas of the Third World, of course, have had more than their fair share of regional conflicts, and quite often the levels of military expenditure of two countries are very much related to each other's strategic behaviour. There are many examples and the obvious ones have already been mentioned. No doubt the reader will remember a few more. It is clear that an important cause of defence spending in LDCs is related to some form of arms race.

It would be foolhardy to ignore international aspects when analysing the causes of military expenditure in Third World countries. Increasing defence budgets are often a direct effect of imported armaments, and the rises are fuelled by the international trade in weapons. The numbers involved are large and often beyond comprehension, except on a comparative basis. Depending on sources, it is thought that between two-thirds and three-quarters of all global exports of *major* arms (principally from the US, the Soviet Union and a few Western European industrial nations) find their way to the Third World. The proportion will be much higher if all minor weapons, specifically those sold through illegal channels, are included. During 1978-82, the volume of weapons transferred increased by about 70 per cent as compared to the previous five-year period.[10]

As we shall see in later chapters, though some of these massive armaments imports were financed by aid, quite a lot had to be directly paid for in some way or other. Thus there can be little doubt that the internationalisation of the domestic economy, and its increasing involvement with the rest of the world, contributes in part to an increase of milex. Military expenditure necessarily rises when imported arms need to be paid for with domestic resources. In an indirect sense, one of the major causes of LDC defence spending is the large amount of weapons transactions in world markets.

International flows of armaments behave in a similar fashion to the flow of factors such as migrant labour across countries. Both 'push' factors (from the supply side) and 'pull' factors (from the demand side) are important in determining the volume and value of traded arms. From the recipient country's point of view, there is a cumulative process involved. Threat, the need for security and higher strategic mobilisation may lead to more inputs of weapons from abroad. But this importation may itself contribute to greater threat (possibly to the other side, abetting retaliation), lack of security and even higher military expenditure since the adversary may respond in similar fashion. Thus, in the presence of imported armaments, an otherwise stable arms race may become unstable, unless the escalation is stopped by embargoes.

Supplier countries contribute in no small way to the internationalisation of military spending and the consequent rise of defence expenditure. There are major economic reasons which will be dealt with later. The political factors can be treated briefly here. These range from influence, control and leverage of clients to maintaining security and stability of particular countries and regions. There are of course major dilemmas involved. Control is uncertain; the US has been powerless, in spite of embargoes, to stop major wars between Turkey and Greece, or India and Pakistan; the Soviet Union was unceremoniously dumped from Egypt in spite of being the major arms supplier. The returns from regional stabilisation policies are often difficult to evaluate. The case of Iran is a prime example of the failure of US arms exports policy, one of whose express objectives was to create a strong military power centre in the Middle East, near the Soviet Union.

The superpowers (the US and the USSR) have tried in recent years to create a regional balance of power, preferably led by a friendly coalition. This often creates more of an unbalanced strategic expansion, with countries trying to outbid each other with foreign arms acquisition. The recipients often play off the superpowers against each other, threatening to buy from one of them if rejected by the other. The exporting countries often encourage LDCs to buy or otherwise import arms, in order to gain economic advantages or political control of an ally. International salesmanship of weapons systems is very sophisticated, and often high-level members of the government (including heads of state) are called in to add their weight to advertisement pressures.

As one country acquires a new weapons system, it becomes 'necessary' for another in the region to buy the same. Arms races, with imported weapons stock, begin. In 1977, forty-seven countries had supersonic combat aeroplanes. Seventeen years ago, in 1960, only four countries had these aircraft. In 1960, only two countries had SAMs (surface to air missiles); by the mid-1970s over twenty-five countries could boast of them. Between 1972 and 1978, the US had supplied over 11,000 supersonic aircraft to LDCs; the USSR had provided 15,745 SAMs to the Third World. The conclusions are obvious.

Table 1.3 gives data on major weapons imported by LDCs, together with figures for the military burden, during the period 1979-81. Except for a few countries like India (which probably got subsidised arms from the Soviet Union), there is a close connection between high imports of armaments and the proportion of GDP spent on the military. The link between the international arms market and sizeable imports of weapons seems to be a close causal determinant of how much a country tends to spend on defence.

1.5 Economic effects of military expenditure: the framework

It is necessary at this early stage to explain the framework within which our analysis is to be considered. It will also be useful to

Table 1.3 *Arms imports and defence burden, 1979-83*

Countries	(1) % of total LDC imports of arms	(2) Military burden
Algeria	2.2	2.2
Argentina	2.8	3.6
Cuba	2.8	7.6
Egypt	7.7	6.1
India	5.5	2.9
Indonesia	1.7	2.8
Iraq	8.9	—
Israel	4.7	20.0
Jordan	1.5	14.4
Korea, South	1.8	6.5
Kuwait	1.2	5.1
Libya	9.2	10.5
Morocco	2.2	6.1
Pakistan	1.3	5.7
Peru	1.8	5.9
Saudi Arabia	7.0	15.0
Syria	11.8	17.3
Taiwan	1.8	8.0
Vietnam	2.0	—
Yemen, South	2.2	13.6

Source: SIPRI (1984) and my own calculations.
Column 1 is an average of figures for 1979-83. Column 2 is an average of figures for those years of 1979-81 for which data was available. Total value of the armaments imported by LDCs during this period was US $ 47,097 million at constant (1975) prices.

mention very briefly some of the earlier discussion within this framework. Each chapter and specific topic will, of course, have its own extensive discussion of the relevant recent literature. A few general observations only are given here.

As mentioned earlier, it is often thought, particularly by economists, that the relation between military expenditure and growth (or development) is essentially a guns and butter or tractor and tank problem. It is 'obvious' that an increase in milex will reduce the resources available to more productive sectors, and thus hamper current investment and future consumption. But that is the price we have to pay for security or freedom – the concept of 'eternal vigilance'.

Even if one agrees with this view, there is still a strong case for knowing relatively precisely the exact costs or burden of defence spending. Quantification of the 'price' of military-related security spending is crucial if we are to work out the value of the services received. Much of the book tries to do precisely that, in a detailed investigation of the various aggregate effects of defence spending. It is hoped that these will give us a complete picture in a formal framework, and will help us in appraising what the military does to the economy. Given our evaluation of the numbers of 'tractors' lost it will be up to policy-makers to see whether the corresponding gain in 'tanks' is worthwhile in terms of the social welfare function which values both goods.

But more is at stake. As pointed out earlier, it has been claimed, and validly so, that there might be a positive association between growth rates and military burdens in LDCs. Given the aforementioned causation between these two variables, econometric evidence seems to suggest that countries with a high military burden may even have higher rates of growth! (See Benoit (1978). A fuller discussion must wait until Chapter 8 on growth, and the Appendix.) The military, through its effect on modernisation and other spin-offs, might have a positive developmental contribution, which will ultimately reflect itself in a higher rate of growth of national product. Further, a reduction in military spending may not necessarily flow into productive channels like investment; rather it may boost unproductive civilian consumption in both the private and the public sector. A tank may protect the country, add to its stability, guarantee the environment within which production may prosper without fear of threats, spread new technology among uneducated peasant-soldiers, inculcate a work ethos among conscripts, and finally, if it is domestically produced, may have inter-industrial stimulative linkages with other industries which may be suffering from excess capacity. The alternative may be a fleet of limousines which will keep local dignitaries happy, but will have less productivity than the weapons expenditure. This is a serious point; it is supported not only by anecdotal evidence as well as some case studies, but also by econometric models which show the positive effects of the defence burden on growth rates in LDCs. A serious analysis, and possible rebuttal, can only be done within a formal framework. A major purpose of the book is to do precisely that.

In reviewing the effects of the military on Third World development, Mary Kaldor (1978) distinguishes between two fundamental approaches to the subject – the developmental approach and the Marxist approach. Both schools analyse the economic effects of military expenditure and study the role of the defence establishment in the development process, in terms of two aspects. Firstly, the role of the military as an organised force is studied. The use of this force in changing socio-economic conditions, creating more 'modern' institutions (including the imposition of an industrial ethos on a relatively primitive society), generating technological progress, and producing linkages with modern industries, should help in fostering development. On the other hand, the military establishment may be essentially conservative in nature, and may hamper the growth of progressive institutions, create an infrastructure which is not helpful to the more productive civilian economy and have insignificant spin-off for industrial development. Obviously, under these latter conditions an increase in military expenditure will have depressing effects on growth and development. Secondly, the military has an important role in the allocation of resources. Once again a clear-cut view is not possible, since the defence sector may divert scarce resources to economically unproductive uses but may also help in the mobilisation of new resources.

The fundamental distinction between Marxist and development theorists lies in their differing attitudes towards the role of institutions. As Kaldor (1978) succinctly puts it, 'for Marxists, institutions are subordinate to class'. Class conflicts produce transformation, dynamics and growth and this is reflected in the prevalent institutions of society. More importantly, LDCs are inextricably connected with the international capitalist system, which is dominated by relatively few developed countries (see Albrecht *et al.*, 1974, 1975, 1976). In this system, military institutions, in particular, are interesting as a specialised organisation within the structure of the ruling class. Thus militarism may have an important role for capitalist accumulation as well as for integration of peripheral economies into the world.

One interesting extension of the Marxist line of thought, as well as certain strands of traditional development theories, would be to link the growth of militarisation in LDCs to the process of unequal exchange that is often said to be produced by international commodity and factor trades. As far as we know, this has not been explicitly done in the non-Marxist literature. A large number of poor countries in the Third World are crucially dependent on the production and export of a few principal commodities. These may be either agricultural goods (e.g. jute for Bangladesh) or minerals (e.g. copper for Zambia). If the sale of these commodities is used to finance the import of armaments, then it is possible for the countries concerned to get badly trapped in the vicious circle of unequal exchange. There is a strong presupposition that developing countries' export product prices have declined relative to the import price of manufactured goods.[11] It is also generally agreed that inflation for military goods has been higher than that for civilian products. Thus the adverse terms of trade effect will be heightened if primary commodities (mineral and agricultural produce) are being exported in exchange for armaments imports. Even the movement of the terms of oil-arms trade seems to have been adverse. Obviously the role of concessional aid will be to mitigate these adverse price movements. However, the volume and value of commercial transactions in arms are rapidly increasing, thus the future forebodes many economic problems for LDCs in the international arena. The global *economics* trade of arms should be a subject for future research.

Without wishing to minimise the importance of the Marxist approach, the primary concern of this book is to analyse the causes and effects of military expenditures in LDCs within the developmental approach towards economic growth. The growth process is conceived of as an economic and social transformation of the existing poverty of the dual economy into a state of industrial-urban wealth. This change in the economic status of LDCs, as reflected in indices such as growth of GDP, or *per capita* income, is stimulated (or hampered) by institutions, which may include the military as an organised force. Our main intention, then, is to analyse and evaluate the growth-stimulating and -retarding effect of military spending within the structure of traditional development theory.

1.6 The structure of the book

The major purpose of this book is to discuss, analytically and formally, the economic effects of military expenditure in less-developed countries. (To avoid repetition we shall often use the term 'milex' to mean military expenditure.) These economic effects are inextricably linked with each other, but for analytical purposes they need to be studied separately. Each chapter will therefore concentrate on one or more specific issues; there will be inevitable overlaps, but we hope to have a clear focus at every stage. However, to put the subject in overall perspective, it may be useful to analyse the structure of the contents in the framework of the growth and developmental process that we wish to investigate.

In a labour-surplus dual economy the amount of labour force available is not a constraint *per se*. Obviously the availability of *skilled* labour is important and there will be an upper limit on its supply. We shall therefore have to deal explicitly with the role of human resources in the developmental process. However, the first focus is on capital formation, since capital is the most important constraint that an LDC will face generally. The relationship between the military, capital accumulation, developmental planning and growth lies at the heart of our analysis.

As mentioned earlier, there are three major issues in the theory of capital planning that confront any developing economy. These are the optimum choices of saving rate, investment allocation and appropriate techniques of production. They have some degree of interconnection but may also be *independent* influences on the rate of growth. In other words, the total amount of saving, the use/productivity of investment and the most profitable technique are conceptually independent with some specific and different effects on the rate of growth. It is analytically useful therefore to study them separately, though keeping the interrelationships at the back of our mind.

Simple one-sector neoclassical growth models tend to lump these three concepts together so that a single decision determines saving, which in turn is identically equal to investment, and which leads to the output-capital ratio given the production technique available to the economy. However, a more general theory of growth has been more careful in distinguishing between these component parts and highlighting the choices required at the three stages of developmental planning. Note that more complex neoclassical growth models do emphasise the difference between aggregate saving, allocation of investment, and the proper capital-labour ratio to be used in different sectors of the economy. In particular, multisectoral growth models or 'disequilibrium' growth theory[12] are quite clear that there are three choice problems involved in aggregative dynamic theory which must be kept conceptually separate even though they are in practice somewhat interdependent.

From the days of Harrod-Domar growth models and the planning literature of the 1950s we know that the saving-income ratio is obviously important for growth of a developing economy. Writing in 1952, Singer claimed that to achieve a reasonable growth rate of just over 3 per cent, LDCs would have to save over 16 per cent of their national income; in reality they were saving about one-third the desired rate. Today, on average, LDCs save more than 20 per cent of their income, so the lesson has been well learnt. Thus the saving propensity is an important ingredient in capturing the essence of a growing economy. In so far as the military has an effect on saving it is bound to influence the growth rate.

Under the usual assumption of market-clearing equilibrium, aggregate saving will be equal to investment. We therefore need a separate body of justification to show how investment will have a separate and independent influence on growth. This occurs in two ways. First the allocation of investment among different sectors (such as those producing consumption goods and those producing capital goods), or between military and civilian industries, will affect the rate of growth. Second, the LDC economy may not have enough co-operative factors which will make the best use of its available capital stock. This lack of 'absorptive capacity' or potential to utilise investment will vary from country to country. Thus two economies with the same rate of saving may have different growth rates due to allocation and utilisation effects. Clearly, high saving leads to high growth *cet. par*. But *separate* investment effects, given the two factors mentioned above, are also crucial in determining productivity of a specified amount of capital formation. Similarly, the sectoral capital-labour ratio or the choice of optimum techniques will in its own way affect the final growth rate over and above that given by aggregate saving and marginal return from investment.

To understand the effects of milex, however, we first need the data. There has been a very large amount of discussion, in recent years, about the quality and reliability of the available data on national defence and international arms transfers. Interestingly enough, the doubts about reliability have gone hand in hand with an increase in availability of data from various sources. This is a healthy sign; passive acceptance of information, particularly if it is considered to be of questionable quality, does not help in improving matters. Chapter 2 gives a detailed summary of the various problems and issues related to the data on military spending. A proper evaluation is essential for our own specific purpose, since the book refers to many econometric studies which rely on useful data.

Coming now to the structure of military spending and its interrelationship with the rest of the economy, the first thing that should be emphasised is that defence is essentially a public good and, inevitably, almost all milex comes from government budgets. There has been some discussion on the degree of 'publicness' of defence spending (see McGuire, 1983; Deger and Sen, 1984a), and empirical tests have been formulated to analyse the issue formally. But the general consensus is in accordance with our intuition, that defence is a public good *par excellence*. Thus its role, within the broad categories of government revenue and expenditure, needs to be specified in some detail. Chapter 3 therefore discusses milex within the government budgetary process and emphasises the short-term allocation effects that result from the government's revenue constraints. The interconnections between overall government revenue, expenditure and defence spending are discussed; so also are the links with taxation, money creation, stabilisation policies and inflation, issues of major policy concern to LDC governments in recent years. As will be seen, the economic effects are best understood within the well-known framework of multipliers or crowding out. Finally, though the emphasis is on short-term allocation, there are also some long-term growth effects of the military within the budgetary process.

Explicit consideration of the factors that contribute to LDC growth takes us on to Chapter 4, which discusses the effect of milex on saving and investment. We emphasise domestic saving from both the private and the public sector; the latter helps us to link national saving with public expenditure. Various channels by which the military reallocates saving but also helps (or hinders) its mobilisation are discussed. The next step is to analyse the alleged trade-off between military expenditure and investment, both directly, in competing for the same funds, and indirectly, competing for the co-operative factors that are needed to make investment productive and milex effective. We show that investment is often constrained more by absorptive capacity than by shortage of resources. The military bids away the ingredients of this absorptive capacity of the economy, and thus may have a more damaging effect on investment and productivity than is apparently perceived.

One of the major components of LDCs' marginal efficiency of investment and the economy's capacity to absorb new capital is the absence (or presence) of co-operating factors. A major input here is human skills and the nature of the relationship between the defence burden and human capital formation could be crucial. We have devoted a separate chapter (5) to this important concept, as a link with, and continuation of, the investment function, as well as to capture independent productivity effects. There is also a connection with human resource investment and public spending, since much of the former comes from the public budget in LDCs. Thus the short-term allocation within government expenditures, faced with inelastic revenues, between defence and other categories such as health, education and welfare, has important long-term implications. They may reduce absorptive capacity and thus lower investment from its optimal path affecting growth in the long run.

We now turn to external factors and the international implications of domestic military spending. This is best done within the context of a small open economy, and Chapter 6 emphasises these issues. We include here a discussion of the world-wide trends in arms transfers. Most of the supplier states (though there are notable exceptions) are rich and industrialised. They include the two superpowers, but also, with increasing frequency, countries like France, the UK, and Italy. Even though our book is concerned exclusively with LDC behaviour, it is important to know the prevalent trends in the international arms market, because these have a direct bearing on domestic economic issues. For example, as we shall see explicitly later, the 1970s have seen a switch from concessional weapons transfers in the form of military aid, to more commercial transactions often paid for by hard currency. Outside of OPEC, this has created extremely large problems for LDCs in general and military-related sovereign debt has increased considerably. Given the behaviour of world markets, we consider in detail the various costs associated with military imports and their prospective effects on the economy. Direct costs, in the form of foreign exchange forgone and balance of trade problems, are compounded by more indirect ones such as the loss of complementary resources. We also discuss the nature and role of foreign military aid which, though less important than in the 1950s and 1960s, can still be helpful in alleviating the economic problems caused by defence-related imports.

High costs of importation have led some LDC governments to go for domestic arms production, particularly in the newly industrialising countries. There are of course political and strategic motives for establishing arms industries. But one of the major reasons must be economic – the desire to reduce imports and save foreign exchange. For some countries like Brazil, the 'export miracle' in arms is as spectacular as that in civilian products. Overall, there is a very close link between strategies for domestic industrialisation policies and arms production. Countries following import-substituting industrialisation (ISI) have done so for both civilian output and armaments. Similarly, countries using the strategy of export promotion (EP) have tried to produce relatively unsophisticated arms in which they are cost effective, and have then exported them abroad. Various case studies supplement the analytical material to show the close links between arms production and the rest of the industrial sector. This comes out clearly in Chapter 7.

The basic question, however, remains. Has arms production led to a reduction in overall import costs and foreign exchange saving? The answer is not encouraging. Even though the direct cost of military imports has fallen, the purchase of intermediate inputs needed for investment in armaments has occasionally been very expensive. Added to this there are domestic resource costs. Finally, given regional arms races, certain countries have been forced to buy unduly sophisticated weapons from abroad because their adversaries did so. This is in spite of producing, domestically, older or less sophisticated vintages of the same type of armaments. Domestic arms production is often based on the maxim 'Necessity is the mother of invention'. In the face of competitive arms acquisition within a region, the maxim often changes to 'Imported invention is the mother of necessity.'

All of the channels considered above have effects on growth. Thus many of the growth effects of military expenditure will already be dealt with in the foregoing analysis. Chapter 8 focuses explicitly on growth, and deals, especially, with some of the broader concepts. It emphasises the role of supply and demand factors and shows how milex can operate from either side of the growth process. Finally, it deals with some interesting non-linearities in the milex-growth relationship. Research here is in its infancy and some tentative conclusions are drawn.

Finally, Chapter 9 deals with the intangibles that integrate growth with other elements of the socio-economic state of the country to produce overall development. We discuss modernisation and entitlements, two concepts which may have a bearing on the way the military may affect development in its broadest sense. Chapter 10 concludes briefly with an overall assessment and some policy conclusions.

The proof of the pudding is in the eating. How do we scientifically test for a statement such as the following: military expenditure increases (or, for that matter, reduces) growth in less developed countries? Case studies are possible, where a selected country is analysed carefully to see the effects of milex. But this is not general. Methodologically, it may be useful first to do a cross-sectional study of selected countries with reasonably common developmental characteristics but also chosen from a sufficiently broad set with relative diversity. In recent years, a lot of interest has been generated in such cross-section analysis which uses *econometric* methods to analyse the postulated relation and tries to answer the important question whether, on balance, defence spending increases or decreases growth. The technical Appendix gives a flavour of such analyses by showing how such an empirical model can be set up, tested statistically with appropriate data, and its results evaluated. There is also a discussion on specification sensitivity, and various pitfalls that researchers should be careful of.

For this econometric model we have chosen a relatively well-balanced sample of fifty countries.[13] Each observation of the variables concerned is a time series average of data from 1965 to 1973. The Appendix gives a detailed discussion for this choice. This is our *control sample set*. Throughout the book there are also illustrative econometric equations which purport to show how different variables affect each other and react with the military burden. They are used to supplement the other types of information provided to support our arguments – based on institutions, countries, case histories and anecdotes. For all of these econometric results we have made use of our control sample set. Those interested in the names of the fifty countries concerned, as well as in knowing the technical details, should read the Appendix first to get an idea of the data source, etc.

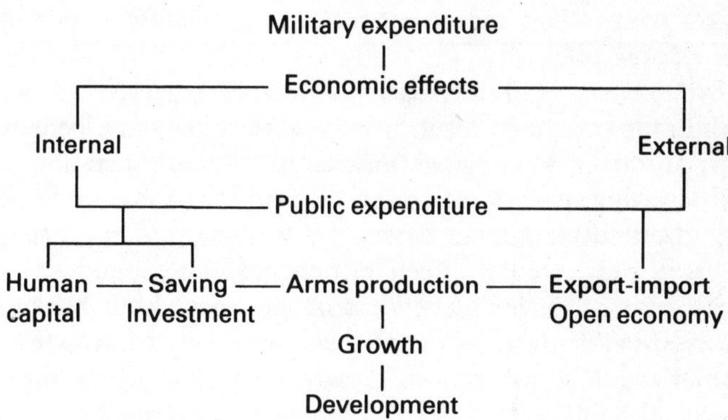

Figure 1.3 The structure of the book

Let me sum up by drawing a schematic diagram (see Figure 1.3), which will help to clarify the interconnections. Security and threat, broadly defined to include domestic, regional and international factors, cause military expenditures to rise. This has economic effects. Short-term allocation effects, particularly within the government budget, are best understood if we concentrate on the public expenditure aspects of milex. However, even here, there will be indirect long-term growth effects. More directly, growth will be affected in the long run by internal and external factors. As military spending reallocates resources away from more productive channels, as well as affecting the mobilisation of new resources, domestic saving will be affected. This in turn will influence investment and the stock of capital. Proper utilisation of physical capital needs more absorptive capacity, which is influenced and affected, in turn, by the human capital stock of the nation. Since the government may be a major provider of human capital investment (spending on education or health), an indirect connection is also established.

External factors lead us to a consideration of the open economy, and the concomitant foreign exchange cost to be borne by the country concerned to finance military imports. To achieve some saving here, domestic arms industries are often initiated. Arms production is also linked with absorptive capacity and investment; it may reduce the former and adversely affect the latter; alternatively, it may stimulate backward and forward linkages with other industrial sectors, providing a potential source of spin-off.

Both domestic and international factors coalesce to affect growth in the economy. Military expenditure has some beneficial effects; it might force governments to increase taxation and domestic saving, part of which can be used for capital formation; it may itself foster human capital by training and modernising people; it may create effective demand and reduce excess capacity; it may have inter-industrial linkages, both backward and forward. All these will contribute positively to growth. On the other hand, it will reduce growth through a whole host of channels. The final effects need to be weighed in balance before a clear-cut judgment can be pronounced.

Finally, the broader question of development remains. Would militarisation and military spending affect development? If so, what is the direction of change? Would security, stability, modernisation, and economic spin-offs increase the quality of life, enhance entitlements and raise capabilities in LDCs? Alternatively, would milex increase repression, remove human rights, reduce consumption and decrease growth through misallocation of scarce resources into unproductive expenditures? The answers are not easy, and often they are based on instinctive biases. We shall try to be more comprehensive, analytical and balanced.

2 The analysis of the data

2.1 Usage of data

It is well known that there are major difficulties involved in quantifying military expenditures, and the data on security-related variables may not be as reliable as researchers would wish. Yet this data is continually being used, for simple comparative statements, more complex analysis of trends, and econometric evaluation of the relationship between defence and other socio-economic variables. It is probably useful to use the available information as intensively as possible, taking due care, of course, of the pitfalls involved. This is definitely one area where demand creates its own supply; the more analysts utilise, refine and demand information, the more there will be an available supply. Nonetheless, the quality of the data is an important question, not only for the purposes of this book (where a large amount of empirical work is cited and discussed), but also for a more general understanding of the issues involved.

Two points must be borne in mind, at the outset, regarding military expenditure data for less developed countries. Firstly, questions regarding data reliability have been raised for *all* categories of variables measuring social and economic conditions in Third World countries.[1] There are of course degrees of reliability; Gross Domestic Product (GDP) can be more accurate than an index of income distribution such as the Gini coefficient. However, the basic problems remain, and it is only with time that things will improve. This is not surprising, since collection and dissemination of information is often positively related to economic development, at least in market-oriented countries. The plethora of publications from international agencies, particularly the recent series of compendiums by the World Bank called *World Tables*, is testimony to the fact that the data base of

LDCs is much better today than in the past, and one can easily expect a secular improvement. Once again, the sophisticated use of information in analysing, forecasting, and planning for development, has been a major contributory cause in the supply of data.

The second point to note at this stage is that defence spending data is bedevilled by certain problems which are common to all countries, not just developing ones. Neild (1981), discussing the secrecy of nuclear weapons purchase and installation in Britain, says: 'Recently, expenditure of £1,000 million on Chevaline, the multiple warhead developed by Britain for her Polaris missiles, was concealed, making it the largest matter in recent years not to have gained a passing mention in the annual defence estimates.'[2] Other instances are cited too, such as the fact that expenditure on warheads is kept secret even though the cost of delivery systems is published. Brzoska (1981)[3] cites the case of West Germany, where three *official* figures for defence spending exist. The range is phenomenal: the proportional difference between the highest and lowest figures for 1979 is reputed to be of the order of 44 per cent. Soviet and Eastern European data on milex are almost non-existent, and there is a continuing saga of data revisions by Western analysts, particularly the CIA, which has gone on for many years. We will come back to these issues again later; at this stage we only note that defence data is a rather grey area in general, and not necessarily for specific countries.

There are many reasons why nations may not be fully honest about their military expenditures. Defence adds to security, protects the economy from enemy threats and actions, as well as establishing stability in some cases. These may all add to social welfare. On the other hand it takes away resources from more productive uses and thus can have high opportunity costs. This may detract from social welfare. Depending on the nature of society's welfare function, the strength of feeling for gains and losses from the military, the position of the military in government and society, and perhaps the agency which is actually collecting and giving the data, there may be tendencies to report lower or higher figures than the actual one. For example, a country which has a strong military, and where feelings about the opportunity cost of defence spending is not high, may have a tendency to claim higher military expenditure than it actually has.

Reporting of data can also be used as a strategic signal for adversaries. Amounts may be inflated if a signal is being given to a belligerent 'neighbour' that the country's security preparedness is high. Deterrence, then, may lead to a higher reported data on defence spending, while peaceful intentions can be signified by a lower announced figure.

The analysis up till now may suggest that there is a dark conspiracy behind milex data, and that governments are intent on misrevealing security-related expenditures. However, this is not strictly true. There are authentic problems in calculating and constructing such series, and it is possible to have incomplete information as well as genuine statistical errors, which will make the data deviate from its true value.

Considerations of security and censorship, together with genuine problems of definition and measurement, may therefore make published military expenditure data from national sources relatively unreliable. It is often believed that experts under international auspices produce better-quality information (see Whynes, 1979). However, even here, there is a lot of controversy, and Brzoska (1981) has recently criticised the fact that 'scientists and the press alike are equally guilty of jumping uncritically on milex figures if only put out by renowned institutions'. We shall be considering carefully the various international institutions responsible for military data and their relative usefulness.

Having said all this, it is still possible to use the data in a relatively rigorous way, provided the researcher handles the information with care. This is of course true of *all* empirical work, but needs to be stressed, particularly in the field of defence spending and the economy, where the use of econometric methods is relatively new. The major point to note is that the *trends* observed for defence spending – whether for major individual countries (in the developing world), or for a cross-section of countries at various periods of time or in different geographical regions – are broadly consistent among different institutions and multinational organisations entrusted with preparing the data. There are differences of opinion about the precise numbers involved, but when it comes to estimating trends most analysts would agree with each other. Thus it is valid to use the data provided it is handled with caution and sensitivity tests are conducted to see the robustness of the results after changes in specification and data source. Whether one is just using the share of defence in GDP or government budgets to show how 'militaristic' a society is, or at the other extreme estimating a complex simultaneous equation model to study the multiple channels by which the military interacts with the economy, used skilfully, the data and results therein can give us both an exploratory description of the problem and a structural analysis of some of the relevant issues.

To sum up, we need to understand the basic limitations of the data, since these will help us in utilising it properly. This is discussed in Section 2.2. The next section gives a comparative evaluation of institutions which collect and disseminate information. The last section concludes with a clarion call that data should be used as fully (and carefully) as possible, since adequate usage may improve the quality and quantity of worldwide information on defence spending.

2.2 The issues

The major issues and problems related to the reporting of military expenditure and the availability of good-quality comparable data can best be understood by looking at the 1975 UN General Assembly discussion, which emphasised four important points. These were as follows: (i) the *definition* and scope of defence spending as well as disaggregated classification within the total military budget; (ii) the deflation for price changes for military expenditure, and the choice of a suitable defence *deflator* to give a proper volume index of the defence effort; (iii) *comparisons* of milex across countries, and comparable measures by which data expressed in national currencies can be converted to a common unit; (iv) the *valuation of resources* used in the defence sector with due emphasis on economic systems and structures.[4]

The fourth issue, regarding valuation of resources, goes beyond the narrow confines of milex data problems; rather it relates to the whole host of questions regarding the consequences of defence for the rest of the economy given *its structural* characteristics. For example, the same amount of military expenditure in an oil-rich economy and capital-poor economy would have vastly different implications. For some countries industrialisation and expenditures on armament production might have spin-off for the civilian sector due to effective demand and R&D. For other countries, this might mean an exhausting drain on resources since the civilian sectors have no linkages with defence production. Thus the problem raised can only be understood in the *overall* context of the book and will not be dealt with here. Instead we concentrate on the first three.

(a) Definitions

The definitions of military and security expenditure as well as its constituent parts may vary from country to country. For example the defence ministry may incur civilian costs while other ministries may have military-type expenditures. Examples of the former may be flood control, civil defence, medical services and even helping in economic development programmes. On the other hand R&D and construction expenditures in civilian departments of the government may be used for security needs.

Of the various international organisations which report on defence spending, the International Monetary Fund (IMF) definition is probably the most comprehensive and explicit. 'Defence', for the IMF,

> covers all expenditure, whether by defence or other departments, for the maintenance of military forces, including the purchase of military supplies and equipment (including the stockpiling of finished items but not the industrial raw materials required for their production), military construction, recruiting, training, equipping, moving, feeding, clothing and housing members of the armed forces, and providing remuneration, medical care, and other services for them. Also included are capital expenditures for the provision of quarters to families of military personnel, outlays on military schools, and research and development serving clearly and foremost the purpose of defence. Military forces also include paramilitary organizations such as gendarmerie, constabulary, security forces, border and customs guards, and other trained,

> equipped and available for use as military personnel. Also falling under this category are expenditure for purposes of strengthening the public services to meet wartime emergencies, training civil defence personnel, and acquiring materials and equipment for these purposes. Included also are expenditure for foreign military aid and contributions to international military organizations and alliances. This category excludes expenditure for nonmilitary purposes though incurred by a ministry or department of defence, and any payments or services provided to war veterans and retired military personnel.[5]

It must be noted, however, that comprehensiveness of definitions does not necessarily mean that the ideal standards will be maintained.

One of the major needs, in the analysis of defence expenditure, is that of disaggregated data. It is useful to know what the military has been doing with its allocated revenue and what constitutes its purchases. This allows cross-checks and permits identification of specific economic effects.

Some of the breakdowns of disaggregated data are particularly important. The UN Centre for Disarmament has analysed a most comprehensive defence expenditure categorisation. These are as follows: (A) OPERATING COSTS (1) *Personnel*: (a) conscripts, (b) other military, (c) civilian; (2) *Operations and Maintenance*: (a) current-use material, (b) maintenance and repairs, (c) purchased services, (d) rent, (e) others. (B) PROCUREMENT AND CONSTRUCTION (1) *Procurement*: (a) aircraft and engines, (b) missiles including conventional warheads, (c) nuclear warheads and bombs, (d) ships and boats, (e) armoured vehicles, (f) artillery, (g) other ordnance and ground force arms, (h) ammunition, (i) electronics and communications, (j) non-armoured vehicles, (k) others; (2) *Construction*: (a) airbases, (b) missile sites, (c) naval bases, (d) electronics, etc., (e) personnel, (f) medical, (g) training, (h) warehouses, depots, (i) command, administration, (j) fortifications, (k) shelters, (l) lands, (m) others. (C) RESEARCH AND DEVELOPMENT (1) *Basic and applied*; (2) *Development, testing and evaluation*.[6]

The details required for the UN mechanism are quite complex, and it is well known that many LDCs would be unable to provide the relevant information even if they wanted to. Some developing countries have been reporting their milex to the UN in the above-mentioned disaggregated form during the last three years, and their numbers are increasing. But the response is also cursory, and many of the elements of the matrix are left blank because they are claimed to be 'not applicable' or 'not available'. It is wildly optimistic to believe, in view of the current state of international tension as well as the inherent problems of LDC data collection, that these desirable standards can be adhered to. However, a start has been made and we hope things will improve. At least the awareness that disaggregated data is important has now been fostered.

What many researchers (including the author) would be satisfied with at this stage is to get reasonable time series for various countries showing disaggregated data regarding total allocation between military forces and industries as well as that of operation cost (mainly personnel) and capital cost (procurement, etc.). These four types of data by themselves would be immensely helpful in tracing out the behaviour of the defence sector over time for a specified country and drawing specific economic conclusions. An example will clarify this.

Table 2.1 *Allocation between military forces and industry: Brazil and India (percentages)*

	Brazil		India	
	(1) Military force	(2) Arms production	(1) Military force	(2) Arms production
1971	98.7	1.3	83.7	16.3
1972	99.4	0.6	83.5	16.5
1973	97.6	2.4	81.8	18.2
1974	97.7	2.3	83.7	16.3
1975	98.5	1.5	81.7	18.3
1976	98.4	1.6	79.0	21.0
1977	98.8	1.2	91.6	8.4
1978	99.3	0.7	97.7	2.3
1979	99.2	0.8	83.0	17.0

Source: Calculated from raw data given in Ball (1984).
Column 1 gives share of total expenditure on military forces for Brazil; similarly for others.

In a recent statistical compendium, Ball (1984) has compiled a very useful set of disaggregated data for many countries which divides security expenditure into military forces and industry and also gives operating and capital costs for each sub-category. Table 2.1 is calculated from the raw data given in Ball, and shows an interesting comparison between Brazil and India – two of the largest arms producers in the Third World. Brazil has devoted a very small percentage of its milex to defence industries, and yet it is the largest exporter of arms in the developing world. Brazil relies on imported blueprints and cheap labour to produce 'appropriate technology', i.e. relatively unsophisticated arms (by superpower standards) which are nevertheless eminently suitable for many developing countries' needs. Its costs are kept low, large-scale investments are not strictly necessary, but its export prices are highly competitive for (relatively) low-quality armaments. India, on the other hand, has followed an import substituting industrialisation policy in armaments production (as we shall discuss more fully in Chapter 7) and this is partly reflected in the high percentage of resources devoted to the arms industry, particularly in capital costs. These types of analyses can only be conducted on the basis of a detailed set. It is expected therefore that a wider availability of disaggregated and comparable data would encourage much more fruitful analysis on the military and its socio-economic consequences.

(b) Price deflators

We turn now to prices. For a specific country, time series data, for military expenditure in nominal or money terms given in local currencies, gives no proper indication of the real trend. We need to deflate the nominal value by a suitable price index before we can get a volume index over time that will give us a measure of the changes in output of the defence sector. With rapid inflation occurring in recent years, this has become particularly important, especially if one is interested in measuring changes in the volume of defence 'produced' by the country concerned.

In principle, the best method for price deflation would be to derive a series of *military price deflators* which could then be used to convert a nominal defence expenditure series into real terms.

In practice, however, very few countries, and even fewer LDCs, have attempted to construct such a deflator series. The reasons are many, and we discuss them briefly.

The first problem is to define a suitable and *objective* 'output' of the military sector, for which a price calculation can be made. There is of course the problem of aggregation – defence may produce output of various kinds and we need to aggregate to get a single price. But this is the least of our worries. More problematic is the fact that defence output is not sufficiently marketable and objective to be defined, even remotely, in a precise fashion. The coal industry produces coal, the steel industry produces steel, and one can easily conceive prices for them. What exactly does defence produce, and how to measure it? It has been suggested that explosive power or destructive power may be used as a proxy for defence output.[7] But quality differences in armaments create insurmountable difficulties. A nuclear bomb may cost the same as supplying conventional arms to a small army, yet the former can have a much higher destructive potential. The output definition is too vague to have a precise price tag put on it.

A better way of dealing with the problem is to analyse the inputs that go into the defence sector and cost them to produce an acceptable price deflator. The final product or output of the military need not be precisely defined; what matters is the price of inputs. An example from consumer behaviour theory may clarify this issue. Suppose a consumer has a utility function

$$U = X_1^{d} X_2^{1-d} \qquad (2.1)$$

where X_1 and X_2 are the two goods he consumes. The utility function is of the special type given by equation 2.1 (log linear in all variables). If the consumer maximises 2.1 subject to his budget constraint, then it is well known that d is the proportion of total expenditure spend on X_1, and 1-d is the proportion spent on X_2. Let the prices be P_1 and P_2. Then the 'ideal' cost of living index[8] is given by P where

$$P = \mathrm{P}_1^{d} \mathrm{P}_2^{1-d} \qquad (2.2)$$

To get the *aggregate deflator P* for the basket of goods consumed by the individual, it is not necessary to define the nature of utility cardinally. For example we could have an alternative utility function

$$F(U) = X_1^{d} X_2^{1-d} \qquad (2.1)'$$

where F is any monotonic function. The main point of the argument is that an overall aggregate deflator can be constructed by implicitly assuming that the 'input' X_1 and X_2 produce an 'output' called utility and d, 1-d are the shares of each of these inputs in the total expenditure.

Now consider the defence sector, which produces an output which may be called 'security'. Security depends on the various inputs needed to produce it, and these may be the specified disaggregated categories of milex. Each input has got a price. If we *assume* that society (or the defence sector) maximises security, and the actual spending on the various inputs that constitute total defence expenditure reflects such an optimisation, then the share of each category can be derived and it corresponds to the d, 1-d mentioned earlier. In principle therefore a price index of the type P can be constructed.

Consider a hypothetical example. Suppose a country spends 10 per cent of its budget on naval ships, 20 per cent on aircraft, 30 per cent on ammunitions and 40 per cent on armed forces pay. It is possible to construct price indices for the four categories P_1, P_2, P_3, P_4, based on the price of ships, aeroplanes, munitions and an index of wages and salaries. Then the aggregate price deflator for the military sector could be

$$P = P_1^{0.1} P_2^{0.2} P_3^{0.3} P_4^{0.4}$$

One major point must always be remembered when discussing price deflators in general. Rising prices should not necessarily mean inflation, since the latter refers to the rate of change of prices for the *same* product, i.e. goods of the same quality being compared for price changes over time. Therefore the secular price rise of military products may reflect an increase in quality in addition to pure inflation. Since 'productivity' increases in defence industries can be high, the rate of change of prices may be reflecting a 'better' product, rather than a more expensive but old-quality good. Once again, in practice, it is not usually possible to segregate the two effects. Thus price deflators tend to overestimate the price inflationary effects by failing to net out quality differentials.

Up till now we have discussed the input-output structure of defence pricing, relating it to the production of security through the use of military armaments and personnel. An alternative method of pricing is to look at the opportunity costs. The former method tries to price defence by asking how much it would cost directly if some specified inputs were used or outputs produced. The latter deals with *indirect* costs; it finds out how much is lost in alternative sectors by the amount of military expenditure in the economy. This measure therefore analyses alternative uses of milex and the cost of opportunities forgone when the country spends a certain amount in current prices. In this case the appropriate deflator is the price index of the alternative category of national expenditure. Two questions are pertinent here. First, what are the alternative uses? Secondly,[9] how does the price of possible alternative uses change from year to year?

Suppose one assumes that a reduction in milex would go for investment, then the appropriate price measure by which we should deflate the nominal series is by the investment goods deflator. On the other hand, inflation correction by the consumer price index implicitly assumes that the resources released by milex would be used by consumers, possibly under lump-sum transfers and similar redistribution of income. If the analyst implicitly assumes that the alternative use of milex has the same composition as the existing GNP, then it is preferable to use the GNP deflator. The differences are not always substantial, as Table 2.2 shows for India and Turkey; on the other hand they may sometimes be large, as in the cases of Sri Lanka and Ghana.

Overall, we have seen that there are three types of price deflators that can be used for the military sector, based on (a) output, (b) input costs, (c) opportunity costs. The first is conceptually problematic; the other two are easier to derive in principle. If the researcher is interested in the economic consequences of military expenditure it is useful to use the third measure to find, at least crudely, what could be done with resources spent on defence. This is also easily calculable, given that relatively dependable series on alternative deflators are

Table 2.2 *Various price indices, 1975-80, for four countries (1975 = 100)*

	1975	1976	1977	1978	1979	1980
Turkey						
CPI	100	117.5	148.0	239.6	391.8	761.1
ID	100	119.5	156.2	230.8	402.3	912.2
GDPD	100	117.7	146.6	210.6	359.3	726.6
India						
CPI	100	96.2	103.5	105.8	115.3	128.1
ID	100	102.7	105.4	114.7	130.5	148.8
GDPD	100	106.7	110.6	112.6	130.2	145.8
Ghana						
CPI	100	156.1	337.8	584.8	903.0	1,355.4
ID	100	109.4	159.9	218.0	361.1	510.0
GDPD	100	128.1	214.2	371.2	518.3	748.7
Sri Lanka						
CPI	100	101.3	102.6	115.0	127.3	160.6
ID	100	106.7	124.7	139.7	169.7	212.9
GDPD	100	125.8	137.7	157.0	185.5	223.0

Source: Calculated by the author from *World Tables*, 1983.
CPI is consumers price index; ID is investment (price) deflator; GDPD is Gross Domestic Product deflator.

available. Like most international institutions which report on volume index or constant price series of milex, we also use the third alternative.

However, security analysts might want more sophisticated and specific military expenditure price series for 'general government final consumption expenditure on defence'. Skons (1983) reports the 1980 UN National Accounts Questionnaire, in which only twelve countries provided a purely defence deflator for 1979, and of them only two, Thailand and Sri Lanka, can be classified as less developed. For Thailand the difference between pure military expenditure and GNP deflators is very small; for Sri Lanka, quite large. The indices for the military were derived by using a set of civil prices of inputs appropriately weighted by their shares in military consumption expenditure, as suggested earlier in the theoretical discussion. Again this should be the subject of further research, and governments must be encouraged to produce appropriate *military* price deflators, so that real output or volume index can be adequately calculated.

(c) Comparisons

If we wish to compare the total military expenditure of one country with that of another (rather than milex as a ratio of other expenditures), then clearly national currency values are useless. This is also true of any other variable that is measured in value terms and stated in terms of the national currency. The usual practice has been to use the official exchange rate to convert domestic currency figures to a common unit, generally the US dollar. If the exchange rate truly reflects the ratio of aggregate or 'average' price levels between the two countries concerned, then it is a useful measure of comparison between like and like. For example if the exchange rates of the Turkish lira and the Indian rupee were 500 TL per $ and Rs 10 per $, then a good costing 500 TL in Turkey should cost Rs 10 in India (in long-term equilibrium), both being equivalent to one dollar. This also implies that the exchange rate changes in line with relative inflation among various countries. Thus if the price of the good becomes 1,000 TL in Turkey, while its price remains unchanged in the US and India, then the TL would be devalued to a level of 1,000 per dollar. Then the lira-rupee rate will change to 100 from an initial level of 50.

However, except probably as a long-term phenomenon, the official exchange rate is rarely equal to the ratio of prices between the two relevant countries. The first reason for this is the simplest. For many countries (particularly in the Third World), the exchange rate is fixed or pegged at a specific level for many years, so that even if domestic inflation is out of line with world inflation, the rate of exchange is not altered quickly, except in stepwise fashion with an occasional major devaluation. Thus under fixed exchange rates, proper convertibility of the same good in value terms is not assured. More important is to recognise that for the exchange rate to be a true indicator of domestic purchasing power, all goods produced in the country are potentially tradables. If few goods are traded, then the exchange rate is at best reflecting the prices of tradables, and not of the whole gamut of products that make up the vector of national output, and whose prices contribute to the aggregate price level of the economy. Finally, even with tradables, there may be various costs and controls specific to the domestic economy which are not reflected in international prices, but find their way into domestic price components. These may be on servicing, indirect taxes, tariffs and quotas; thus they are not adequately reflected in exchange rates.

To devise more reliable comparative price-quantity figures, it is better to use (domestic) purchasing-power parities (PPP) as suggested by the UN International Comparison Project (ICP). The project essentially provides figures which can be used to connect local currency values to a common current unit – the US dollar. The PPP is defined as 'the number of units of a country's currency required to buy the quantity of goods and services that can be bought in the United States with one US dollar'.[10] The PPP therefore provides a better measure for comparing volume indices of output, since it reflects the relative purchasing power of domestic currency and the dollar. One advantage of the ICP calculated PPPs is that they are derived from a system of multisectoral comparisons, where all the countries in the specified sample are compared simultaneously. Comparisons of price levels and quantity indices are therefore transitive as well as base-country invariant.[11] This is useful, since with simple binary comparisons it is not always possible to have transitive relations. For example, with the ICP numbers, it is possible to say that if country *X* has a higher PPP than country *Y* and country *Y* has a higher PPP than country *Z*, then *X* must have a higher PPP than *Z*. Finally, disaggregate PPPs have also been calculated so that we have indices not only for GDP but also for its three major components, consumption, investment and government expenditure.

Converting milex in local currency figures to a common unit, viz. the US dollar, can therefore be done using official exchange rates as well as the various PPP indices. The results are usually vastly different. Table 2.3 gives relevant figures for a number of countries. As is clear the differences between the values can be very high for LDCs; this is much less so for a developed country like the UK. However, it should also be noted that this is a common characteristic of *all* components of GDP as well as GDP

Table 2.3 *1975 milex in US million dollars using various PPP indices and the official exchange rates*

	(1)	(2)	(3)	(4)	(5)	(6)
India (rupee)	23.822	2,844.0	9,528.8	5,768.0	16,429	9,198
Kenya (pound)	19.9	54.0	110.0	64.2	144	105
S. Korea (won)	465,000.0	960.7	2,435.0	2,163.0	3,163	2,447
Brazil (cruzeiro)	11,220.0	1,367.0	2,113.0	1,876.0	3,243	2,158
Mexico (peso)	6,740.0	539.2	936.0	793.0	991	911
Iran (rial)	452,000.0	6,682.0	12,951.0	8,480.0	11,801	11,385
UK (pound)	5,165.0	11,475.0	13,380.0	9,895.0	13,884	12,722

Col. 1 gives national currency value of milex from SIPRI.
Col. 2 gives the value of milex in US $ millions converted at official exchange rates for 1975.
Col. 3 gives of the value of milex in US $ millions converted at the PPP index for consumption goods.
Cols 4, 5 and 6 are similar, but using PPP's capital formation, government expenditure and total output respectively. All these are calculated by the author from figures given in *World Tables* (1983).

itself: there is nothing inherent in milex *per se* that produces differing estimates using alternative PPP figures.

Let us consider Table 2.3 a little more carefully. Column 1 gives national currency figures for seven countries, six of them developing ones, while the UK is kept as a comparative standard. These numbers are of course not comparable with each other. In column 2, the domestic currency milexes are multiplied by the official exchange rates and thus transformed into US $ millions – a set of comparable figures. We can now, for example, say that India's military expenditure in 1975 was more than double that of Brazil – both measured in a common unit. But remember that exchange rates are not a 'true' measure of domestic purchasing power of expenditure across countries. Thus the fact that India had twice the defence expenditure of Brazil does not necessarily mean that twice the quantity of goods was bought with the military budget or that the opportunity cost of expenditure forgone in other fields is twice as much. This is over and above the standard problem of aggregation; the issues would exist even if all goods could be satisfactorily aggregated.

Consider, for example, column 5. It has been calculated by using the government expenditure PPP (local currency per dollar). The latter is a relative price; if it is, to take the Indian case for 1975, Rs 1.45 to the dollar, then the index tells us that the Indian government can buy for Rs 1.45 what the US government can buy for one dollar. Note that the official exchange rate for 1975 was Rs 8.38 per dollar. Using the PPP measure, then, consider the opportunity cost of milex. Thus if India had no public expenditure on defence it would release a certain amount of resources *directly* (i.e. without any multipliers), equivalent to about $16,429 (see column 5). Alternatively, without any milex, the Indian government could purchase a set of goods *worth* $16,429 *in the US*, the composition of the goods being similar to what the American government actually buys. Looking at the Brazilian entry we see that it is of the order of $3,243 million. Thus the authorities in India, in pursuing their defence spending, are losing, in the worth of *alternative* goods, about *five times* more than the Brazilian authorities.

The hypothetical examples show the type of issues involved. If defence spending in India were stopped completely and all military expenditure were used to buy other goods in the government consumption basket, then this would purchase in principle, $16,000 millions' worth of goods at American prices. If the Brazilians did the same they could purchase about $3,000 millions' worth of goods. The opportunity cost in 'real' terms is about five times as much for India; the usual exchange rate calculation shows a much lower differential.

At present, expenditures on the military budget comprise spending on all categories of aggregate output, viz. consumption, investment and government expenditures. Thus none of the available PPPs are fully efficient for comparative estimates of defence spending across countries, though each has its own specific merit. What is really needed is a *specific* PPP for military expenditure alone, but this will have to wait, given the current paucity of data. Again we may identify an important area for further research. In the absence of such sophisticated methods, we are in practice constrained to use official exchange rates for international value comparisons of defence budgets. Once again let me stress that this is not unique to cross-sectional analysis of military expenditure alone; similar problems remain with studies related to other variables.

2.3 The sources

The first major source of military spending data is the national government, which is usually in a better position to know its own domestic security expenditure than other agencies. Serious allegations have been made about developing countries' reporting of defence budgets.[12] We discuss the various methods reputedly used for such underestimates. It is possible that multiple figures may exist for the total military expenditure of the same country, and these are attributable to the clientele for which the data has been prepared.[13] For example, among some NATO countries the domestic public gets the lower figure while the Alliance receives the higher figure. Budget manipulations, euphemistically called 'creative book-keeping', are possible. The very nature of defence, with its emphasis on secrecy – for justifiable reasons, of course – implies some form of manipulation.[14]

Five methods are allegedly used to misreveal defence data. These are (a) double book-keeping, (b) aggregation, (c) extra budgetary finances, (d) unidentified use of foreign exchange, and (e) military aid. All of these would lead to *under*reporting, thus published national data would be expected to be less than actual.

Double book-keeping occurs when the government keeps two sets of accounts, one used for published budgetary statistics and the other for internal use by ministers and civil servants. The case is not entirely dissimilar to the experience of West Germany and other NATO countries mentioned earlier, except that, for LDCs, the second account is not published. Thus fear of manipulability increases. Highly aggregate data can also effectively hide the true cost of expenditure on defence. It is easier to check for internal consistency, as well as gaps in the data structure, when a greater level of disaggregation is provided. However, detailed breakdown *per se* is no check on reliability, for it is possible that government statisticians have done a 'better' job and managed a more efficient obfuscation.

Extra-budgetary accounting is possible when the military is heavily involved in the civilian economy, for example as heads of state economic enterprises. Then the civilian sector or enterprise may be asked to contribute to the defence effort or to special funds set up for the military. On the other hand, the nexus may operate the other way round too. The military may be engaged in 'civic action' programmes which have little or no connection with security or threat. The military budget may thus contain items which are not strictly security expenditures, yet may be difficult to disentangle. Unidentified use of foreign exchange is similar. A part of government export earnings is not entered into official accounting systems, but used to import weapons (or, for that matter, luxury cars!). Finally, military assistance data may not be fully reported, or may be obscured by other forms of economic aid.

One of the major difficulties with these allegations is that, in spite of the attention that they have received from researchers, there is currently very little in the way of hard evidence or concrete case studies always to support them. Military expenditures are *intrinsically* liable to be misrevealed. Therefore it is widely believed that they must be false. Yet such assertions are rarely documented as strongly as the vehemence of the allegations would warrant. Critics of the data do a good job when they point out *in principle* the problems inherent in defence facts. However, when it comes to providing evidence about the underestimates, the general feeling seems to be that where there is smoke there must be fire! Even Ball (1984), who has given more evidence than most about unidentified expenditures, has recourse to statements like 'Such an allegation is, of course, extremely difficult to substantiate.'

It is necessary to be objective about the degree of belief (or disbelief) that one may have for milex data emanating from national sources. There is little doubt that bias exists. However, if it is small or always in one direction (as alleged, there has been underreporting, not *over*reporting), then precautionary statistical measures can be taken in empirical work. Further, *long-term trends* in time series data, or *steady state properties* in cross-section data, may be relatively immune from these criticisms.

Thus empirical analysis using the properties of trends or averages is reasonably satisfactory provided the researcher uses the information carefully.

Turning now to international sources, there are a number of agencies which publish annual military expenditure data in some form or another. The best-known are: (i) the International Institute of Strategic Studies (IISS), (ii) the US Arms Control and Disarmament Agency (ACDA), (iii) the Stockholm International Research Institute (SIPRI), (iv) The International Monetary Fund (IMF), and various UN publications. ACDA publishes the *World Military Expenditure and Arms Transfers (WMEAT)*, SIPRI publishes the *World Armaments and Disarmaments Yearbook (WADY)*, IISS publishes *The Military Balance (MB)*, IMF publishes its *Government Finance Statistics Yearbook (GFSY)*, and the *UN Statistical Yearbook (UNSY)* also has data on milex. In addition, Ruth Sivard edits an important annual publication entitled *World Military and Social Expenditures*, which in addition to defence has other categories of social and economic expenditures for a large number of countries (142 in the 1983 edition). We discuss the relative coverage of the first four given by IISS, ACDA, SIPRI, and IMF, since these are the ones most often used.

The Military Balance published by IISS is useful if compact information for particular countries is sought for a particular year. Each issue provides, for the most recent year for which data is available, information regarding population, years of military service, total armed forces, estimated GNP, defence expenditure in local currency current prices, exchange rate, as well as strategic details about the army, navy and air force. For country studies specifically related to defence only, the book is appropriate and thus widely used. However, if one is interested in a time series or historical data, the data is rather inadequate. Only the current (or recent) local currency value is given; this is often an estimate and not updated. A summary table does give a series on dollar values of military expenditure (as well as its *per capita* level, proportion of government spending and GDP), but these are quite short, and various issues often having significant changes have to be compared. It is sometimes suggested that *MB* data uses intelligence sources in London, but this cannot be checked and anyway does not guarantee reliability. Finally, for defence expenditure, 'the latest available budget figures are quoted', which means national definitions are used, restricting comparability among countries. The *MB* is candid about the government share figures: 'This series is designed to show national trends only; differences in the scope of the government sector invalidate international comparisons.'

The *World Military Expenditure and Arms Transfers* published by ACDA has much more comprehensive information and its milex 'data are generally the expenditures of the Ministry of Defence', with manipulations. Various sources are used, a prominent one being the files of the US Agency for International Development. A vast array of figures is produced which in addition to milex in current and constant dollars also includes central government spending disaggregated into public health and education expenditure, as well as the number of people (population), armed forces, teachers, physicians. In addition to country-by-country data, geographical, regional, political and economic groupings are reported. Finally ACDA gives arms transfers data, both imports and exports, by country and year as well as selected groups.

In terms of sheer volume and comprehensiveness of data, ACDA publications of *WMEAT* are particularly useful. But it has its own problems, specifically those related to pricing and exchange rates. *WMEAT* does not give local currency figures either in constant or in current prices. It also changes its base year for the constant dollar series from volume to volume, not indicating very clearly the methods of conversion. Since the data in each volume is for about ten years only (more of course than IISS), it is difficult sometimes to construct a long enough consistent series if the researcher is interested only in military expenditure. Again ACDA uses confidential sources in addition to government budgets, UN publications, internally circulated IMF/World Bank country reports and those from US embassy officials. But there is no detailed information regarding sources of milex data collection and methods of data preparation – thus it is difficult to have any independent checks on the accuracy of the figures. More important, since restricted government information is used, one may suspect manipulation, particularly if manipulability serves the interests of the informer. Further as Brzoska (1981) points out, 'the ACDA system of reviewing national milex figures generally produces smaller figures. If this is the case and credit is given to controllability the use of ACDA figures should not be encouraged'. However, this seems to be a 'Catch-22' situation. On the one hand some 'hard' information can be got from unverified sources, yet a lingering suspicion remains about its authenticity.

SIPRI is remarkable in that it is probably the one international institution which uses *only* open sources when calculating milex data. Thus data can be readily verified and checked. 'The NATO definition is used as a guideline for all countries, especially when choosing between alternative series. Thus the figures published in the *Government Finance Statistical Yearbook (GFS)* are preferred to those given in other sources, since the definition which the *GFS* uses by and large agrees with the NATO definitions' (SIPRI, 1982). In practice therefore SIPRI uses *GFSY* figures with adjustments made from alternative published sources. Two advantages have been claimed for SIPRI in comparison with the two organisations previously mentioned. It gives a very detailed accounting of its sources, so independent verification is possible. Further it publishes an updated local currency series, so that comparisons with other items of national expenditure can be made easily. The coverage, though not as wide as *WMEAT*'s, is nevertheless good; it gives three large tables for milex in constant US dollar price and current local currency price as well as the military burden (milex as a proportion of GDP). In addition data on arms exports and imports is provided for major exporting countries and major importing regions.

The IMF gives current value defence spending in local currency and, as mentioned earlier, has the best definition of milex possible. Both SIPRI and ACDA make use of *GFSY* data to publish their own estimates. It is thought that the reliability of *GFSY* data is relatively 'high', though again independent checks are difficult.

We end this chapter with a brief discussion about problems inherent in arms transfer data. These are similar to the ones analysed for milex. The use of suitable deflators for price changes, accounting for quality increases over time, comparability, adjustments to a common currency, etc., are all present with equal force, when one is considering the trade in weapons. The problem is complicated by smuggling,[15] transfer of small arms, nongovernmental trade and so forth.

SIPRI gives constant dollar figures (for each year) for the value of trade in *major* weapons with the Third World; exports are classified by country, and importers in LDCs by region. In addition, an important register of arms trade between industrialised and developing countries is provided which lists major weapons systems on order or delivery during a given year. Much useful information can be gleaned from this table, though the absence of weapons prices makes it less tractable for economists, who are usually more concerned with the value of trade. ACDA defines arms transfer as the 'international transfer under grant, credit or cash sales terms of military equipment usually referred to as "conventional" '. Thus tactical guided missiles are included but strategic missile systems are excluded, as also are nuclear, chemical and biological weapons. Almost everything else for pure military use (including equipment for defence industries) is considered in principle.

Again, arms transfer data must be analysed carefully. In the mid-1970s ACDA wrote:

> much of the international arms trade involves barter arrangements, multi year loans, discounted prices, third-party payments, and partial debt forgiveness. Thus, acquisition by a nation of some given quality of armaments does not necessarily impose the burden on its economy that is implied by the estimated equivalent US dollar value of the shipment. Therefore, the economic value of arms imports should not be related in detail to the local economies. (ACDA, *WMEAT*, 1967-76)

As we shall see in a later chapter, things changed radically during the 1970s, particularly the latter half, and the burden of imports could be related more closely to the quantity, since the payments system become more rigorous. However, the basic point regarding careful handling of data remains.

To sum up, the best sources of defence-related data, in terms of both coverage and reliability, seem to be SIPRI and ACDA. The former has the added advantage of open sources. Short-term variations in milex, particularly for recent years (which may only be estimates rather than actual expenditures), are not very trustworthy, though using long series, averages over time, large cross-sections of data, and trends, will give reasonably satisfactory empirical results. Finally we must mention, and emphasise, that the use of the military *burden* (milex as a percentage of GDP) as a primary measure has many attractions. First, it does not require the use of either exchange rates or price indexes in its construction, being a ratio of current price figures in national currencies. Second, since it is unit free, it can be compared across countries without conversion or deflation. In what follows, empirical analysis is quite often conducted using military burdens. This gets rid of many of the problems discussed earlier.

3 Military spending and public expenditure

3.1 Defence and the budget

Invariably almost all military expenditure comes out of government budgets. Other items of public expenditure, such as those on health and education, have their counterpart in private consumption expenditure. But defence spending is predominantly a public good and its macroeconomic effects are inextricably connected with government spending. Further, the share of the military in total budgetary allocations can be quite high in LDCs relative to developed economies. Table 3.1 gives the share of defence expenditure in government total *revenue* for LDCs as a whole as well as distributed according to income categories. As is clear, since defence is simply one item among a vast array of public expenditure categories, the relatively high values of this share show the importance attached to it as a purely public good.

There are a number of important issues which one may consider when analysing the impact of milex within government budgets. First we analyse the relationship of the growth of the

Table 3.1 *Military spending as a share of government revenue (percentages)*

	1965	1970	1973
All less developed countries (LDCs)	17.6	19.0	16.5
High income LDCs	15.5	16.7	11.6
Middle income LDCs	25.9	23.9	20.6
Lower income LDCs	19.3	21.1	21.9
Oil producing countries	15.4	19.4	19.5
Industrialised economies	18.8	16.2	12.7

Source: *World Tables* (1976).

public sector with economic development, giving special emphasis to military expenditure. This is discussed in Section 3.2. Secondly, we analyse the impact of defence spending on the size of the budget deficit, specifically whether higher milex leads to an equivalent amount of taxation. The possibility (or otherwise) of balanced budgets at the margin has a variety of implications. We need to analyse (a) the tax effort consequent to a rise in defence spending, and the possible mobilisation of additional resources for non-defence needs; (b) the implications of budget deficits in the monetary process via the governments' financial constraints; (c) short-term multiplier effects consequent to an increase in any form of government expenditure. These are dealt with in Sections 3.3, 3.4 and 3.5. Finally, the allocation of government budgets between defence and other, more productive categories of expenditure is discussed in the last section.

3.2 Economic development and government expenditure

Various theories have been proposed regarding the relationship between government expenditure and economic development, and it may be useful to review them briefly here. The nineteenth-century political economist Alfred Wagner proposed the now classic 'Wagner's Law', which postulated a positive and rising relation between state activity and economic growth. He believed that the continuous growth of society and the economy would cause an expansion of government activity. There are three basic reasons for this. First, the internal and external aspects of law and order become more important with an increase in national wealth, so that the government is obliged to increase its activities in the fields of policing and defence. It is expected that richer nations will be more security conscious, thus the share of defence in GDP may rise with *per capita* income. Second, social welfare spendings will rise with increased development, since these are superior goods whose demand rises with income. Third, the government may need to participate more fully in the production process owing to technological reasons. With the growth of large-scale technology, high set-up costs and the necessity to exploit increasing returns to scale, it is preferable for the government to enter the field of production directly, since its very size and ability to spend more than atomistic private sector industrialists will make it more efficient. Government expenditure either by itself or as a proportion of GDP is postulated to be a positive function of *per capita* income, and further, the elasticity may even be greater than unity. Thus the growth of public spending is greater than the growth of output (income) per head. Wagner's theory therefore makes long-term factors, such as population, income and growth, the major causes of a secular rise in state activity with development.

Though Wagner believed that the revenue constraint was important for developing countries' governments in the short run, he thought that in the long run 'the desire for development of a progressive people will always overcome these financial difficulties'. This may be true in principle, but in practice LDCs may find that the budget constraint may be of paramount importance in the expansion of government expenditure. The second major explanation of state spending in LDCs, then, is in terms of their capacity to raise resources. Empirical studies have shown[1] that government revenue is relatively inelastic in developing economies, and this may be the binding constraint in limiting aggregate expenditure to specific levels.

The third theory is in terms of displacement effects. (See Peacock and Wiseman, 1967.) For relatively long periods of time, the share of government spending in the national product remains stable. The value of this share is a compromise between the concepts of 'tolerable burden of taxation' and the 'desirable level of expenditure' that the citizens and the authorities have when formulating the socio-economic role of the state. A major structural change or crisis will induce a basic re-evaluation of the share, and cause it to shift to a different level, which will then become the new (semi-permanent) one. 'Such disturbances may create a displacement effect, which in turn may shift public revenue and expenditure to new levels. After the disturbance is over . . . a new plateau of expenditure may be reached, with public expenditure again taking a broadly constant share of GNP, though a different share from the former one' (Peacock and Wiseman, 1967). Thus government expenditure as a share of GDP is determined by social consensus on revenue and spending, as well as the occasional displacements caused by major structural disequilibrium.

Though the foregoing analysis has been conducted in terms of *overall* government spending, it can easily be adapted to military expenditure *per se*. The three major determinants of the defence burden are therefore: (a) long-term developmental factors such as *per capita* income; (b) the total budget constraint; (c) displacement variables such as wars or structural shifts like an oil price rise for oil-exporting countries. It must also be stressed that these three determinants affect military expenditure as a public good which produces 'security'. In an earlier study, Whynes (1979) has used the concept of Wagner's Law to discuss the relationships between security expenditure, government budgets and indices of economic development. It is hypothesised that the total government budget (as a proportion of GDP) increases as an economy becomes more developed. Further, with economic development, the role of the state in providing both security and welfare expands, thus the defence share in the national product rises. Finally, the military burden is positively related to the ratio of government expenditure to aggregate national income. The latter relation may simply be a spurious one since defence itself is a category of state budgets. Alternatively, if the government is considered a rational agent and defence is not an inferior good, then defence spending is expected to be a positive function of the total outlay incurred in government budgets.

Various empirical studies have been conducted to analyse the postulated relations. Two are particularly exhaustive and important. Lotz's (1970) work is one of the first formal analyses to isolate the determinants of defence expenditure (as well as other functional categories of national budgets). Tait and Heller (1982) use data for 1977 and a massive sample of eighty-four countries to analyse the nature of variables that affect government functional expenditure categories (as a share of GDP). Their results for the military burden are given in column 2 of Table 3.2. Column 1 reports the estimates given by Lotz (1970). Columns 3 to 6 are my own estimates using the control sample of fifty countries (see also Deger and Sen, 1984b).[2] A comparison of the three sets is revealing and will illustrate some important issues.

Lotz uses two indices of economic development, *per capita* income (y) and degree of urbanisation (u). The coefficient of u (urbanisation as a proxy of development) is significantly positive,

Table 3.2 *Economic estimation of military burden*

	(1)	(2)	(3)	(4)	(5)	(6)
Constant	0.02	−7	2.63	2.30	1.50	1.34
	(0.1)	(−2.27)	(2.77)	(1.55)	(1.26)	(1.16)
y	−0.006	−0.04	0.17	0.15	0.24	0.15
	(−3.5)	(−0.32)	(2.32)	(1.59)	(3.43)	(2.44)
MO	0.02					
	(1.8)					
u	0.048	0.05		0.013	0.075	
	(2.6)	(2.25)		(0.29)	(2.42)	
GR	0.081				0.16	0.15
	(2.19)				(2.48)	(2.59)
POP 14		0.16				
		(2.17)				
GR(net)		0.10				
		(2.48)				
N					0.0052	0.0055
					(1.38)	(1.45)
D					−0.65	−0.22
					(−3.23)	(−1.94)
*D*1					3.5	3.98
					(2.35)	(3.33)
*D*2					9.1	11.35
					(6.4)	(9.96)
R^2	0.366	0.15	0.1133	0.1151	0.8734	0.8712

Sources: Col. 1 from Lotz (1970), his equation 3.
Col. 2 from Tait and Heller (1982), their Table 3.
Cols 3-6, my own computation.
(*t* values in parentheses).
Definitions: *m* is military burden, *y* is *per capita* income; MO is exports of minerals and petroleum as percentage of total exports; *u* is share of population in urban areas; GR is government expenditure as a percentage share of GDP or GNP; GR (net) is the same, net of defence; POP14 is the percentage of population aged 14 or under; *N* is total population; *D* is the index of internationalisation as explained in the text; *D*1 and *D*2 are oil and war dummies.

thus development produces an increase of the defence burden (*m*). However, the negative and significant value of the *y* coefficient casts doubt on Wagner's Law, since the Law would claim a positive association between these two variables. As expected, higher government expenditure (GR) causes defence spending to rise.

The negative (and significant) coefficient of *per capita* income in column 1 of Table 3.2 is disturbing, for it contradicts the relatively plausible hypothesis that the defence burden may rise as the economy gets more prosperous on average. But one has to be careful about the results. The two variables, y and u, are highly correlated. Thus, the existence of multicollinearity may make the single equation estimates relatively unreliable. The presence of such a correlation between independent variables is admitted by Lotz (1970) himself when he claims (for a separate equation in the same paper) that 'The standard error for the urbanisation variable increases when any of the other variables is included, because of multicollinearity.'

Leaving aside the formal econometric problems, it is also not clear from an economic point of view why urbanisation *per se* should influence a nation's military burden. As an indicator of development, there are more valid socio-economic indices, such as the literacy rate, or health provisions, or consumption of electricity. To select a variable of dubious economic significance, which also raises substantial estimation problems, seems odd.

Tait and Heller (1982) also use an index of urbanisation (see column 2, Table 3.2), and are content with the following explanation: 'It seems reasonable to consider that urbanized societies must spend more on defense and are willing to do so.' It is unclear why urbanised societies are more prone to defence expenditures, since there seem to be more pressing and imminent reasons for spending money on the military. Consider, for example, the three major countries of the Indian subcontinent, India, Pakistan and Sri Lanka. They have similar levels of urbanisation (about a quarter of the population), but very different levels of defence spending and military burden. (Military expenditure as a percentage share of GDP in 1979 was 2.6, 5.0 and 0.8 respectively.) Latin American countries in general have higher urbanisation ratios, but on average a lower military/GDP share. Argentina's defence burden in 1979 was of the same magnitude as India's, but the proportion of the total population in urban areas was much higher, of the order of 50 per cent. Brazil has 65 per cent of its people living in towns and cities; on the other hand it spends less than 1 per cent of its GDP on defence. It is difficult to be convinced by the urban-military links, *a priori*, for LDCs.

The insignificant (and negative) coefficient of *per capita* income found by Tait and Heller (1982), reported in our column 2 of Table 3.2, is also disturbing. One reason for it may be that they took countries with a *per capita* income below $1,750, which leaves out countries like Argentina, the Bahamas, Barbados, Israel and Malta, as well as all of OPEC, from their sample of LDCs, even though these should be included using broader indices of underdevelopment. The other independent variables, such as the age distribution of population, are relatively *ad hoc*. The fit too is not good, witness the very low R^2. Overall therefore an independent analysis is required to identify the causes, determinants and structure of the defence burden.

Columns 3-6 of Table 3.2 report various empirical equations that I have estimated with the defence burden as the dependent variable. Observe the first of these, reported in column 3. *Per capita* income is significant and affects the defence burden positively. The fit of the equation is reasonable considering we have only one independent variable. Observe that the Tait and Heller equation (in column 2) does only marginally better with many more variables. Adding the urbanisation variable in column 4 does not change the basic structure: both coefficients are positive and *per capita* income is still significant (though urbanisation is not). Adding more independent variables (the rationale for their inclusion will be explained later) improves the fit dramatically, and almost all variables are now highly significant (see column 5). Note particularly the positive sign of *per capita* income in accordance with standard theories. Though we do not believe that urbanisation is a 'good' variable to include in a military equation, it is still kept for comparison, in column 5, and the positive effect could be spurious. Government budget affects defence positively, as expected.

Let us now consider the various variables I have used to explain defence, in addition to *per capita* income. One point not often noted in the literature, must be stressed; defence is essentially a major public good, therefore its share in national income is explained by any variable that reflects the 'publicness' aspect of military spending. This could be *per capita* income, the total government budget or the level of total population (*N*). In addition, the earlier theoretical discussion suggests that economic development, resource constraints and 'displacement' are important central factors in explaining defence shares in national income. The first of these factors may be proxied by *per capita* income and/or growth rates; the second by government expenditure as a share of GDP. Finally, country-specific dummy variables such as those for oil revenues or war economies would be helpful in explaining the military burden, precisely because they cause structural 'displacement'.

The international aspect of military expenditure and economic development could also be useful in explaining LDC defence burdens. One interesting formal method (used in Deger and Smith, 1983) can be briefly analysed here.[3] Kravis *et al.* (1978) have found for developing economies that national income *per capita* measured at official exchange rates (y) can vary significantly from that measured at purchasing power parity (q). The difference between the two (i.e. $q - y = D$) is an index which can be interpreted as measuring the degree of integration that the domestic economy has achieved with the rest of the world. This could be used also as an index of development in general: more developed countries are usually more integrated into the international economy. In general it has been found that as an economy becomes more open to the world market forces and the importance of trade grows, the difference between q and y ($q - y = D$) shrinks.

Column 6 of Table 3.2 then gives my final estimates. The econometric test assumes that military expenditure is for a public good providing security (reflected by variables y and N). The defence burden also depends on the index of development (reflected by y and D) and is affected by country-specific structural shift factors (two dummies for oil surplus and war countries). The revenue constraint is captured by the share of government expenditure in total national output. Finally, higher international integration (lower D) should increase military burden. Observe the substantial improvement in R^2 as compared to the findings of Lotz and of Tait and Heller as well as the significance and right signs (as expected) of all variables.

We also experimented with a large number of alternative domestic economic variables such as growth rates, but these failed to give any significant coefficients. Thus a simple validation of Wagner's Law may not be possible empirically. Economic development raises growth rates but this in turn does not necessarily increase the share of the military in GDP. Rather, as argued previously, the causation seems to be the other way around; it is military expenditure that affects growth rates and not vice versa. The proponents of a secular increase of the military burden with economic development would be disappointed empirically if they tested the hypothesis using growth rates as a proxy for development. Yet, as we have seen, when *per capita* income is used in the regression, the coefficient is significantly positive. The main reason for this seems to be that income acts as a portmanteau variable, transmitting the effects of development, government budgets and even possibly structural change. In a way the regression equation in column 6 is in accord with all three theories discussed above, but it is difficult to distinguish their effects separately.

We have emphasised cross-section results, since the postulated theories are all for long-term steady states, and coefficients derived from cross-country variables tend to exhibit long-term properties. However, the fact that the military burden does not depend on growth, but is strongly influenced by *per capita* income, has also been observed in time series analysis for a single country. Results reported for Morocco by Fontanel (1982) also show that in general the military burden is not well explained by economic variables except income per head. To sum up, therefore: the main emphasis in explaining military spending must be on its capacity as a public good influenced somehow by stages of development but also by government's capacity to increase its budget as well as by noneconomic factors such as security, threats or wars.

3.3 Taxation

Military expenditure can be increased and financed by additional taxation. This may have a number of direct and indirect effects. If the budget deficit consequent to additional military expenditure remains the same, then extra domestic money creation is not necessary to finance the defence effort. As we shall see in the next section, this may avoid certain undesirable problems.

If the improvement of the tax effort is for the long run, in the sense that additional taxes are available even if the military burden goes down in later years, then the total saving potential may have been increased for the economy. It is possible, though, that the extra revenue may be used in financing government consumption expenditure in other fields as well as, of course, adding to fixed capital formation.

Thus additional defence expenditure can have fiscal effects which may lead to the mobilisation of resources. Both long-term and short-term changes in the economy are induced through the interrelationship between defence, taxation and saving. If the government has raised taxes (say as a proportion of GDP) to finance increases in defence shares, then it may be willing to keep tax levels at their previous high even when military expenditure is reduced. This may give a long-term boost to the economy, since increased tax efforts may cause national saving as a proportion of income to rise, *cet. par*. Further, if the government can manage to siphon off some of the extra revenue collected, in the first instance, for strategic purposes, and use it for developmental effort, then clearly even in the short run extra resources will have been mobilised for productive purposes.

The foregoing analysis implicitly assumes that the implicit transfer of resources from the private to the public sector is beneficial for the economy. The private sector has a lower disposable income due to extra taxes; this reduces its saving. The government has a higher (tax) income, and provided its propensity to save is greater than the private sector's, the economy has more investable resources. Of course, it may be still be argued that the private sector is more 'productive' in its investment, thus the net transfer will not increase aggregate efficiency. However, for LDCs, as we have already mentioned in Chapter 1, state intervention in investment is often essential for sustained growth.

Gandhi (1974) has made a serious study of the Indian tax effort during the Sino-Indian and the (two) Indo-Pakistan wars, i.e. 1962-64, 1965-66 and 1971-72. These were periods of national crisis when defence spending went up substantially and the government could raise taxes by exhorting people to be more patriotic. His conclusion is pessimistic. Even though the government raised tax rates and made valiant fiscal efforts to finance the war, it rarely maintained the momentum after the conflicts ended. In the short run, negligible surplus was generated for the domestic economy and almost all the additional revenue collected was exhausted in the 'war effort'. Rather, physical shortages appeared to throw the planning mechanism out of gear and the inter-industrial effects of the war economy created substantial problems (see Mathur, 1963). Despite the fact that the tax effort was raised during periods of national security crisis, the 'revenue effort slackened substantially after every year' (Gandhi, 1974). Moreover, overwhelming parts of the additional revenue 'was always absorbed by defence' not only during the war years but 'surprisingly even in later years' (Gandhi, 1974). The study of these special years for India, coinciding with the war effort, seem to imply that an additional tax burden to help defence does not have much of a spin-off in getting more resources for the rest of the economy.

It may be argued that analysing specific years may be misleading, since the effects are expected to continue for some time beyond the relatively short period in consideration. One may use time series data for the Indian economy to test the hypothesis as to whether defence expenditure increases (or decreases) the government budget *deficit* (expenditure minus revenue). Noting that additional military expenditure will probably lead to an increase in both budgetary revenue and spending, it is the deficit which matters in the final analysis. If deficits actually go down, then clearly the changes in the tax effort have been higher than the defence burden.

Using time series data again for India from 1960 to 1981 we have, using the Cochrane-Orcutt (CORC) procedure, the following estimated equations:

$$BD = \underset{(1.78)}{15.5} - \underset{(-2.58)}{0.099}\, ME \tag{3.1}$$

$$R^2 = 0.4016$$

$$NBD = \underset{(1.73)}{659.23} - \underset{(-3.92)}{0.077}\, NME \tag{3.1'}$$

$$R^2 = 0.6219$$

(*t*-ratios in brackets)

where *BD* is budget deficit and *ME* is military expenditure both in real terms and *NBD*, *NME* are their nominal values. (The variables *BD*, *NBD* have *negative* values when there is a *deficit*.) It is clear from the estimated equation that defence spending manages to *increase* the deficit in the central government budget, thus raising spending more than income. The additional tax effort, if any, is used up for defence and a further amount of resources needs to be directed towards the military sectors. Rather than creating extra resources, military spending seems to be reducing resources available for civilian use.

A cross-section study using part of our total country sample also revealed an interesting similarity to that reported for the single country. A tax effort (t) equation is estimated, where t is defined as total tax revenue as a proportion of GDP. It is assumed that the tax effort depends on the saving rate (s), military burden (m), growth of manufacturing (g_f), foreign capital inflow (a), exports share in national income (e), as well as *per capita* income (y). It is expected that manufacturing and export sectors of the economy have a high potential for tax collecting and this justifies the variables (g_f) and (e). Foreign capital inflows often lead to slackening of the tax effort and thus (a) is expected to have a negative coefficient. Saving propensity (s) and *per capita* income could have a positive effect on tax effort while the inclusion of the defence variable (m) is self-explanatory in the light of our previous analysis. The estimated equation is:

$$\underset{}{t} = \underset{(.68)}{4.206} + \underset{(.98)}{.417s} + \underset{(2.77)}{.858m} - \underset{(-.250)}{.065g_f} - \underset{(-.81)}{.3112a} + \underset{(1.88)}{.202e} + \underset{(.02)}{.003y}$$

$$R^2 = 0.4676 \qquad (3.2)$$

(The estimates are based on observation from twenty-seven countries from our original sample, for which data was available.)[4]

There is a definite positive effect of the defence burden on the tax effort. Note that a £1 increase in military expenditure (given GDP) raises tax revenue by £0.858. However, this also shows that the budget deficit also rises (of the order of £0.142) implying that the net effect on government revenue is not positive. Even though revenues rise consequent to extra milex, it is not sufficient to finance the additional defence burden.

This inability to meet defence expenditure from taxes has two implications. On the financial side, the monetary authorities need to be activised to meet the financial or nominal needs of the defence planners. On the real side, there is a diversion from other areas of government or private resources to meet this spending. The next section deals with the first problem while the second problem is analysed in later sections.

3.4 Budget deficit and money creation

The financial aspects of governments' attempt to increase military spending without a countervailing rise in taxation is important, since it may be the major conduit through which defence-induced inflationary pressures are generated in the economy. The links between budget deficit and money creation are worth analysing in some detail to understand the process.

The Central Bank in any economy controls the stock of high-powered money (H) which constitutes the monetary base. This consists of currency and commercial bank deposits to the Central Bank. Money (MN) may be defined as the sum of currency and deposits (both demand and time deposits). The relation between H and MN is given by the money multiplier m_1 where

$$MN = m_1 H \tag{3.3}$$

Thus money supply, as given by equation 3.3, is determined by the monetary base controlled by the Central Bank and the money multiplier which is a function of the reserve and currency behaviour of commercial banks and the public. The money multiplier is not a constant over time, since it in turn depends on various factors, including the rate of interest (Dornbusch and Fischer, 1978). The multiplier showing the increase in money stock for a unit increase in base is greater than unity and often larger than two.

The high-powered monetary base is linked with the budget deficit in the following way. Consider the government with two departments: the Treasury or Finance Ministry, which deals with budgets; and the Central Bank, which operates the monetary side of the financial system. For most LDCs, in practice, the two departments are closely linked so that they can be consolidated into one sector. However, for analytical purposes and taking account of their functional roles, it is preferable to keep them separate. Let the money value of the budget deficit (DF) of the Finance ministry be

$$DF = P(G-T) \tag{3.4}$$

where P is the aggregate price level and G and T the real value of government expenditure and tax revenue. This deficit can be financed in two ways, by borrowing from the Central Bank and by sale of bonds to the private sector. Since most LDCs have underdeveloped financial markets, the second method is generally inapplicable, thus the major and often the only way of financing the Finance Ministry budget deficit is to go to the Central Bank. The latter lends to the ministry by creating high-powered money. Thus we have

$$DF = P(G-T) = \Delta H \tag{3.5}$$

where ΔH is the change in H.[5]

Equation 3.5 is the government's financial constraint. An increase in G not financed by T must lead to a corresponding increase in the growth of high-powered money and the expansion of the monetary base. Assuming for simplicity that m is constant in the short run we have from equations 3.3 and 3.5,

$$P(G - T) = \Delta H = (1/m)\Delta(MN) \tag{3.6}$$

so that the deficit in turn increases the actual money stock in the economy. Monetary expansion in LDCs leads to or 'causes' an increase in the inflation rate. The effect may operate with lags, and the central relation between money and inflation is of course a matter of some controversy and debate (see Kirkpatrick and Nixson, 1976a). However, the basic point is accepted by both sides of the controversy, that an expansionary money supply is often associated with high inflation.

Equation 3.6 can then be used to trace out the inflationary

effects of military expenditure, through the budget-money link and the monetary nexus that operates in financially backward developing economies. If military expenditure is not fully financed by taxation, then an attempt to increase milex will raise the budget deficit. Since the scope of selling bonds to the public and conducting an open-market operation is very limited, most of the deficit is 'monetised' in the sense that it leads to an increase in the monetary base. This works through the money multiplier in increasing the actual stock of money (or its rate of growth) in the economy. Increased growth of monetary expenditure by the private sector increases the rate of inflation. Thus real military expenditure is potentially inflationary if the government financial constraints are taken into account.

A large number of case studies have demonstrated quite conclusively that defence spending can have inflationary effects in the absence of countervailing measures taken by the monetary/fiscal authorities. Fontanel (1982) gives empirical estimates for the wholesale price index of Morocco, which is strongly affected by milex: 'Military expenditure is the cause of very strong inflationary tensions.' Terhal (1981) and Gandhi (1974) produce evidence for the Indian economy in the 1960s, when high defence spending financed by successive deficit budgets was the cause of rapid price increases within the economy. A number of studies done for Latin America give similar results. Del Pando (1983) believes that the massive increase in military expenditure in Peru between 1971 and 1975 was a major cause of high price rises during 1977-80. Carranza's (1983) paper on the role of the military in the development process of Argentina also highlights the inflationary potential of additional milex.

The effect of inflation will be dealt with elsewhere in the book. What is undoubtedly true is that defence spending through the financial channels of monetary and fiscal policies is a major contributory factor towards inflation. This may be true for any item of public expenditure. But even when monetarist governments, like that of Chile between 1973 and 1980, try to reduce government spending *overall*, they maintain high military expenditure for reasons of security. Thus the ever-present threat of inflation remains.

3.5 Multipliers

Government expenditure can potentially stimulate aggregate demand, and if supply responds to additional demand then output will rise. The Keynesian multiplier formalises this concept. Given excess capacity in production, underutilised capital stock, less than fully employed labour and possibly other resources, as well as relatively stable prices, an increase in autonomous demand, generally emanating from the government, can increase output over and above the amount of the initial stimulus. Thus, under the postulated assumptions, a one-unit increase in government spending *cet. par.* may increase aggregate national output by *more* than one unit. Since military expenditure *is autonomous demand creation par excellence*, its increase is expected to add to total output.

There will be not only a short-term multiplier effect as predicted by Keynesian theory, but also the possibility of long-term growth. If producers have idle installed capacity due to lack of demand then they are not achieving the profit rate they should get by a more effective utilisation of capital. An increase in demand leading to a more efficient capacity (capital) utilisation may lead to an increase in the profit rate which will stimulate investment and ultimately increase the growth rate. As Faini, Arnez and Taylor (1984) so clearly state: 'A military twist on the basic Keynesian model is the most cogent argument in support of a positive impact of increased arms spending.'

Multiplier effects have been used to support the claim that a security-based autonomous increase of milex can have expansionary effects in developed countries.[6] On the other hand, LDCs have often been considered unsuitable for such analytical models. Essentially, given the *lack* of capital stock (rather than excess capacity), it has generally been thought that LDCs are supply-constrained rather than demand-constrained. It has been argued in the literature that aggregate demand is not an essential problem in developing economies. It is the short-term inelasticity of aggregate supply that is the source of low output. Thus government expenditures (including defence), rather than adding to output, only seem to fuel monetary inflationary pressures (as analysed before) or to increase the real inflationary gap. Incidentally, this has been the view generally taken by the IMF in its advocacy of contractionary stabilisation policies, claiming that credit restrictions and reduction in budget deficits will reduce inflation, but not output, since the aggregate supply is given by (fully utilised) capital and abundant labour.

Recent theoretical work done by the neo-structuralist school at MIT (see Taylor, 1980), as well as neo-Keynesian analysis for developing economies (see Chakravarty, 1984), has repeatedly shown that even in less developed countries there may be structural rigidities which can make output less than its potential level due to aggregate demand deficiency. Thus stimulating demand through say public spending (defence or otherwise) may increase total national output, though invariably at the cost of some price rises.

In practice LDCs may be either demand- or supply-constrained depending on the specific features of the country concerned. A simple analytical model taking both types of economies into consideration will now be discussed briefly. Consider an economy where aggregate demand is given by the sum of private consumption (C), investment (I), government civilian expenditure (CG), military spending (M), and trade surplus, exports minus imports ($X-R$). Assume for simplicity that trade is balanced, thus $X = R$. Then in equilibrium

$$Y = C + I + CG + M \quad (3.7)$$

where Y is national income (output).
Assume that private demand $C + I$ is a linear function of Y such that

$$(C + I) = bY + B \quad (3.8)$$

Similarly assume that CG is a linear proportion of Y while M is autonomous.

$$CG = gY + G \quad (3.9)$$

Then using equations 3.7, 3.8 and 3.9

$$Y = (1/1 - b - g)\ (M + \mathrm{A}) = (M/x) + (A/x) \quad (3.10)$$

where x = 1/1 − b − g is the usual Keynesian multiplier and $A = B + G$ the *autonomous* components of consumption, investment and civil government expenditure.

Now consider the case where the economy has a capacity constraint $Y = \bar{Y}$, such that national output cannot increase in the short run beyond $\bar{Y}$. The corresponding level of autonomous demand for milex that the economy can sustain at full capacity is clearly $\bar{M} = x\bar{Y} - A$. This is shown diagrammatically in Figure 3.1.

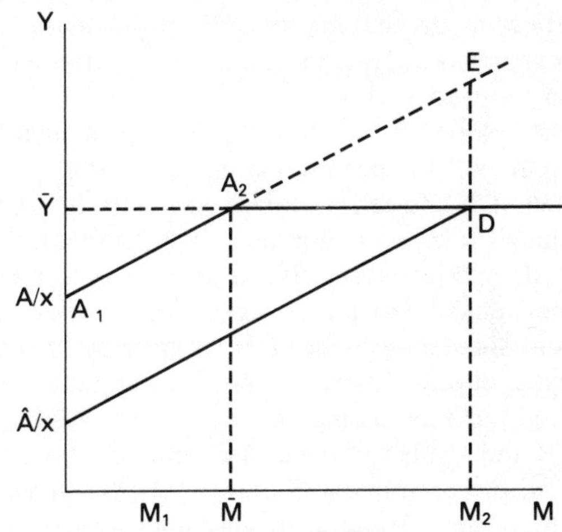

Figure 3.1 Capacity constraints and the multiplier

Now it is clear that if military expenditure in real terms is at M_1 less than $\bar{M}$, then any increase will give rise to the multiplier effect and output will rise along the A_1A_2 segment. However, if real military spending is sought to be raised above $\bar{M}$, say to M_2, then output is at its potentially maximum level $\bar{Y}$ and thus something must give in the short run.

There are two possibilities if the government persists in its effort to raise real military expenditure. If nonmilitary autonomous expenditure remains at its old level A, then clearly real M cannot increase. An inflationary gap will develop and prices will rise to increase nominal military expenditure without a corresponding change in real defence spending. The inflation that occurs here is conceptually different from that discussed in the previous section, though the actual mechanics could be related to each other. The inflationary gap is of the order of *DE* in Figure 3.1, which causes the price level or rate of inflation to rise (Keynes, 1940).

The alternative is that the civilian component of aggregate autonomous demand will be reduced from A/x to $\hat{A}/x$ so that $\bar{M}M_2$ amount of milex can be accommodated. This is the resource allocation effect in the short run. The effect on aggregate output is the same: GNP remains at $\bar{Y}$. However, the composition changes with extra milex substituting civilian spending A. The precise effect of the substitution will obviously depend on what the original A was intended for, and some of these effects will be studied in the next section.

The theory shows that LDCs can either be demand constrained with output at Y_1 corresponding to milex M_1, or supply constrained at $\bar{Y}$ and milex initially at $\bar{M}$. In the former case, an increase in M_1 causes a multiplier shift of output by $1/x$ times the change in defence spending. In the latter case, either an increase in $\bar{M}$ is not tenable but pushes up prices, or alternatively, if the government succeeds in raising M, it must be at the expense of civilian expenditures. There will be 'crowding out' and its precise effects need more investigation.

What is the evidence regarding demand stimulating by the military and the consequent multiplier, if any? Precise estimation is difficult, principally because it is not easy to identify which country is in which regime – demand- or supply-constrained. Further, a large number of other factors usually impinge on the volume of output in LDCs, therefore it is not always possible to isolate the effect of autonomous multipliers since the *ceteris paribus* condition is difficult to implement. Finally, some components of government expenditure are used for counter-cyclical stabilisation policies. An *expected* drop in household demand (due, say, to a bad harvest) may force the government to increase its own demand to stabilise output. It will then be difficult to separate out cause and effect and note precisely the effect of government spending.

With these difficulties in mind, the empirical evidence using time series and institutional data for at least two developing countries shows that some demand effects are discernible from military spending. Fontanel (1982) shows for Morocco that the military expenditure GDP relation is positive *only* if the multiplier effects are considered (though overall it has a negative impact taking other elements together): 'Military expenditure has a . . . direct impact on GDP . . . as an item of public expenditure it has a positive role.'

Benoit comes to the same conclusion using an Indian case study for the 1950s and early 1960s. Between 1950 and 1961 the government conducted contractionary stabilisation (monetary/ fiscal) policies, thus keeping demand growth in check. The war with China in 1962 forced very high budget deficits by historical standards and the aggregate demand effect operated to increase output and indirectly also growth. Terhal (1981), using a macroeconometric model for India, also shows that between 1962 and 1967 defence spending (as well as other categories of government budgets) had a positive effect on output through demand stimulation. But remember the warning by Olof Palme (1982), who observes that 'military spending adds to demand but unlike spending on roads, schools, hospitals it does little to improve productivity in the long run'.

The short-term aggregate demand effects on supply-constrained regimes will obviously be quite different and less beneficial. The IMF model mentioned earlier applies mostly to Latin American countries, where aggregate supply is the binding constraint, and demand creation does not raise actual output much above the potential level. Argentina, for example, during 1976-81 saw a rise in military expenditure, which increased from 2,424 million new pesos (at constant 1970 prices) in 1976 to 3,464 million new pesos in 1981, an increase of about 43 per cent. On the other hand real GDP rose by only 10 per cent while the aggregate price index (GDP deflator) increased by a staggering 134 per cent during these five years.

To understand the short-term multiplier effects of defence spending, therefore, one has to study the economy concerned and determine the specific aggregate constraint within which it operates. If GDP is determined by supply factors, then military spending as a component of government budgets might have undesirable real and inflationary effects. The precise nature of the real effects will clearly depend on the components of aggregate demand that are crowded out, and it is to these that we now turn.

3.6 Crowding out

When aggregate supply is near its potential capacity level with full employment of resources prevailing, an increase in milex will tend to displace other items of aggregate demand without creating the desired multiplier effect on output. This phenomenon of 'crowding out' is important when one wishes to study the macroeconomic impact of additional defence spending.

Crowding out may occur *within* the government budget so that milex reduces other items of net government spending. Alternatively, the size of the budget deficit increases in line with milex, and the axe falls on demand generated by the private sector such as investment or exports. We deal with each in turn.

Consider now the case in which additional defence spending is incurred at the cost of other forms of government expenditure. Total government spending can be subdivided into four major categories, consisting of defence, economic services, social services and welfare (development budget), and the rest (usually called 'other' in World Bank publications). Economic services comprise spending on agriculture, industry, electricity, gas, water, transport and communications, as well as tourism, flood control, etc. Social services consist of expenditures on education, health, social security and welfare as well as housing and community amenities. The relation between defence and social services is best left to Chapter 5, on human capital formation. It will also be dealt with in the context of overall development and the enhancement of the capabilities of the people of LDCs (see Chapter 9). The main trade-off that we are concerned with here is that between defence and economic services. It is possible that much of government investment for national growth is concentrated in the expenditure categories grouped under economic services. Further, the productivity of public expenditure may be quite high here. Finally, private sector expenditure, particularly for capital formation, may not be forthcoming in some sectors, and government intervention may be the only way for vital sections of agriculture, industry or transport to develop. As we shall see in Chapter 8, on growth, the development of the agricultural sector in particular may be quite crucial for overall growth rates. If there is a potential trade-off between defence and economic services, development may be retarded.

Development theories and practitioners have generally noticed a reluctance on the part of private enterprise to invest in agriculture, because the rate of return is low from the individual's point of view (the social rate of return may of course be high). In particular, backward agriculture, characterised by interlinked markets (Braverman and Stiglitz, 1982), may never get the full benefits of output-augmenting technical progress. The reason is simple. Traditional rural economies are often based on share-cropping, where the landlord and tenant-farmer share the total produce in a predetermined ratio. Innovations which increase total output would normally benefit both landlord and tenant in proportion to their shares. However, as Bhaduri (1973) has pointed out, the landlord is quite often the moneylender too, giving consumption loans to the tenant at usurious rates of interest, thus having a second source of income. After the landlord has introduced output augmenting technology (as during the Green Revolution), it is clear that his crop income will go up. But the tenant may borrow less or retire accumulated debts from previous loans, thus the interest income of landlord may fall. It is possible that total income, from crop share and interest, may be less than before the introduction of new technology. Thus important disincentives exist for private agents like rural landlords to invest in agriculture (S. Sen, 1983).

The foregoing analysis highlights the need for government intervention in agricultural investment to increase the productivity of the primary sector. As has been increasingly pointed out in a two-sector growth theoretic context (see Kaldor, 1975), growth of manufacturing is often constrained by the growth of agriculture. If agricultural productivity increases slowly while industry grows fast, the terms of trade (price of manufacture as a ratio of price of agriculture) will move *against* manufacture, since there is a relative excess supply of manufactured goods. A decrease in manufacture's term of trade will eventually slow down its progress because capitalists will have little incentive to invest when faced with declining relative prices. Ultimately the growth of the whole economy will suffer.

Economic development since the early Lewis dual economy models has been increasingly identified with industrialisation. But it is now recognised that industrial growth *needs* agricultural growth too and the essential complementarity of the two is crucial. Manufactures in LDCs need primary products as *inputs* which can be processed into industrial goods. In turn industrial outputs need to be sold to the primary sector where income (and saving) must be sufficiently high to absorb the sale of manufactures (as agricultural investment). If this interdependence is carefully scrutinised one sees the necessity of a more balanced approach to dual economy development.

We therefore have two interrelated concepts. Investment in agriculture is important for its own sake, for the development of the industrial sector and also for overall economic growth. However, private agents like landlords are not always willing or able to make this investment. The inescapable conclusion is that government intervention is needed on a relatively large scale. Thus government developmental expenditures, particularly agricultural investment, become an essential part of the whole process of economic growth.

We believe that one of the most pernicious effects of defence spending is when it potentially crowds out agricultural investment. As noted earlier, there is some evidence that even though tax effort rises with milex, the deficit rises even more so that the additional tax revenue is less than the extra defence spending. Thus some crowding out is inevitable, and in so far as that falls on agricultural expenditure, it has a much more undesirable effect than many other items of aggregate demand. Alternatively, if reduction of milex leads to an increase of rural investment and productivity increases in agriculture, then a virtuous cycle can easily be set in motion.

Lotz's (1970) study identified some trade-off between defence and developmental expenditures (he calls the latter 'economic services'). He estimated that a £1 increase in available resources to the state will raise defence spending by 8 pence while development categories will gain to the amount of 37 pence. Thus his data set showed that a more elastic revenue ceiling will help 'economic services' relatively more than the military. However, the major issue is different. The question is whether there is a negative relation between the same £1 being allocated from one item of budgetary expenditure to another. Lotz's correlation matrix shows that defence spending is negatively correlated to development spending – both as proportions of total government expenditure. The precise quantitative nature of the negative relation needs more research. But overall it is clear that some crowding out of government expenditure (both current and capital) in agriculture and other productive areas occurs, with undesirable consequences for the long-term prospect not only of the primary sector but of the whole economy including manufacturing.

Of the fifty countries in the control sample, data for the share of agriculture as well as defence in government total expenditure for 1967 and 1973 was available for thirty-four countries, in *World Tables* (1976). Comparing these two years, twenty countries showed a negative relationship between the two shares, eleven countries showed a positive relationship, while for three the relationship was indeterminate. Therefore for those thirty-one countries for which a clear relationship emerged, 65 per cent (twenty out of thirty-one) showed that as the defence share in government spending went up (down), the share of agricultural expenditure went down (up). A substantial majority of cases thus showed a negative trade-off. More generally, we can analyse the relation between economic services and defence, and try to see whether or not one increases at the expense of the other. Since we refer to, and analyse, a large number of cross-sectional econometric studies later on in the book, it may be fruitful to do a formal analysis of a single country at this stage.

We consider the case of Iraq during the period 1950-80. As oil revenue increased steadily during the 1960s and jumped to phenomenal levels after 1973, both defence and economic services gained in absolute terms since total government expenditure and revenue increased substantially. Thus there was no absolute trade-off between these two functional categories of state spending. In this respect, of course, Iraq is not typical of LDCs in general. However, we can still investigate the relationship between the *shares* of these two variables in total budgetary allocation. Since Iraq is surrounded by relatively hostile neighbours, defence has always had a high priority in governmental expenditures. We assume therefore that the share of defence in total spending (SDEF) is determined first, given the needs of security and threat. It is interesting, therefore, to note how the share of economic services (SES) responds to the prior levels of military allocations. It is also postulated that current levels of

Table 3.3 *Relation between economic services and defence share in government budgets in Iraq, 1950-80*

	(1)	(2)
	SES	SES
Constant	0.48	0.49
	(4.27)	(3.77)
SDEF	−0.86	−0.92
	(−3.64)	(−3.28)
SESI	0.34	0.45
	(2.54)	(3.10)
*D*1	0.11	—
	(4.73)	
R^2	0.9099	0.8526
Rho	—	0.38
		(2.29)

Sample size 31 (*t* ratios in parentheses).

SES are dependent on its past value, i.e. SES lagged one period (SES1). Table 3.3 gives the econometric estimates. The first equation in column 1 also includes a dummy variable *D*1 for the years 1973-80 when oil revenues were extremely high. The second equation (column 2) leaves out the dummy. No autocorrelation was observed for the first equation, so it is estimated by OLS. The second equation, on the other hand, showed evidence of first-order autocorrelation, and the estimation accounts for that. (Rho is the first-order autocorrelation coefficient, and its statistical significance should be noted.) The fit is good for both equations and all the variables are significant. The coefficient of SDEF is very high, implying that a unit increase in the share of defence *reduces* the share of economic services in the total budget by 0.9. There is a negative trade-off between defence and developmental expenditure by governments, of the order of (almost) one to one.

As mentioned earlier, even though Iraq will not be typical of LDCs who are generally more resource-constrained, it is instructive to see how high the trade-off can be potentially. When government revenue and spending are generally inelastic and do not change substantially, there may be an absolute decline of economic services when the defence burden increases. The 'crowding out' will then be quite harmful.

The second aspect of demand reallocation in the face of relatively rigid supply of the national product takes us out of the narrow confines of government budgets and on to other categories of aggregate demand. Recall the equilibrium condition

$$S = I + (G - T) + (X - R) \tag{3.11}$$

or

$$S = I + CG + M - T + X - R \tag{3.12}$$

Equation 3.11 is derived from 3.7, noting saving $S = Y - C - T$ where S is private saving, T is total tax paid and G is total government expenditure civilian and military. If now M rises without a countervailing change in CG and total revenue (T), then for a given level of output (and saving) there must be a trade-off with investment or exports. For LDCs, exports and military spending are generally autonomous with each other, thus investment demand must bear some of the pressure of change in milex. It is of course true that import R will rise, but clearly by not as much as M (only part of the domestic military burden is used to buy foreign defence products). Thus some reduction or crowding out of I is inescapable, though as we show elsewhere more fully (see Chapter 4) the effect is definitely not one to one for LDCs. Fontanel (1982) reports econometric evidence from Morocco which shows that an increase in the defence burden reduces investment, increases imports, and keeps exports relatively stable.

Overall, therefore, we expect that an increase in military spending does have some crowding out effects for many LDCs, particularly those that are predominantly supply-constrained. In particular, government's civilian expenditure, specifically investment in agriculture, may be reduced. This will have long-term adverse repercussions within the economy. The effect on private sector investment might also be negative. Unless the multiplier effects are very strong, overall the military's influence will be negative, since it will have short-term adverse effects on the economy and will also reduce future growth prospects and bring unnecessary inflation.

The discussion in this chapter has mainly concentrated on short-term resource allocation effects of military spending with special emphasis on the government budgetary process. But, as we have seen, there will also be indirect long-term effects, particularly if defence starts crowding out investment. The next chapter concentrates on the long-term effects via the saving and investment process.

4 Saving, investment and military expenditure

4.1 Capital formation

The importance of saving and investment in the growth process cannot be overemphasised. One of the most commonly used indices of economic development is a high *per capita* income. But *per capita* income can only rise if the growth of the national product is greater than the growth rate of population. Raising growth rates *per se* may not be the panacea of all developmental problems – this much is clear from the discussion in Chapter 1 – but it is certainly a major consideration. As is well known, increases in physical capital formation are an essential ingredient of raising growth.

The classical view of development would stress prior saving which would be translated, under equilibrium, to investment. This model therefore emphasises the supply side of resource creation. A more Keynesian view would be to stress investment demand, which if sufficiently high would pull up saving. An independent increase in investment raises national income which in turn produces more saving. The causation is relevant, but the basic point is more important. Saving and/or investment is important for development. This chapter therefore looks at this problem from the point of view of military expenditures.

As we have seen in the short run, the national income equilibrium condition gives us

$$Y = C + I + M + CG + X - R \tag{4.1}$$

Again defining

$$S = Y - C - T$$

we get in equilibrium

$$S = I + M + (CG - T) + (X - R) \tag{4.2}$$

or

$$(R - X) + (T - CG) + S = I + M \tag{4.3}$$

The first term $(R - X)$ is the excess of imports over exports, thus giving us the foreign capital inflows (foreign saving) required to finance the trade deficit. The second term $(T - CG)$ is the civilian budget surplus (total tax minus civilian government expenditure) and therefore a proxy for public sector saving. The third term on the left-hand side of equation 4.3 is domestic private sector saving. This is constituted of personal saving (from households) and corporate saving (from firms). Equation 4.3 therefore tells us that domestic investment and military expenditure are financed by three forms of saving: that emanating from the foreign sector (overseas saving), government fiscal surplus, and private or nongovernmental surplus of income over expenditure.

Already, the resource allocation effects of milex are clear from equation 4.3. If aggregate supply is fixed at its potential level, then an increase in military expenditure may crowd out investment (or other forms of government civilian spending (CG)). On the other hand, with a demand-constrained system, an increase in milex will have a multiplier effect, raising income and thus potentially also investment. Then there is little trade-off between investment and defence in the short run; rather milex may indirectly help investment.

In Chapter 3 we had a first look at aggregate demand creation by the military which could either have beneficial multiplier effects or adverse crowding out of productive expenditures. The emphasis there was on the government budget. We now discuss, in much more detail, the implications of these mechanisms for the *whole* economy. There will, inevitably, be some overlap in the analysis, but it is important to stress and clarify the issues as fully as possible. The short-term effects of strategic expansion on the economy will lead naturally to the long-term consequences related to capital formation, a study of which is the primary purpose of the present chapter.

LDCs are generally thought to be characterised by surplus labour (Lewis, 1954) and shortage of capital. Inadequate aggregate demand essentially means excess capacity, thus capital is not being fully utilised. This can occur in the short run due to rigidities in the system. It is difficult to envisage an economy on the long-term growth path not making full use of its capital stock. Thus we would expect long-term equilibrium to be characterised by full capacity production.

The reason for the foregoing statements is essentially quite simple. Consider a dual economy with a traditional sector, producing a subsistence good, and a modern sector. Since there is labour surplus, the real wage rate of labour is fixed at the subsistence level given by custom, tradition or law. In effect the modern sector can draw on this reserve of labour if they pay the fixed real wage. The crucial question is whether the given capital stock (in the short run) will be fully utilised or not. The answer depends on the type of rigidities that the system faces. Consider Figures 4.1 and 4.2, representing the modern sector. Aggregate output is produced by capital and labour and the production possibilities are given by the isoquants. Aggregate demand Y_m^D for modern sector output restricts the isoquant on which the economy will actually lie. The current rental wage ratio is given by the tangent to the isoquant at E_1 and E_2 and this is the short-term equilibrium. The difference between the two figures is that the first represents a fixed coefficient technology while the second gives perfect substitution between the two factors. Labour is unlimited, but capital is fixed at $\bar{K}$ (w is the fixed real wage, r is the rental price of capital service).

For the economy depicted by Figure 4.1, production takes place at E_1 and capital is underutilised to the order of K_1K essentially because of the fixed coefficient technology. Since the isoquants are L-shaped, the most efficient point of production is given by the vertex of the isoquant. Output is demand constrained at Y_m^D, so the specific isoquant is determined, giving production at E_1. Production at $\bar{E}$ would mean producing at potential output capacity, but low aggregate demand prevents this from occurring. For the economy shown in Figure 4.2, there are no rigidities in technology. If demand determines the isoquant Y_m^D, production could just as well take place at E_3,

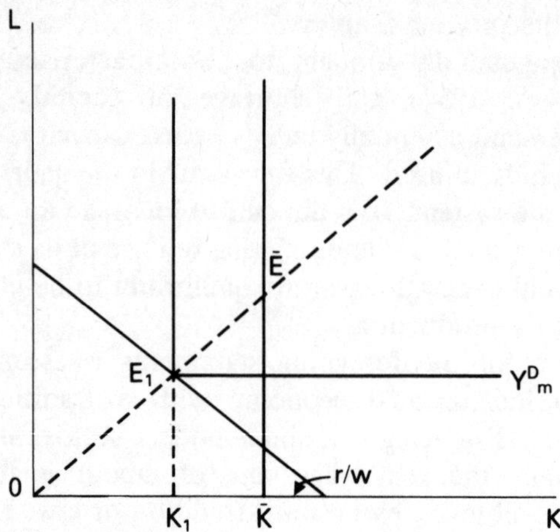

Figure 4.1 Underutilisation of capital stock: fixed coefficient technology

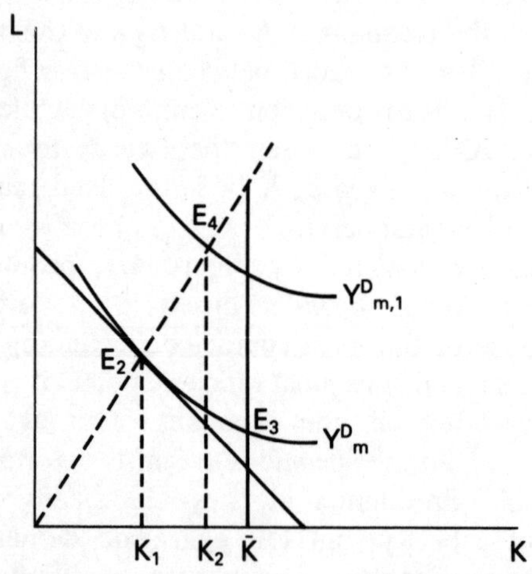

Figure 4.2 Underutilisation of capital: the possibility of factor substitution

provided the factor price ratio is right. Since there is excess supply of capital to the order of $K_1\bar{K}$, the factor price of capital service, i.e. r, should fall, capital intensity should rise, and the optimum point would be E_3. If therefore the underutilisation of capital stock persists, then clearly the price ratio r/w is rigid, thus production continues at E_2.

Under these circumstances, an increase in aggregate demand will boost production and raise output, since we have a demand-constrained system. Capacity utilisation will increase and so, under normal circumstances, will the amount of profits. If the *rate* of profit is given by total profit divided by the fixed capital stock, then this will rise too. A higher rate of profit may mean more investment and higher growth. The reasoning can be expressed more clearly by some simple algebra. Assume that output in the modern sector Y_m is determined by demand ${Y^D}_m$. The production function is

$$Y_m = F(K, L) = {Y^D}_m$$

The real wage rate w is fixed by the surplus labour economy at w. If the production function obeys constant returns to scale, then we have

$$F_1\, K + wL = {Y^D}_m$$
$$P + wL = {Y^D}_m$$

where P is total profit, and wL is total wages paid. Now consider a change in ${Y^D}_m$. We get, taking total differentials,

$$d{Y^D}_m = dP + wdL$$

(d represents the differential operator).

$$dP = d{Y^D}_m - wdL$$

Under plausible assumptions, dP will be positive, thus profits (P) will rise. The rate of profit is given by $k = P/\bar{K}$, where $\bar{K}$ is the fixed amount of installed capacity. Thus an increase in demand will cause the profit rate to increase.

This can easily be seen in Figure 4.2 if we continue to make the assumption that factor price ratio remains constant. Since w is fixed, this implies that r is a constant. Then increasing demand to $Y^D{}_{m,1}$ shifts the isoquant to the right and production takes place at E_4 (see Figure 4.2). The total profit earned goes up to rK_2 and the *rate* of profit is now $rK_2/\bar{K}$, which is greater than the previous rate $rK_1/\bar{K}$. Note that the profit rate is defined as total profits divided by installed capital stock ($\bar{K}$), and not capital in use.

Thus, if military expenditure rises, it can give a demand boost to domestic output, particularly in the modern sector. To quote Faini, Arnez and Taylor (1984, p. 488) once again: 'In an economy with excess production capacity, increased aggregate demand from the military or any other source will drive up output, capacity utilisation and (under plausible assumptions) profit rates. Investment may respond to higher profits increasing to put the economy on a faster growth path.' Aggregate demand effects work through increases in rate of profit and thus investment, provided, of course, there is unutilised capacity. This is specially true for the industrial sector, where lack of effective demand may be particularly important in LDCs. Econometric investigations reported in Faini, Arnez and Taylor (1984) for a large sample of developing countries show that a rise in the defence burden of about 10 per cent, in aggregate, could increase the share of industry in GDP by about 2 per cent. This is clearly a short-term multiplier effect of the type we described above. However, in their model the effect of defence is also strongly negative for investment in the long run. We now turn to a discussion of longer-term issues.

It is expected that in the long run both types of rigidities discussed earlier (technology and factor price ratio) will become less important. If capital has been installed, then not using it entails a cost to the economy. New technology will evolve and factor prices will ultimately change to eliminate the costs attached to underutilised capital. Thus we would have production taking place on the vertical through K.

With full utilisation of capital and output being at its potentially maximum level, the allocation costs of the defence burden increase in the long run. Multiplier effects are eliminated, but crowding out remains. Consider equation 4.3 once again. Assume that investment obeys the accelerator relationship so that

$$I = v\dot{Y} \tag{4.4}$$

(where $\dot{Y} = dY/dt$ is the rate of change of output with respect to time and v is the incremental capital-output ratio, ICOR, assumed fixed). Let us, for simplicity, take the case where the civilian budget surplus $(T - CG)$ and trade balance $(R - X)$ are a constant fraction of national product. Therefore

$$(T - CG) = xY \tag{4.5}$$

$$(R - X) = zY \tag{4.6}$$

Assume a constant long-term saving propensity $s = S/Y$. Putting equations 4.4, 4.5 and 4.6 into 4.3 and simplifying we have

$$g = \dot{Y}/Y = s/v + (x - z)/v - m/v \tag{4.7}$$

or

$$g = a + bs + cm \tag{4.8}$$

(g is growth rate and m military burden; $a = (x - z)/v$, $b = 1/v$, $c = -1/v$).

Equation 4.7 shows the long-term effect of the military burden on growth via the saving and investment process. Military spending, by reducing saving 'available for investment', has a long-term pernicious effect on the economy. If m rises, given all other parameters at their constant levels,[1] investable resources are less and growth falls. Equation 4.7 is an adaptation of the famous Harrod-Domar model of growth.

In the original Harrod-Domar framework, the incremental capital-output ratio (v) is held to be a constant. Thus the effect of saving propensity on growth, given by coefficient b in equation 4.8, reflects the productivity effect of additional capital formation. In other words, additional capital (through saving) creates additional output through the capital-output ratio and this contributes positively to growth. In the context of embodied technological progress (see Hahn and Matthews, 1969, and Dixit, 1976), an additional and important role can be ascribed to the saving propensity. Since technical progress occurs only through new machines (or the most recent vintage), in a vintage capital model additional saving will mean not only *more* capital stock but also *better* capital stock. The improvement in quality of vintage will have an independent growth-stimulating effect in addition to the standard one given by v. Even if one assumes fixed coefficients in technology, i.e. a fixed input-output structure as in a clay-clay vintage capital model, higher saving will lead to higher growth (i) through capital formation *per se* as well as (ii) through new machines embodying the latest technological inventions.

The role of the military in reducing investable resources is even more damaging from this point of view of growth. If an increased defence burden means that the amount of new capital formation reaches a lower level than it could have attained, then the economy suffers in a lowering of both the *quantity* and the *quality* of its capital stock. This could have potentially even more damaging effects on growth rates as compared to a state where no embodied technical progress takes place. Thus equation 4.8 should be rewritten as

$$g = a + b's + c'm \tag{4.9}$$

where b' and c' now represent the productivity of physical capital as well as the vintage effect of efficiency capital.

Overall, saving and investment behaviour are important for growth and development. Thus any analysis of the economic effects of military expenditure will have to dwell intensively on the supply of investable resources. The next two sections analyse in turn the relationship of military spending with saving and investment respectively. The reason for keeping them separate is because, in LDCs, not all saving is automatically converted into productive investment. A rise in saving does not necessarily mean a rise in investment, because the latter might be constrained by the absorptive capacity of the economy which sets an upper limit to the optimum level of investment. Conceptually it is better to treat them separately, since the effect of military spending works through different channels.

4.2 Milex and domestic saving

In short-term equilibrium, domestic investment is financed by private saving, public saving and the balance of trade deficit (proxy for foreign savings). In what follows we shall concentrate on the first and show its relationship with military expenditure. Government budget surpluses have already been dealt with, and the trade balance will be analysed in Chapter 6.

There are two major ways in which defence spending may influence the average propensity to save of the private sector (i.e. both corporate and personal saving), and thus help or hinder the mobilisation of new resources. First, structural change induced by the military may alter the rate of time preference which in turn will affect current consumption and therefore saving. Second, government expenditure caused by defence will contribute to inflationary forces which in turn may lead to 'forced saving'.

The rate of time preference is crucial in determining households' consumption and saving function. It is expected that in LDCs the rate of time discount will be high, thus causing a low propensity to save. It can be formally shown that a decrease in the rate of time preference will increase the average propensity to save.

There exist a number of ways by which military expenditure can affect the rate of time preference and thus influence the saving-income ratio. If the primary purpose of defence spending is to maintain security and protect the country from threats (as proposed in Deger and Sen, 1984a), then a rise in military budgets should increase domestic stability. In principle, a higher defence outlay should contribute to 'peace' and security, thus allowing people to take a longer intertemporal view of the consumption/saving decision-making. Military expenditure may be necessary to guarantee the conditions under which production and consumption can proceed in an orderly fashion through military influence on administration, social structure and international security. However, the opposite may also be true. By conducting an arms race with neighbours, increasing belligerence, plus greater exploitation and ruthless subjugation of internal dissent, the military may heighten the degree of insecurity. In that case, military expenditure will certainly increase the rate of time preference and decrease saving propensities.

Another line of reasoning that links defence spending and saving rate through time preference should be emphasised. When LDC governments decide to increase military outlay given relatively inelastic total budgets (Lotz, 1970), they have to reallocate resources away from other uses. It is expected in the light of our previous discussion that the axe will fall on items of government expenditure which constitute the 'social wage', public spending on education, health, transport, social services and transfer payments. Given the state of underdevelopment and the lack of institutional protest from society (from say powerful trade unions or consumer associations), it is much easier for the authorities to reduce the social wage. Private agents will therefore have to compensate for the lack of state-sponsored amenities, by increasing their own expenditure on these items of the household budget. Essentially, a reduction or withdrawal of provision for public goods will mean some rise in consumption as a share of income. Thus the propensity to save may fall. If time preference is low, then there might be a tendency to provide more for the future. But given household expenditure at the edge of subsistence, where most LDC inhabitants reside, the rate of discount will be high and it would be considered preferable to spend now on these essentials rather than save for the future. Consequently a rise in the defence burden may lead to a fall in the saving ratio.

Private saving is essentially income minus expenditure. If the rise in milex implies a lower provision of goods which were being provided by the government, then the private sector must increase its expenditure to accommodate this withdrawal of public services. However, individuals are usually not myopic and have some form of intertemporal optimisation. The question is whether they will spend more in the current period (the present) on the services crowded out by the military, or leave it for a future period. If they take the latter decision, then their saving will rise, since saving is essentially for spending in the future. However, with many households at the edge of subsistence or very poor, these decisions may not be taken in optimum fashion. People may be *forced* to spend now, rather than save for the uncertain future. It is highly probable therefore that milex causes a decline in the private sector's saving-income ratio.

Let us now consider the defence burden, inflation and saving.

All forms of public expenditure can be potentially inflationary. This may be because the initial resource situation is tight and the economy is operating near full capacity where an increase in aggregate demand causes an inflationary gap. Governments may have recourse to deficit financing and increase monetary growth as a means of financing additional spending. Further, such spending can exert an upward pressure on wages and other costs which induces a cost push inflation. An increase in the defence burden therefore may cause inflation, as was repeatedly emphasised in the previous chapter.

The effect of inflation on mobilisation of resources is more problematic. Leaving aside the special cases of hyperinflation, it is possible that inflation may cause 'forced saving' and provide an incentive for new resources to be forthcoming. Faced with rising prices, transactors might decide to save more for the future, deciding that their real earning accruing in later periods should be protected from the ravages of inflation. If real saving takes place because agents wish to achieve a certain targeted real wealth, then in any period people will save when the target exceeds their current wealth and dissave otherwise. Thus saving is dependent on the difference between target and actual wealth. Suppose that the private sector holds some nominal assets (such as cash, bonds denominated in money, etc.), as part of its wealth. When inflation occurs, the price level rises and the current *real* value of these nominal assets fall. Thus the difference between target and actual wealth widens, and current saving rises. Here inflation increases savings.

However, there are three important reasons why inflation may cause the saving-income ratio to fall and thus impede the mobilisation of resources. Firstly there may exist money illusion, thus a rise in nominal (money) income due to a rise in prices will cause real consumption spending to increase. Consider the simplest possible case, where real consumption is a function of money value of income:

$$C = a + b[PY]$$

where C, Y, P are aggregate consumption, real income and price levels respectively. Define real saving as

$$S = Y - C - T = -\mathrm{a} + [1-bP]Y - T \qquad (4.10)$$

where T is total tax payment net of transfers. Thus a rise in the price level causes a rise in real consumption and a corresponding fall in real saving. The example is simple but highlights an important concept for LDCs, where people may have money illusion and assume a rise in nominal income, with offsetting price rises, as a signal to increase real consumption.

Secondly, if current inflation contributes adaptively to an expectation of a high rate of inflation for the future, people may decide to consume currently rather than later, when prices may be prohibitively high. This could be particularly relevant for consumer durables. Finally, the saving propensity is positively related to the real rate of return (r). By the Fisher equation we have

$$\begin{aligned} i &= r + p \\ r &= i - p \end{aligned} \qquad (4.11)$$

where i is nominal interest rate and p is rate of inflation. Remember $p = (1/P)(dP/dt)$, or the proportionate rate of change of price P with respect to time. For a given nominal interest rate i an increase in p will cause the real return r to fall and thus the saving-income ratio will decline. There are good reasons for believing that inflation *per se* may not be helpful in raising saving.

Evidence on inflation, saving and growth is so contradictory that it is difficult to pass a clear-cut judgment. Inflation might lead to 'forced saving' or to an increase in profitability which induces higher investment. On the other hand, expectations of continuing inflation might cause a spending boom, conspicuous consumption and investment in low-priority sectors which clearly have no growth potential. Cross-section studies reported by Thirlwall (1974) reveal no strong bias in either direction.

Looking at an individual LDC and its historical development might be more useful. But the paucity of relevant data makes it again a hazardous exercise. It is probably more instructive initially to consider, analytically, the case of inflation and growth in a theoretical framework of a Lewis (1954) type model of economic development with unlimited supplies of labour. Lewis considers the case of an agricultural LDC with untapped reserves of labour whose current marginal product in agriculture is almost zero and who can be transferred (relatively costlessly) for employment elsewhere. The main constraints on such an economy are capital and land. It is difficult to employ this reserve army of labour in the consumption goods industry without reallocation of existing capital and productive land which are fixed. But certain forms of capital formation such as construction or road building are extremely labour-intensive and require very little of the scarce resources. Surplus labour is used therefore for capital formation. They are paid wages and generally financed by credit creation (increase in money supply), which has been termed as 'liberalisation of monetary fiscal policies'. This by itself is inflationary and is a direct route by which inflationary finance is used for investment and growth. But the effects are short-term and we are more interested in longer-term analysis. Since the supply of wage goods is relatively inelastic, the price of such goods rises faster than that of capital goods. It becomes more profitable to invest in the consumption goods industry and this drives scarce resources away from more productive areas of the economy. Conspicuous consumption increases as some sections of the community take advantage of rising income due to inflationary profits. Imports of luxury foreign products rise with a reduction in exports. The recent history of Iran and Turkey shows evidence of such inflationary effects going against growth and development.

The solution is to have a strong government which can capitalise on this spiral. Lewis gives an example of the Soviet Union where during the crucial years when the economy was being transformed from a 5 per cent to a 20 per cent net saving-income ratio, hyperinflation took place simultaneously. But the inflation profits largely went to the government in the form of turnover taxes. It is unlikely that in most present LDCs the government has the power or inclination to mop up this surplus with politically unpopular measures. The alternative to believing in such government action is to assume the existence of a capitalist class which uses these high inflationary profits to invest in the capital goods industry and has a long-term perspective on economic development. Once again most LDCs rarely have a class with such entrepreneurial motivation; rather 'animal spirits' are used for quick profits in a wage goods industry which has little growth potential. In any case, landlords, rentiers and hoarders will probably take a large share of inflationary profits and will use it for conspicuous consumption.

The prototype model just analysed may not be the only one that developing countries face; it is used for exposition only, and too much should not be read into it. The point is that, for long-term growth, inflation may have undesirable effects and one cannot pass judgment easily on these issues.

The relationship between defence, inflation, saving and growth has been stressed often in the literature. Benoit gives the example of India after the Sino-Indian war in the early 1960s:

> A possible link . . . was through inflation. I had originally supposed that, even if heavy defence burdens caused inflation, this could only pull resources away from civilian uses, not increase their total. I observed, however, that in India the mainland Chinese attack of 1962-63 resulted in rapid increases in defence spending, a liberalization of monetary fiscal policies, a considerable rise in prices, and a substantial speed up in the rate of real increase in civilian goods and services – until the very bad harvests of 1965 and 1966. (Benoit, 1978)

The causation that he emphasises is straightforward. An increase in defence expenditure as a share of GDP raises the rate of inflation. This in turn brings unutilised resources into economic use, and is thus helpful to economic development.

> It seemed likely that the need to finance heavy defence burdens had induced certain countries to relax their strict monetary fiscal policies, leading to more inflation than would otherwise have occurred – but this inflation, unless extreme, had succeeded in pulling into economic use unused or underutilized resources which contributed to real growth. (Benoit, 1978)

The first link in the chain of reasoning is beyond question. What remains doubtful is whether the second line of reasoning holds good. Defence spending is usually inflationary and the various budget-money links emphasised in the previous chapter show it to be true. But the major question is whether national saving is positively affected by inflation.

Empirical evidence is clearly required.[2] Investigation with our fifty-country sample showed that when the saving-income ratio is regressed on inflation, defence and other exogenous variables, a negative and often highly significant relation emerges. This can be seen with the econometric specification given below, which makes saving-income ratio (for the whole economy) (s), a function of defence burden (m), growth rate (g), rate of inflation (p), foreign capital inflows as a proportion of GDP (a), and *per capita* income (y).

Thus we have

$$s = a_0 + a_1m + a_2g + a_3p + a_4a + a_5y \tag{4.12}$$

a_1 gives the influence of military spending on saving through stability, structural change and time preference. a_2 shows the influence of growth rate via the life cycle theory of consumption; so also does a_5; a_3 emphasises the role of inflation on saving as discussed earlier; while a_4 represents the foreign capital effect on domestic saving which is postulated by Weiskopf (1972) as negative.

The regression results are as follows:

$$\underset{(10.95)}{s = 12.3} - \underset{(-3.23)}{.34m} + \underset{(4.67)}{.77g} + \underset{(6.01)}{.32y} - \underset{(-2.35)}{5.77p} - \underset{(-9.38)}{.65a}$$

$$R^2 = .8963$$

The coefficients for growth and income are positive as expected from theoretical considerations. Similarly, foreign capital has a negative impact on domestic saving-income ratio. The coefficients on inflation and the military burden are interesting. Both inflation and the military burden *reduce* saving for a given level of income, and the average propensity to save falls. All coefficients are significant; R^2 is very high.

The military burden thus has two reinforcing negative effects on the supply and mobilisation of resources. It reduces saving (as a ratio of national income) directly, given our cross-sectional sample results. It also increases inflation, which in turn *reduces* saving once again. Thus from the structural and time preference, as well as from the point of view of inflation defence has a negative effect. Even though theoretically we cannot say which direction the effect of the defence burden on savings income will go, empirical results show the adverse consequences.

Curiously enough, the literature on the military burden in LDCs has been generally silent on this important issue.[3] Most of the analysis has stressed the demand side of resource creation, concentrating on the role of investment. The latter is important, and we deal with it in the next section. However, more attention and more research, we believe, should be devoted to the supply of investable resource, and how the military may be having a detrimental effect on resource mobilisation *in addition* to the standard reallocation effects.

4.3 Investment

The previous section noted that military expenditure may have a negative effect on private sector saving and can thus depress the aggregate saving-income ratio. However, this is not sufficient by itself to postulate that investment will also be adversely affected. Benoit (1973) has claimed that there is no necessary trade-off between investment and defence spending, thus a reduction in the latter does not necessarily mean an increase in capital formation; rather the extra resources released may be frittered away on conspicuous consumption. Therefore countries which have a low defence burden do not necessarily have a high investment rate and thus a high growth rate for national output. There is an element of truth in this explanation. However, as we shall see, even though the relationship between milex and fixed capital formation is complex and not amenable to simple explanations, overall there is a growth-depressing effect via reduced investment when military expenditures are increased.

Investment can be viewed from the demand or supply side of aggregate resource mobilisation, as we have mentioned in Section 1 of this chapter. On the demand side both investment and military spending are competing for the national product in the short run. If milex rises and there is excess capacity as well as a surplus of labour then output will increase and there need not be a reduction in other components of aggregate demand such as investment. Rather, the increase in national output will *cause* investment to rise also, if of course we make the reasonable assumption that investment is a positive function of output. This is the standard operation of the 'multiplier'.

If, however, there are supply bottlenecks and output cannot rise commensurately with the autonomous expansion of the defence sector, then some component of aggregate demand will have to fall to accommodate the rising milex. This is the opposite extreme, that of 'crowding out', where relatively rigid aggregate supply in the short run needs reallocation among various categories of national demand. This much is well known.

Smith (1980) has suggested that, for *developed* economies, there may be a one-to-one trade-off between military spending and investment shares in Gross Domestic Product (GDP). For a given level of GDP, the share of the 'social wage' (private consumption and publicly provided goods for social consumption) is relatively inflexible. Public opinion expressed through the ballot box, and institutional pressure from the trade unions and other such bodies, prevent governments in these countries from reducing the proportion of the social wage in national income. Thus an increase in the share of the military in aggregate demand comes necessarily from an equivalent reduction in the investment share. Note that this analysis is conducted in terms of the proportion of national product that is devoted to each category of expenditure. Thus we can have both investment and milex rising together and no absolute crowding out. However, in terms of ratios, if the social wage hypothesis is right, there is a one-to-one trade-off between defence and capital formation.

It is difficult to apply these hypotheses to LDCs. A spirit of 'militarism' on the one hand and nondemocratic internal repression on the other help the establishment to increase defence budgets at the expense of the social wage. Econometric evidence exists (see Deger, 1981) that there is a significant negative relationship betwen the defence burden and the share of national output going to education (one major part of the social wage). It is quite feasible for policy-makers to pass the cost of a rise in defence spending on to other components of the social wage. As Sivard (1983) claims: 'The military impact is most direct and unambiguous in the allocation of public funds. Military and social programs must compete for shares of limited national budgets.' Thus it is highly unlikely that a £1 (or 1 per cent) increase in milex (or the defence burden) will reduce physical capital formation equiproportionately. There are many ways in which LDC governments can spread the impact of defence spending.

At this stage it may be instructive to look at the data and conduct some preliminary econometric investigations. For our cross-section sample of fifty countries, we investigated the nature of alternative investment equations with defence as an independent argument. Table 4.1 summarises the results. In every equation, the growth rate (*g*) and the share of defence in GDP (*m*) appear as explanatory variables. Other important variables such as exports (*e*), imports (*r*), balance of payments (*b*) (all as proportions of total output) are included too.[4] Note that in every single case the estimated parameters for the defence share in the investment equation is significant and negative. There can be little doubt empirically that an increase in defence spending leads to a reduction in investment as a proportion of GDP. However, the absolute value of the coefficient of defence is well below unity. This is unlike the results for OECD countries as shown by Smith (1977, 1980), and reflects the negative effect on the social wage in LDCs.

Table 4.1 *Investment equations with defence as an independent variable*

C	11.31	10.08	15.19	11.76	12.49
	(7.70)	(8.10)	(10.82)	(7.3)	(10.9)
g	0.489	0.794	0.503	0.473	0.831
	(2.8)	(4.9)	(2.5)	(2.6)	(4.85)
m	−0.239	−0.322	−0.172	−0.238	−0.433
	(−2.3)	(−3.7)	(−1.6)	(−2.3)	(−2.0)
y	0.258	0.292	0.293	0.264	0.315
	(4.38)	(5.9)	(4.5)	(4.4)	(6.2)
e		0.196	−0.04		
		(−4.6)	(−1.0)		
b					0.297
					(−4.0)
*D*1					1.25
					(0.407)
r			−5.211	−2.08	−4.8
			(−1.6)	(−0.7)	(−1.9)
R^2	0.5533	0.7002	0.4977	0.5583	0.6920

The analysis from the demand side and for the short term shows that there is an inevitable reduction in the investment share as the military burden goes up. However, the impact is quite small (about one-third) compared to the OECD results. If our concern is purely for the short-term effect on physical capital formation (investment) of increased national security-related milex, then there is not much to worry about.

But there is also the supply side. In a classical world, where all saving is automatically invested, there is little need to discuss the aggregate volume of investment separately. It has been noted already that an increase in the military burden can reduce the saving rate and thus the investment rate from the point of view of resource supply. However, in LDCs, all saving may not be *productively* invested, not because of lack of demand as in the Keynesian model, but because of extraneous constraints on the investment process. These constraints have been termed the absorptive capacity, and it is this absorptive capacity of the economy to utilise investment properly that finally sets the upper limit on investment, independent of the total saving that the economy may generate.

Therefore the problem for LDCs is that even if sufficient funds are available, the amount of investment is often limited by the economy's ability to absorb capital. This has been analysed by Horvat (1958), Adler (1965), Chenery and Strout (1966), Marris (1970) and many others. To quote Marris (1970), absorptive capacity relates to a 'growth rate constrained by factors *other* than either "saving" or "foreign exchange", in other words by factors such as the supply of skilled labour, administrative capacity, entrepreneurships, social change etc.'. Development theorists generally agree that two countries with the same rate of capital accumulation (as well as similar vintages), may have widely different levels of growth due to a difference in their potential for utilising investment, given by absorptive capacity.

This concept can be formally understood by considering the technical progress function as proposed by Kaldor. We have a relation between the growth of capital stock *per capita* ($\dot{k}/k$) and the growth of income per head ($\dot{y}/y$), given by

$$\dot{y}/y = p(\dot{k}/k) \tag{4.13}$$

The restriction on the technical progress function is given by

$$p'>0,\ p''<0,\ p(0)>0$$

Note that when $\dot{k}/k = 0$, $\dot{y}/y>0$. In other words, an economy with no capital accumulation *per se* can still have a positive growth rate of output. This could happen because of disembodied technical progress which affects existing capital stock and increases its productivity with time. However, for LDCs we could interpret this phenomenon as an increase in absorptive capacity. If co-operative factors such as skill, familiarity with machines and knowledge of how to use them, management expertise, etc., increase, then the same capital can be used to produce more output. Thus, the intercept of the technical progress function can be used as an index of measuring absorptive capacity. The two curves in Figure 4.3 relate to countries I and II and it is obvious that the latter has a higher absorptive capacity. Thus at the same level of capital formation say $(\dot{k}/k)_1$, output growth is higher for country II.

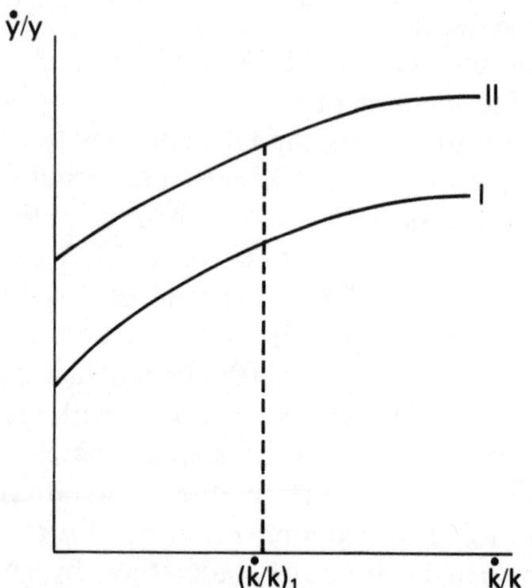

Figure 4.3 Technical progress function and absorptive capacity

It is difficult to predict *a priori* how the military might affect the stock of co-operating factors which increases the productivity of existing capital and raises the capacity of the economy to absorb new investment. Benoit (1978), Kennedy (1974), Johnson

(1962), Pye (1962a), and others claim that the military has a strong 'modernisation' effect, adds to the infrastructural base of the country, trains people in new skills, allocates resources towards R&D, creates effective demand for underutilised industrial capacity, maintains security, instils discipline and work ethos – all of which will increase absorptive capacity and have growth-stimulating effects. On the other hand, given stringent resource constraints, the military will reduce the amount of co-operating factors going to productive civilian enterprises and so have a detrimental effect on investment and growth. Further, military spending is geared to strategic considerations and thus may not have any economic productivity. Roads may be built in inaccessible regions, the infrastructure created may be unsuitable for civilian use, trained personnel may not return to their original occupations and the spirit of 'militarism' may be used for external adventures and internal repression. All of this will certainly reduce absorptive capacity and negatively affect investment.

In a little-discussed paper called 'The optimum rate of investment', Horvat (1958) gives one of the earliest and possibly the clearest exposition of the concept of absorptive capacity. It is interesting to note that he leaves military expenditure out of his analysis,[5] and thus the interconnections of the military with absorptive capacity is totally ignored. We will come to the defence aspect later; let us first see what the concept entails. The economy is conceived of as a large productive enterprise which, given the volume of investment, has a *maximum* potential capacity for growth. It can of course grow at a slower rate, but never faster than the maximum. The ratio between additional output and investment is called the 'production coefficient' (p). Thus p is a productivity variable, and is a function of the level and changes of investment (I) and absorptive capacity (A). We therefore have

$$p = f\,(I, dI/dt;\ A, dA/dt)$$

(where dI/dt is the rate of change with respect to time, etc.). 'Investment has to be absorbed by the economy. How well this will be done depends on the factor A' (Horvat, 1958).

According to Horvat the variable A denoting absorptive capacity depends on four more variables – personal consumption, health, knowledge, as well as the overall organisation of the economy, both political and economic. Consumption has essentially an incentive value for individuals in poor societies. It may also have direct nutritional effects: a man who eats well works well, particularly if he was undernourished before. Health, of course, has a direct productivity effect which is difficult to deny. The role of these variables in increasing the marginal product of *labour* has been noted elsewhere in the efficiency wage literature. Horvat is here emphasising that the marginal return to *capital* will also increase if the co-operating factors are better fed, well-nourished and healthy. Note the close connection between his concepts and that of human capital. The role of knowledge and the technological frontier are obvious candidates for inclusion here. Finally comes the institutional set-up, the socio-cultural, political and economic organisations within which investment has to be carried out. Political independence, a social revolution, internal and external stability will all increase absorptive capacity and improve the productivity of investment.

It is obvious that the saving that an economy generates, and potentially wishes to invest, may not be equal to the amount that it can absorb. Clearly, the absorption of investment, giving a positive marginal product, is relevant; simply investing because one has the savings is not good enough. Thus the concept of absorptive capacity drives a wedge between actual savings (which are equal to actual investment, by definition) and *effective* investment, i.e. the investment capable of generating positive marginal returns. Potentially there is a maximum to effective investment for a given economy at any point of time. 'Investment is . . . relative, it is the share of investment in social product which is analytically meaningful. Given enough time, the share of investment may be increased as far as we like (short of 100%). The question is only whether the economy will absorb it' (Horvat, 1958).

There are also obvious interrelationships between I and A. At any point in time, investment is limited by absorptive capacity. However, as the former takes place, the frontier of the latter moves out, so that the economy's capacity to undertake more investment in the future is enhanced; the potential ability or will to work, the number of skilled technical workers and scientists, as well as the institutional infrastructure, are all interrelated with investment; the former constraining the latter in the short run, but expanding in the long run.

We believe that the role of the military in changing or influencing absorptive capacity is quite crucial in understanding the long-term impact of defence on supply and use of resources for investment and finally growth. Later chapters will emphasise separate categories of absorptive capacity. One component is human capital, and Chapter 5 deals exclusively with this. Further, much of the 'spin-off' that the military provides (and for that matter the 'kick-backs'), can be slotted under the generic heading of absorptive capacity also. In Chapter 9, on economic development, we discuss many of these relevant issues in the context of modernisation. Finally the analysis of arms production also has an indirect bearing on these concepts. The theme of absorptive capacity is extremely important in understanding the economic position of the military.

If we look specifically at the four basic factors that Horvat mentions as constituents of absorptive capacity, we find the effect of military expenditure ambiguous *a priori*. It has been claimed that military spending by repressive regimes reduces personal consumption. The military government of General Videla in Argentina (1976-81) engineered a severe economic recession in attempting to curb inflation by reducing liquidity, imposing credit controls and cutting back on aggregate demand. However, defence spending rose, possibly due to the prospect of war with Chile over the Beagle Channel and later due to the Falklands/ Malvinas conflict. GDP fell by about 3.5 per cent between 1977 and 1978; all categories of aggregate demand were affected. But private consumption expenditure was probably hardest hit. Carranza (1983) claims that consumption in 1978 in real terms was the same as that of 1972. Data from *World Tables* (1980) also shows a sizeable drop in personal consumption in the first two years of military rule in Argentina. Thus there is some evidence for the hypothesis that milex might force a reduction in consumption. However, countervailing evidence can also be shown for other countries. Consider the case of Peru, where the left-leaning military government increased military expenditure quite substantially from around 1972-73. The establishment of right-wing governments in various countries surrounding Peru (Bolivia, Ecuador, Argentina, Brazil) increased the sense of insecurity felt by the Peruvian junta. But foremost consideration was probably given to the overthrow of the Allende regime in a military coup conducted by General Pinochet in Chile,[6] who also happened to be at the opposite end of the politico-economic spectrum. The trend reversed from about 1976-77. Table 4.2 uses the figures for defence expenditure and the defence burden for Peru taken from del Pando (1983) as well as consumption and GDP data from World Tables. Though the bases are different only the trends are relevant, and they clearly show the movement of consumption and milex.

Table 4.2 *Milex, consumption and GDP for Peru, 1973-76 (constant prices ml. of soles)*

	1972	1973	1974	1975	1976
Milex	8,474	11,009	9,420	12,356	9,256
Defence burden (%)	3.3	3.8	3.1	4.0	2.9
Consumption	266,665	280,600	293,197	303,375	313,773
GDP	376,501	392,559	421,933	441,073	449,987
Consumption-income ratio (%)	79.9	71.5	69.5	68.8	69.7

Source: Rows 1 and 2 from del Pando (1983); cols 3, 4 and 5 from *World Tables* (1980). Milex is in 1970 prices while consumption and GDP are in 1973 prices.

Over the period, milex went up substantially in 1973 and 1975, but consumption expenditure generally rose throughout, almost independent of defence spending. In 1973 both the defence burden and the consumption-GDP ratio rose; they both fell in 1974. Milex showed a cyclical pattern, giving evidence of inertia. Real consumption increased steadily. Thus the apparent conflict between milex and consumption is not clear-cut. Our theoretical discussion in the previous section would suggest that it is possible that recorded consumption spending actually *goes up*, since the extra defence burden may reduce the supply of civilian public goods.

Again on health, education and technological progress the role of the military can be to reallocate the stock of absorptive capacity so that less is available for the more productive civilian sectors. Chapter 5 shows that government spending on human capital formation is negatively related to the military burden, thus some components of absorptive capacity must suffer as a result of higher milex. It is highly unlikely that households' private expenditure on those items can compensate for the reduction in government effort. However, the military may itself contribute to civic action programmes, training and medical facilities as well as R&D, which will have a positive effect on absorptive capacity. At this stage no conclusions will be drawn, since this is the subject matter of a future chapter.

Finally comes organisation, the fourth basic factor of Horvat. Here too opinions differ sharply. Military institutions and organisational structures are in the vanguard of modernisation at the one extreme, and bastions of institutional inertia at the other extreme, with many shades of opinion in between. Again case studies supporting either point of view can be given and a final judgment is problematic. We shall return to these issues later.

To sum up briefly, LDC military expenditure may not crowd out investment from the demand side in the same way as in OECD countries. Benoit (1978) is quite right when he claims that in developing countries 'only a small part of any income not spent on defence is put into highly productive investment'. Thus an expansion in milex may not mean an equivalent fall in investment, and similarly for a decrease in milex. However, adverse effects may be present primarily through the absorptive capacity constraints that LDCs habitually face. If military spending reduces the absorptive capacity of the civilian sector, then investment will suffer even though investable funds are available. There is evidence that although the military contributes somewhat to absorptive capacity, its net effect in reducing health and education expenditure, and thus reducing human capital formation, might ultimately cause more harm to investment and growth than simply crowding out.

5 Human capital formation

5.1 The importance of human resources

The development of human resources or human capital formation is an important policy objective of governments in less developed countries. The obsessive interest shown in the past towards physical capital accumulation leading to high growth rates *per se*, has given way to policies which look at a much wider definition of the 'capital' or 'wealth' of a nation. There are two principal reasons for this. It is now generally agreed that physical capital (or its change – investment) is only one of a number of inputs that are required for a higher national output. Thus even to achieve sustainable high growth rates one needs human capital as an independent factor of production. Further, there may be cross-productivity effects such that better human capital may also increase the productivity of the physical capital stock. If we conceive of an aggregate neo-classical production function with three factors – capital, labour, and technological progress – then the last may be crucially dependent on human resources. The earlier discussion on absorptive capacity is also relevant here. In addition to the saving-investment gap (domestic capital) as well as the export-import gap (foreign capital), LDCs may have insufficient ability to benefit fully from whatever investment they may already have. This absorptive capacity gap may well be due to lack of well-developed human capital. The second reason for the emphasis on human resources is conceptually different. As we have argued previously, it is increasingly clear that growth and development cannot be automatically equated with each other. The trickle-down effect, whereby high growth rates would automatically, and within the medium term, affect the poorer and more deprived section of society, does not seem to have materialised in many countries. There are obviously notable exceptions like South Korea and Taiwan where high growth coexists with a more egalitarian distribution of income (A. Sen, 1981). But there are a large number of countries where a more frontal attack is necessary to foster human capital formation specifically to improve the quality of life generally.

One of the major ways in which human capital accumulation can be stimulated in LDCs is through public education expenditure as well as government spending on health and other social services. It is imperative to realise that, in LDCs, *governments* are by far the most important agencies in this area and can do much more than private enterprise could ever hope to achieve. Government initiative in this area can be judged from the fact that in the mid-1970s, 3.5 per cent of all LDC GNP was spent on public health and education expenditure. This is quite a superior performance relative to historical standards.

However, as we have noticed so often throughout this book, LDC governments also have extremely strong commitments to military expenditure to bolster security and counter threats. Aggregate defence expenditure is almost always state-induced, and the consumption of scarce resources to support the military machine as well as reallocation of valuable inputs into armaments production must generally be provided for in national budgets. Comparable data shows that 6.3 per cent of LDC GNP was spent on defence in the mid-1970s and this is almost double that of expenditure on health and education.

It is clear that education and health expenditure to foster human capital and defence spending to buttress security are both major publicly provided goods in less developed countries and need state participation to function effectively. The relationship between them must be quite important given the interest in development strategy which emphasises human capital and the quality of life. The trade-off may appear simple. It is expected that, for a given government budget, a £1 increase in military expenditure will crowd out an equivalent amount of all other spending, and education and health will be reduced according to their proportion in the total. As we shall see, this analysis is simplistic, since there are numerous feedbacks of the hypothesised change in defence spending and the final effects are quite complex. Econometric results reported in Deger (1981) show that there exist a large number of simultaneous channels by which these effects and counter-effects operate and the final causality is not clear-cut. This chapter is intended to throw some light on this issue and also give a flavour of the quantitative results of the econometric model.

In spite of the relative importance placed on human capital in developmental planning, we cannot of course ignore the role of growth. After all, equitable growth is one of the best channels through which LDC can escape from the vicious circle of deprivation and underdevelopment. Therefore, our interest will focus on the *interactions* between defence, human capital and growth in the context of an interdependent model.

One of the major stimulating effects of defence programmes claimed by the literature is in human capital formation. The military may provide 'education and medical care as well as vocational and technical specialities.'[1] If the military does have this type of spin-off, there will be a substantial role for the organised force in the developmental process. Under these circumstances the trade-off between budget allocations of different types of public goods (defence and state education) may become less acute. If the military independently is providing services in these areas, there may be a lesser need for government agencies to spend large amounts of resources on education, etc. The military establishment might take on some of the roles of the civilian authority in human resource development and ease the task of the state education sector.

In the absence of such factors, however, there may be considerable negative effects on human capital formation due to high defence spending, since the major agency in LDCs responsible for both these activities is the government. Given an upper limit to national budgets, an increase in the military burden could be at the expense of education of health spending and thus have adverse consequences on the human capital of the nation.

To understand the interrelationships, consider a simple hypothetical framework. The government decides to spend more on the military and allocates money out of social expenditures on, for example, education or public health. This induces private agents to spend more on these services, which increases consumption expenditures and reduces saving. A reduction in savings causes the growth rate to fall. There are implications for the government budget since revenues may not rise sufficiently. If defence has prior claims on state expenditure, then there may be a second round effect on public education and health services. Whether private spending under these categories is sufficient to compensate for public expenditure is difficult to quantify, but given the importance of the government in the provision of a social wage, it is possible to see the nature of the trade-off between defence and human capital.

It may be instructive at this stage to compare the case of developed countries (DCs) again. As mentioned earlier, Smith (1977, 1980) demonstrates that there is a trade-off in DCs between military expenditure and investment, of almost equivalent amounts. Thus defence spending does not significantly affect the social wage (including education, health, social security, benefit, transfer, etc.), and the burden primarily falls on investment.

However, the same is not true for LDCs. It is much easier for governments to reduce the social wage for human capital expenditure to fuel an increase in defence. There are few institutional obstacles (such as powerful trade unions or consumer protection groups) in decreasing the social wage. Further, the first priority of national planners is usually high growth, and a reduction in investment is always an unacceptable alternative. If the military establishment has any say in the matter, it will generally prefer its spending to be financed by cuts in the social wage rather than a reduction in investmnt. The dream of most military regimes is a powerful industrial complex helpful to indigenous defence production, and this cannot be achieved by sacrifices in investment. Thus it is difficult to evaluate *a priori* the ultimate impact of the defence burden on the development of human resources. The purpose of this chapter is to clarify some of the complex interrelationships between defence spending and human resources. We do this by emphasising public education expenditure.

Basically we wish to study two important issues. The first is the relation between two major aggregate goods provided by the state in LDCs – defence spending and social wage expenditure. Since the latter contributes significantly to human resources in a poor country, the potential trade-offs are important. Second, we wish briefly to discuss how the interrelationships can be quantified, what sort of empirical results one can obtain and what their implications are.

5.2 Human capital formation and defence

The formalisation of the effects of defence on human capital accumulation will depend crucially on our understanding of the channels through which an autonomous increase in defence spending influences the growth of human resources. For analytical purposes, we shall focus on four channels separately, even though there may be interconnections. These may be termed (a) spin-off, (b) social attitudes, (c) growth effects and (d) the government revenue constraint.

(a) Spin-off

There are a number of direct and indirect ways in which high defence expenditure may have spin-off effects on employment and the creation of human capital. We consider them in turn.

First, the military may help in mobilising labour and increasing employment. Since the days of surplus labour (dual economy) models, development theorists have placed little emphasis on labour shortages. Rather, production planning has always focused attention on the two other binding constraints to growth, i.e. physical capital stock and foreign exchange. Though there is a great deal of merit in such an analysis, it may not be applicable to all LDCs and at all times. Surplus labour may be potentially present but may not have access to centres of employment. Further the socio-cultural ethos may not be conducive to the work ethos. Finally, there may be a pool of voluntary unemployed persons content to live on the extended-family-owned marginal farm or even on the fringes of the urban economy. In all these cases the military may be a potent instrument in mobilising human resources, imposing discipline and work ethics in turn, as well as aiding in the development of rudimentary skills.

Even if the economy is characterised by a vast reserve army of surplus labour in general, there can be no doubt that skilled labour is usually in short supply and may be an important constraint to growth. Blitzer (1975) has given a detailed survey of how such constraints may be incorporated in a planning model. Consider skilled labour of a certain type as an input in the production process. Suppose we can characterise the technology by means of skilled labour input-output coefficients which are fixed. Then the demand for skill category s type of labour (E_s) is given by

$$\sum_i a_{si} x_i = E_s$$

(where x_i is output of activity i, and a_{si} is the amount of skilled labour type s needed to produce one unit of x_i).

If the available supply of such labour is fixed at L_s, then

$$\sum_i a_{si} x_i = E_s = L_s \text{ (for all } s)$$

These inequalities therefore define the constraints within which the economy has to operate.

It is obvious that if military activity uses labour from any skill category s then the amount available for civilian output will be reduced. Thus there will be a reallocation of resources to the military from the civilian economy and this may have adverse consequences.

These models, however, have serious theoretical shortcomings. As Blitzer (1975) points out, the shadow prices corresponding to these constraints frequently have unreasonable values, display considerable instability, and fluctuate widely in response to small parametric changes. Human capital formation or the creation of an additional labour supply in different skill categories should be made endogenous to the system, rather than fixed as an upper bound. The structural equations of the economy will then have L_s as an endogenous variable. The educational planning model analysed by Blaug (1970) gives an excellent review of this methodology.

The military may have an important role to play in adding to the skill content of the existing labour force. As mentioned earlier, Benoit (1973) and others have pointed out that technical training is an important part of military service and thus adds to human resources. Even though the main purpose of the military is not skill creation, it can help substantially in that activity. In military colleges, for example, the standard of vocational and technological education is usually very high in LDCs.

On the whole, therefore, the defence establishment may be helpful in enhancing the reservoir of skilled labour and shifting outwards a binding constraint on growth. In the absence of such dynamic considerations, however, it may compete for scarce available human resources with the more productive civilian economy and so have adverse effects.

(b) Social attitudes

Social rigidities have been a major inhibiting factor for human capital accumulation in LDCs. For example, many developing countries have promoted the growth of secondary and higher education at the cost of neglecting the provisions of basic and technical education. This phenomenon is intimately related to the hierarchical and immobile structure of society. University or high school diplomas have become the new status symbols. An Arts graduate may have little productivity from a social point of view, yet his socio-economic position is always higher than that of a technician even though the latter has much more to contribute to the industrial growth of the economy. Thus the social problem of hierarchy and the educational problem of valueless higher degrees are fundamentally connected with each other.

Diplomas in further education are one set of qualifications (there may be others, such as family connections, patronage or caste) intricately tied in direct ways to the reward system operating in society. The higher the title conferred by a degree (whatever its intrinsic worth), the higher the potential benefits to its holder. As Blaug (1979) puts it, 'the recruitment and promotion policies in Asia and Africa have done much to foster diploma disease'. There is also a misuse of vast amounts of resources in factory-style universities, etc., producing graduates with little chance of using their expertise.

Blaug suggests a possible remedy for this non-optimal state of affairs: 'A more potent indirect means of reducing the attractiveness of upper secondary and higher education is that of squeezing earnings differentials in labour markets.'

It has been suggested that the military in LDCs is a progressive institution and therefore tends to break up social rigidities. Whynes (1979) goes so far as to say that 'the military represent the major and possibly the only "Gesellschaft" element in the predominantly "Gemeinschaft" LDC society and, by means of the dissemination of its ideology . . . will contribute towards the process of cultural development'.

Even a cursory glance at military structure brings out the weakness of this point of view. Many LDCs operate some form of temporary conscription or short-term obligatory national service. Almost all of them (including relatively high income nations like Turkey or Greece) have different tenures for graduates and others. It is generally valid that people with university degrees usually do less military service than people without. Thus the static, hierarchical, socio-educational structure we mentioned earlier is imported *in toto* within the military organisation. The military behaves exactly like any other institution in perpetuating Blaug's 'diploma disease'. Further the inequality in pay structure between the highest and the lowest ranks could be even greater than in civilian employment.

The army may see itself as an institution separated from and perhaps superior to the parent society. Then the military simply adds another class to the already hierarchical system and will contribute little to its decay. It has its own rules of the game, which can be as conservative, myth-ridden and rigid as those of any civilian groups. In effect, the difference between the military and other institutions is one of degree and not of kind.

Some studies have also remarked on the 'modernisation' effect that military regimes are supposed to have (Pye, 1962b). Specifically, a 'modern' society dispenses with its feudal and social obligatory system and moves towards some form of market-oriented, monetised industrial-capitalist system. This has obvious beneficial implications for the stock of human capital in the country.

Once again we find it difficult to believe that the army is intrinsically any more modern than many other institutions, such as the civil service, the judiciary, the business community, etc. Individual case studies are necessary to make a specific judgment, and it is impossible to generalise from Pye's (1962b) categorical comment. We have to be agnostic on this score at this stage; a detailed discussion is provided in a later chapter.

(c) Government revenue constraint

The expenditure function of an individual consumer will have income as an important exogenous variable. It is generally not possible to vary income (except within narrow limits). It is not always clear why government demand should also be a function of its income or revenue earned. Intuitively, one expects the government to be able to expand its revenue constraint, in order to meet desired levels of expenditure on different activities. But as Lotz (1970) points out, the case for LDCs is substantially different. The sum of governmental expenditure equals the 'financing which is available', and this is not an elastic function. Thus the government has an upper limit on its total revenue (= income = expenditure) and budgetary allocations become important. The different variables which may set upper limits to the government's total finance available are the following: (i) tax revenue dependent on *per capita* GNP, sectoral output and foreign trade activities; (ii) domestic borrowing which is dependent on the size and strength of the financial sector as well as the degree of monetisation; (iii) creation of high-powered money by borrowing from the Central Bank; and (iv) foreign aid which is exogenously given. We briefly discuss each in turn and show why the overall revenue function is rather inelastic.

Given low *per capita* income, direct tax revenue (for example, from income tax) is not substantial. Further, an increase in marginal tax rates leads to large-scale tax evasion and is often counterproductive. Similarly, indirect taxes such as excise duties cannot be easily increased, since the burden of tax is passed on to the consumer, who suffers, and also because the revenue itself may fall due to high elasticity of demand. Customs duties are important too, but once again the prevalence of smuggling, and the importance of intermediate imports for domestic capital formation, makes it unfeasible for the government to increase tax rates substantially.

Given the backward and weak financial sectors in LDCs, the

lack of monetarisation and the prevalence of barter, the government has little ability to borrow to finance its deficit. As Taylor (1980) states, 'since there is no serious market for equity and prudent investors find government bond too unreliable, the public's only options for holding wealth are loans to firms and money'.

The budget deficit usually feeds into money creation almost on a one-to-one basis in LDCs. The simplest and often the only way for the state to increase expenditure is to borrow from the Central Bank and thus expand the nominal monetary base. This in turn increases the stock of money and could produce inflation as discussed earlier. Since developing countries have become increasingly worried about inflation in recent years, this channel to finance additional spending by the state has become a dangerous one to use. Finally, foreign aid is determined elsewhere and may not be controllable at will. However, foreign resources and their fungibility add a whole new dimension to the problem and will be dealt with in Chapter 6 of this book.

The overall conclusion seems to be that there is not much flexibility for a low income, rural-oriented LDC with backward financial institutions to increase its total budget rapidly. Given this constraint, there will invariably be an allocative trade-off between different parts of the government, budget-defence expenditure and human capital investment being important constituents. As we found in the first section of this chapter, unlike DCs, LDCs' governments will find it difficult to resist a cut in human capital expenditures. Given a powerful military regime and strong demands for physical investment for growth, LDCs invariably economise on welfare and human resource openings. One may thus expect a negative correlationship between defence and human capital within the government revenue constraints. It is also clear that this negative relation will be modified or reduced if governments can expand their budgets or finance their additional deficit (due to defence spending) by various means briefly discussed earlier. However, this is of limited help in the light of our discussions in Chapter 3.

(d) Growth effects

On a national scale, LDCs with high growth rates can generate a high enough surplus to foster human capital accumulation. Fast-growing countries can *afford* to have more inputs transferred to long-term activities such as the development of human resources. Countries growing at a very slow rate might presuppose that it is a 'luxury' to divert resources from say investment in physical capital to investment in human capital. Given that planners prefer to spend more on human resources, *cet. par.*, high growth rates may be a sufficient condition for them to do so. However, it must be stressed that fast growth is not a necessary condition for high expenditures on education or health – witness the case of Sri Lanka or Tanzania – but it may be sufficient to tip the balance. Further, a high growth rate, increasing *per capita* income, may mean that individuals in society themselves spend more on these categories of expenditure and add to the investment in human capital over and above what the government provides.

If defence expenditure has growth-stimulating effects, then there is a powerful reason for claiming that defence aids human capital (albeit indirectly) via growth. A high growth rate may lead to high human capital (note the reverse causation). Then there is a positive influence running from military expenditure through growth rate to human resource investment. However, a large amount of literature in recent years has shown econometrically that defence spending reduces the national saving or investment rate and this in turn reduces growth rates in LDCs. If, as we expect, there is a positive relation between growth rates and human resource development, then military spending may have an adverse effect on human capital formation on this account.

5.3 Quantification

In this section we will briefly discuss how the types of interrelationships discussed in the previous section can be quantified in the framework of an econometric model. The final results from an analysis done earlier (see Deger, 1981) will be reported and its implications noted.

The major problem lies in finding a suitable operational proxy for human capital. We use the ratio of public education expenditure as a proportion of GNP. In addition to the fact that data for such a variable is readily available, we also assume implicitly that public education spending as a proportion of national output is a crucial and probably overwhelming determinant of human capital formation. In other words, if this ratio falls as a result of an increase in the defence burden, then the rate of growth of human capital will, in all probability, fall too. The spin-offs from other aspects of military spending will not be able to compensate for any decline in education expenditure. However, these spin-offs are also integrated into the model so that the final multipliers will reveal all the interconnections.

The empirical model uses a set of simultaneous equations to find the interconnections between military burden (m), government education expenditure as a ratio of GDP (e), growth and saving rate. The model is formally similar to that used in the Appendix except for the inclusion of the human capital index e. The essential task is to *estimate* the value of the *multiplier*, de/dm, i.e. the effect of a (marginal) change in m on the value of e when all the interrelationships between the four variables have been accounted for.

The calculated value of this multiplier using the results reported in Deger (1981) came out as −0.4528. The negative sign implies that the defence burden reduces education spending taking *all independent effects* together and is probably strongly detrimental to human capital formation.

An approximate idea of the elasticity of education to military expenditure (as shares of GNP) can also be derived using data reported in ACDA (1978). The average m/e ratio for 1967-73 came out as 2.52, which when multiplied by the multiplier de/dm, gives us the elasticity of e with respect to m as equal to −1.1426. This means that a 1 per cent increase in government military spending as a share of GDP reduces the education budget by 1.14 per cent as a share of GDP, when we account for all interdependent variables such as growth, savings and other exogenous variables. There seems to be little doubt about the negative effects of defence spending.

These numbers are approximate, but are nevertheless extremely revealing about the magnitude of the trade-offs involved in this area. But what do they actually mean in an operational context? We give some concrete meaning to the abstract analysis conducted hitherto.

ACDA (1978) reports that in 1976 *all* developing countries together spent 6.3 per cent of their GNP on defence and 2.6 per cent of their GNP on education. The total amounts spent were $86.6 billion and $35.6 billion, respectively on military and education, out of a combined sum of $1,380 billion for the GNP of all LDCs taken together. Consider now a 10 per cent reduction, for only one year, in the share of military spending ratio, i.e. from 6.3 per cent to 5.67 per cent. In absolute terms this is not much and amounts to a decrease of only $8.4 billion. Given our elasticity measure derived in the previous section, the foregoing change in defence spending will increase the education expenditure ratio to 2.9 per cent of GNP. In absolute terms the amount of *increase* will be $4.4 billion per year. This is the extra amount of education expenditure that is releasable from a small 10 per cent reduction in the military share in GNP for each year, after taking account of all interdependent effects.

Some idea of the actual impact of this sum of money can be seen by the following figures reported from Sivard (1977).[2] To get a major increase in the number of primary schools with an addition of 100 million new places for children we would need $3.2 billion. A massive programme to extend literacy to all adults (700 million) in LDCs by the end of the century would require $1.2 billion. A preventive and community-oriented training programme for a sharp increase in the number of medical auxiliaries to take care of 85 per cent of all village health requirements would need $0.25 billion. All three projects would cost the exchequer a sum of $4.95 billion. As is clear, a 10 per cent reduction in defence spending would be almost sufficient to cover the additional expenditure for these important human resource projects, and all these can be completed in *just one year's* decrease at 10 per cent of the military budget. An 11 per cent reduction will be exactly sufficient. This is *not* a high price to pay for the corresponding gains in human capital and the physical quality of life.

It has often been argued that developed countries should divert a minute fraction of their massive armaments expenditure as development aid for human capital in LDCs. The moral of the previous calculation is that developing nations can and should do a lot for themselves in these areas. It is generally accepted that defence has a high physical resource cost. What we have demonstrated is that the human resource costs are exceptionally high too. Ultimately, this may prove to be much more of a burden than anything else.

6 The military burden in the open economy

6.1 Arms exports

Recent years have seen a substantial increase in the value and quantity of international arms transfers. This has been caused by various factors; an increase in the cost and sophistication of defence technology; a large OPEC oil surplus which generates additional revenue to buy arms; an increase in credit facilities to finance military imports; and competitive arms races in the Third World on the basis of armaments stocks bought from a few developed countries. For an open economy, the macroeconomic costs of weapons imports may be quite substantial, and we will now deal with some of the relevant issues in this context.

Our major concern is with the domestic economy and the implications of arms transfers either through purchase or through foreign aid. However, the analysis is best understood from an international perspective, and therefore some discussion of military trade will be included.[1] This will concentrate on the economic aspects of the problem, though we also believe that the political overtones are quite important.[2] Most arms are sold or given by developed countries (including the Soviet Union); many of them are bought by developing countries. Thus there is a clear north-south division here. As is to be expected, opinion is sharply divided as to the nature and impact of arms transfers and trade. One group of analysts believe that it is destabilising, not essential to the needs of LDCs, an inappropriate or even unjust method of recycling petro-dollars, that it fuels unnecessary arms races which may erupt into wars when critical stock levels are surpassed, and that it should therefore be curtailed or stopped. Others think that the arms trade is like any other form of trade but may have externalities attached. Thus if countries wish to buy or sell at appropriate market prices, taking into account the specific nature of the product, then the trade should go unhindered. Clearly the truth lies somewhere in between, and most governments have taken the middle path; some restrictions have been imposed either through quantity rationing or prohibitive prices but a lot of arms transaction have been allowed to continue unimpeded.

From the post-war period till recently, the international armaments market has passed through various important phases. The 1950s were a period of military alliances and aid. Most arms transfers were done on a concessional basis. The 1960s were the period of the superpowers, when the US and the Soviet Union dominated the world trade in arms; the importance of aid remained, though it was slightly less than before. From the early 1970s, particularly after the first major oil price rise in 1973, we observe the oligopolistic period, when more countries started entering the markets, though the numbers were not very high. The relative importance of the major exporters changed; the two superpowers sold the maximum, but France and Italy improved their positions dramatically, while Britain fell back. Concessionary transfers were reduced drastically and hard currency payments gained favour. The current period, the 1980s, will probably see much more competition, with LDC governments themselves entering the market as exporters, headed at this stage by Brazil. Increased competition and commercialisation have been integral parts of this market.

Two features stand out in the international market for arms nowadays, both of them quite recent phenomena. The value of arms imports *at constant prices* by LDCs has increased extremely rapidly during the 1970s. From $2,506 million in 1970 (at constant 1975 prices), arms imports reached a staggering $9,841 million in 1980, taking into acount all developing countries (except Vietnam).[3] This more than fourfold increase in the quantity of arms bought by less developed economies is truly large, and the rate of growth of defence imports far exceeds the rate of growth of other macroeconomic indicators such as exports, total imports, GDP, etc. Secondly, the amount of weapons purchased either through cash sales or credit facilities has increased tremendously, relative to outright grants or gifts. Thus military aid in the strictest sense of the term is declining rapidly, and LDCs have now to 'pay' for their weapons. In 1971, the grant component of total US military exports was 66 per cent while cash sales and credit took up the rest. In 1979, the position had reversed dramatically. Only 5 per cent of total US arms transfers were in the form of grants while 61 per cent were direct cost transactions and 34 per cent were financed by credit. These two features – a 'jump' in the volume of weapons purchased by LDCs and a larger proportion of cash and credit sales with less emphasis on pure aid – should be noted in any discussion of the domestic costs and benefits of military expenditure in an open economy.

There are many reasons why arms transfers take place, but most can be categorised as political and economic motives. Arms sales which try to promote the security of allies and ensure the stability of friendly governments fall firmly in the political domain. So also do attempts by the supplier nations to gain influence and control recipient nations, both politically and strategically. The United States' determined efforts to sell arms to the Shah and modernise the Iranian army were dictated partly by the need to help an ally against hostile neighbours (Iraq, the USSR) and also to ensure that Iran became the dominant power in the region and to guarantee her strategic stability. The Soviet Union became the main supplier of arms to Peru, with 41 per cent of that country's total imports during 1975-79, chiefly in order to oust US influence and establish a political base in South America. Political motives were dominant at least until the early 1970s and they are still quite important in dictating the nature and direction of global arms transfers.

However, recent years have witnessed a growth in importance of the economic rationale behind arms sales. Troubled by rising oil prices and balance of trade deficits, many DCs have tried to find new and profitable outlets for arms exports. Further, arms products have very high set-up costs, particularly with respect to R&D, thus high sales are often important in reaping the benefits of increasing returns. With a decline in domestic demands for conventional weapons, exports may become essential for profitability and survival. In recession-ridden DCs there is a high incentive to export arms, one of the few buoyant world markets in the 1970s. SIPRI emphasies this point strongly:

> When an economy is in crisis, more weight is allocated to economic than to political arguments. With high unemployment, foreign trade imbalances and budget deficits,

> this is now particularly evident in the West European arms manufacturing countries. Financial constraints have caused cuts, postponements and cancellations in most domestic defence procurement programmes. This has, in part, contributed to rising unit costs, thus inducing further cuts . . . the major arms producers are pushing military sales particularly to Third World countries, more than ever before . . . arms exports improve the balance of payments, lower unit prices through the advantages of scale, and ensure employment in the arms industries. (SIPRI, 1982)

European countries have reduced the grant component of their arms transfers to an absolute minimum, so that their exports are predominantly for cash and credit. Table 6.1 gives selected export data for the four major European nations in arms production during 1970-80. In addition to the first and last years of the decade (1970, 1980), 1974 is given since it was then that the effects of the first oil price rise filtered through to the market, and 1978 is chosen as the year of the highest arms exports (in the decade) by developed economies to the Third World.

It can be seen quite clearly that arms exports are rising significantly, partly in exchange for petro-dollars, but also for the hard-earned export revenue of many poor LDCs. To this we shall return later.

It has been argued, notably by Pierre (1982), that the economic motives can be overemphasised. After all, if one looks at aggregate data, then arms sales comprise a small fraction of foreign revenue. For the US and France, approximately 5 per cent of total exports come from armaments, while for Britain the

Table 6.1 *Volume of exports of major weapons (selected years) to LDCs (US $ million 1975 price)*

	1970	1974	1978	1980
France	203	449	1,236	1,008
U.K.	185	579	488	431
Italy	43	139	553	516
W. Germany	1	116	87	159

Source: Condensed from SIPRI (1982).

figure is of the order of 3-4 per cent.[4] However, this misses the point. The importance of the firms engaged in defence production and their concentration in oligopolistic industrial structures make them far more important than such macroeconomic ratios would suggest. The leading French aircraft manufacturer Dassault-Breguet exports nearly 70 per cent of its total turnover. Three hundred thousand highly unionised workers are employed by the French arms industry. French arms deliveries as a percentage of oil imports (vitally necessary for an economy with small petroleum reserves) amounted to a massive 24.7 per cent on average during 1970-80. In 1980, France had a balance of trade deficit without arms of $20.1 billion. Arms exports of $5.8 billion helped reduce the overall deficit to $14.3 billion, thus arms contributed to a large 40.5 per cent *improvement* in the trade deficit. A leading analyst on the French arms trade is very clear on these points. Commenting on weapons production and exports he writes in SIPRI that

> the transfer of arms and technology is a critical component of an overall economic strategy. This strategy has as its main elements the modernisation of the French economy; the preservation of full employment, with particular emphasis on employment in sections of advanced technology; the pursuit of economic growth; the importance of France's international competitive position, so as to avoid balance of payments deficits; the development of a global market for French goods; and adequate access to raw materials, especially oil. (SIPRI, 1983, p. 372)

Even the superpowers are not immune to the lure of the marketplace in arms sales and the attractions of foreign exchange earnings. The three major sources of hard currency earnings for the Soviet Union are gold, energy and arms (Deger, 1984). Commercial motives have become increasingly important for the USSR. Cardesman (1981) points out the case of the recent sale of Soviet jet fighters to a poor economy like Zambia, in which only seven years' credit was offered, at commercial rates. Compared to the open-handed behaviour regarding gifts of defence equipment in the past, this is almost niggardly. The US, as already noted, has also cut down its grant elements in arms exports, and direct sales have gone up from about $1.1 billion in

1970 to $15.8 billion in 1975 and $16 billion in 1981 (Pierre, 1982).

The message is clear. From the perspective of DCs, economic motives are becoming more important than in the past, and, concomitantly, sales and credit arrangements are now more crucial in securing arms purchases than military 'aid'. Thus many of the analyses of quite recent vintage[5] seem rather dated. In the next two sections we shall investigate briefly the nature and trend of the international arms markets from an LDC perspective and then analyse, in some depth, the costs of arms transfers.

6.2 Trends in arms transfers

The international transfer of defence products (both capital equipment and labour services) can take place through a variety of channels. Historically, the US has relied on the following categories to supply weapons and military services: (a) Military Assistance Programmes (MAP), which consist of grants and soft loans to buy arms and services; (b) Foreign Military Sales (FMS), which give credit and other forms of financing for commercial transactions; (c) International Military Educational and Training Programmes (IMETP), for training and personnel; (d) the Foreign Assistance Act, which provides assistance to regimes threatened by destabilising forces; and finally (e) Excess Defence Articles, this last category being relatively nonoperative in recent years. From the point of view of LDCs, though the specific form might vary, there are essentially four major methods by which defence-related transfers take place. These are (a) direct grants of equipment or financial grants for the purchase of arms; (b) preferential credit arrangements (including the facility to pay in local currency or barter); (c) imports at 'market' prices either through hard currency or commercial credit; (d) training facilities in supplier countries and/or military advisers and personnel in the relevant LDC itself.

Whatever may be the formal method by which arms sales are conducted, the essential question for an economist is how these are financed. There are three ways. First, the recipient nation can get weapons *free* or through grants, the purest form of military aid. Second, arms imports may be paid for by *cash*, earned from export revenue, say, or occasionally, as in the case of the Soviet Union's sales to India and Egypt, payments are made in the form of barter. Third, imports are financed by *credit*, which may be concessionary, thus having an element of aid in it, or it may be at commercial rates, the LDC therefore bearing the full burden of future payments including interest.

The first major feature of weapons imports that has become crucial in recent years, particularly from the viewpoint of the Third World, is the decline in military aid relative to more commercial transactions. Brzoska (1983) estimates the distribution of payments for all Third World arms imports into (approximately) the three categories mentioned above: grants, export surplus, credits. Table 6.2 presents some of his results as averages.

Table 6.2 *Distribution of payments for arms imports in LDCs (percentages)*

	1970-72	1973-75	1976-79
Grants	57.7	53.0	28.5
Export revenue	12.0	20.0	19.3
Credits	30.3	26.7	51.3

Source: Brzoska (1983). Totals may not add due to rounding errors.

Comparing the early 1970s with the end of the decade, grants declined considerably in importance while 'payments' in the form of credit and those made out of export revenue increased substantially. Between 1970 and 1972, over half of all arms imported by LDCs were concessionary and reflected military aid. By the late 1970s, this had fallen to almost a quarter and over 70 per cent of arms had to be paid for in some form or other.

A related feature, again a product of the 1970s, is that a predominant share of the global arms trade now goes as LDC imports. Until the mid-1960s, weapons transfers were mainly between NATO and WTO allies. Vietnam started changing the trends, but the floodgates were truly opened with the oil boom and the Middle East conflict. It is estimated that over three-quarters of all international weapons transfers now go to the developing world. Coupled with this is the fact that there are only a few major supplier countries. These are the US and the USSR, the two largest; France, the UK, Italy, West Germany, the medium-sized arms exporters; and some smaller ones such as Canada and the Netherlands.[6] The market therefore exhibits all the characteristics of an oligopoly, with higher than competitive prices, and the quantity of sales usually set by the demand functions of Third World buyers at the postulated price. Things may be changing though, with the future possibly seeing an increased degree of competition and lower (more competitive) prices.

Table 6.3 gives more evidence of the explosion in arms imports. It should be emphasised that these values are only for major weapons and are much below the total value of arms imports, which include large quantities of minor armaments and spare parts. These are divided by regions so that the 'hot spots'

Table 6.3 *Imports of major weapons and their annual growth rates (US $ million constant 1975 prices; five years' moving averages)*

	1970	1971	1972	1973	1974	1975	1976	1977	1978	1979	1980
Middle	1,353	1,544	1,869	2,282	2,653	3,475	3,837	3,980	4,260	4,394	4,266
East	0.15	14.1	21.1	22.1	16.3	30.9	10.4	3.3	7.0	3.2	−2.9*
North	116	126	157	285	444	602	841	1,158	1,294	1,327	1,353
Africa	5.5	11.2	21.7	81.5	55.8	35.6	39.7	37.7	11.7	2.5	1.96*
Far	341	348	281	354	478	579	989	1,347	1,400	1,309	1,255
East	−2.0	2.0	−19.2	25.9	35.0	21.1	70.8	36.2	3.9	−6.5	−4.12*
South	363	362	374	349	332	383	541	586	689	796	840
Asia	8.0	−0.2	3.3	−6.6	−4.8	15.4	41.2	8.3	17.5	15.6	5.5*
South	209	238	296	392	490	593	665	745	768	809	798
America	20.8	13.8	24.3	32.4	25.0	21.0	12.1	12.0	3.0	5.3	−1.3*
Sub											
Saharan	94	113	176	199	258	470	693	676	791	840	697
Africa	2.1	20.2	55.7	13.0	29.6	82.1	47.4	−2.4	17.0	6.2	−17.0*
Central	21	31	46	72	75	80	90	89	110	176	225
America	23.5	47.6	48.4	56.5	4.1	6.6	12.5	−1.1	23.6	60.0	27.8*
South	52	51	96	117	127	164	207	176	158	138	103
Africa	−17.4	−1.9	88.2	21.8	8.5	29.1	26.2	−14.9	−10.2	−12.6	−25.3*
Total	2,551	2,816	3,295	4,050	4,858	6,344	7,864	8,760	9,471	9,792	9,542
		10.4	17.0	22.9	19.9	30.6	23.9	11.4	8.11	3.38	−2.5*

Source: Calculated from SIPRI (1983), p. 290. (Vietnam and Oceania are excluded.)
*Annual rate of change of arms imports for each region.

such as the Middle East can be isolated if required. Five-year moving averages are reported since they smooth out erratic fluctuations in annual data.

The growth of military imports is compared to the growth of other major macroeconomic variables in Table 6.4. The choice of years, averages for 1970-77, is dictated by the availability of data from *World Tables* (1980). Military imports data in this table excludes the Middle East to make it roughly comparable with World Tables figures which exclude capital-exporting oil-producing countries. It is clear that armament flows increased at a much higher rate than total imports, GDP, and other macro indicators.

Certain other aspects of the new trends in the arms trade are worth mentioning. There has been a marked change in the qualitative dimensions of weapons imports which has matched the quantitative expansion. Current sales are often the most sophisticated weapons in the armoury of the supplier, unlike the past when second-hand and often very old vintages tended to be sold. There were cases in the 1960s when World War II vintage weapons were still being purchased by LDCs. Today, instances can be cited of armies in the Third World using armaments which the supplier countries have failed to provide even to their own armed forces. The US sale of AWACS (Airborne Warning and Control System) aircraft to Iran was completed even before the producing country had made the final decision regarding its own procurement.[7] The Soviet Union's exports of T-72 battle tanks to Libya and Syria have reportedly delayed their introduction into the WTO armed service. The supply by the UK of Chobham armoured tanks to Iran is also a classic example. SIPRI reports

Table 6.4 *Growth rate of macroeconomic variables of developing countries*

	(1)	(2)	(3)	(4)	(5)
	Arms imports	All imports	Exports	Invest-ment	GDP
1970-77	16.64	9.0	5.2	8.1	5.7

Source: Col. 1 calculated from Table 6.3, row 10; cols 2-5 from *World Tables* (1980).

that in its arms registers for 1981, covering major weapons on order or being delivered, 94 per cent of the contracts were for new weapons systems, 2 per cent for second-hand equipment and 4 per cent for refurbished weapons.

Co-production or licensing arrangements for armaments have also mushroomed with the trade in recent vintages, and arms industrialisation seems to be expanding in line with new imports. Third World countries, as they increase domestic fabrication of arms, are also slowly but steadily entering into the export markets. Even though in relative terms LDCs as a whole export only 4 per cent of total world exports, the absolute value is increasing fast. Again, within the Third World, only a few countries are able and willing to export arms, the outstanding examples being Brazil, Israel and South Korea. Chapter 7 deals exclusively with arms production.

Overall, therefore, the nature of arms transfers and the concomitant trends signal fundamental changes in the last decade or so. A quantum increase in weapons imports (particularly, though not only, for oil surplus countries); more sophisticated arms being purchased in the world markets; weapons increasingly being financed out of credit and export revenue rather than from aid; arms races being conducted on the basis of weapons supplied by a few oligopolistic sellers – these are some of the features that characterise today's world market for arms. All of these trends involve higher expenditures and resource costs, particularly in terms of scarce foreign exchange – and it is to these costs that we now turn.

6.3 The cost of military imports

Before discussing the various ways in which military-related imports can be a burden on the economy, let us briefly consider whether there are some advantages in the transfer of weapons and personnel into LDCs. Again the analysis must be conducted in terms of spin-off. Familiarisation with sophisticated imported weapons might lead to learning-by-doing as well as adapting the technology to domestic uses. However, given the nature of military technology, serious questions must be raised regarding its suitability for use in LDCs, particularly in the civilian sectors.

Chapter 7 gives numerous examples where even arms-producing NICs (newly industrialising countries) may not find today's advanced weaponry suitable for domestic use. As regards the training of personnel under military assistance programmes and the dissemination of information when soldiers trained abroad return to their native armies, again major doubts can be raised regarding appropriateness, adequacy and the nature of the training received. Whynes (1979) refers to the Draper Report issued by a US Presidential Committee in 1959. This indicated that military assistance had been instrumental in providing for civic action programmes and further education for LDC armies. However, subsequent analysis showed that 'most of the educational programmes revolved around possible solutions to communist aggression and techniques of dealing with extremist guerilla movements'[8] – not necessarily the knowledge most conducive to economic development!

Turning now to actual costs, the foreign exchange component of total military budgets depends on various categories of expenditure on imports. These are the direct import of armaments, the requirement for consumption expenditure of the military, and finally, for arms producers, the import needs of domestic defence production. The burden will obviously be lower if the country receives foreign military aid which pays for part of the import costs.

The case of India is instructive. Since the partition of the subcontinent and the gaining of independence in 1947, the perceived threat from Pakistan has always been a major reason for bolstering defence. However, the 1950s did not see any major increase in real (constant price) military expenditure. The share of GDP spent on defence remained consistently below 2 per cent. As the importance of the government increased during these early planning years, the share of the military in central government expenditure fell from 35.6 per cent in 1950 to 22.6 per cent in 1960.[9] However, the foreign exchange component of the defence budget increased substantially, mainly because of arms imports. Table 6.5 gives the data for foreign exchange requirements, of direct weapons imports and military production, as well as the total value of imports – all as shares of the military budgets.

The war with China in 1962 was the great watershed in Indian

Table 6.5 *Foreign exchange components of Indian defence expenditures (percentages)*

	(1)	(2)	(3)
1950-51	6.9	1.2	11.9
1951-52	6.9	1.7	12.3
1952-53	7.1	2.6	13.4
1953-54	5.2	3.3	12.1
1954-55	8.8	4.0	16.3
1955-56	15.9	5.0	24.3
1956-57	20.7	5.1	29.1
1957-58	16.7	4.3	24.5
1958-59	22.4	4.8	30.5
1959-60	27.1	5.5	35.7
1960-61	26.1	6.0	35.1
1961-62	18.3	5.7	27.1
1962-63	6.3	3.9	13.4
1963-64	6.3	3.9	13.4
1964-65	2.9	4.0	10.1
1965-66	1.6	3.9	8.7
1966-67	6.6	4.5	14.3
1967-68	3.0	4.9	11.0
1968-69	4.2	5.0	12.5
1969-70	4.4	4.4	12.8
1970-71	4.2	5.1	12.2
1971-72	4.7	4.8	12.6
1972-73	5.4	6.1	14.3

Source: Calculated from Terhal (1982), table III.
Col. 1 is the share of direct defence imports of weapons in total military budgets.
Col. 2 is foreign exchange needs of domestic defence production as a percentage share of total military spending.
Col. 3 gives the ratio of total foreign exchange spent by the military as a proportion of total defence budget.

military history. The total military budget increased rapidly. In 1960 it was US $776 million (at constant 1972 prices). By 1970 this had increased to $1,734 million dollars, a rise of about 123 per cent.[10] However, the foreign exchange payments changed moderately, showing almost no increase at all. Terhal (1982) has made an intensive research effort to estimate the actual import values of Indian military expenditures since little precise data is available. His figures, on which Table 6.5 is based, show that the foreign exchange burden was commensurately less than was warranted by the rapid rise in military allocation.

Part of the reason why the foreign exchange burden did not rise appreciably was that India received massive aid from the Western powers in the wake of the Sino-Indian war. Until about 1965 (when India spoilt its record by going to war with Pakistan – a US ally!), large amounts of military aid poured into India, and this must have alleviated external costs considerably. Even though the West reduced its aid to India by the 1960s, the Soviet Union became a staunch supporter and friend of India, thus military imports could be subsidised using Russian aid. Note the structural break in column 1 of Table 6.5 around 1962-63. The sharp downward movement in arms imports as a share of the total defence budgets can clearly be accounted for by the influence of foreign capital. It is also easy to see the vast difference between the late 1950s and the 1960s, in the behaviour of the ratios, particularly in columns 1 and 3.

The other reason, of course, for the nonincrease of import costs, at a time when total military budgets were rising rapidly, was the domestic production of arms. One of the aims of an import-substituting (defence) industrialisation strategy, which India followed assiduously, is precisely to reduce the foreign exchange burden of military imports. However, here the situation is more complex, since a reduction in direct weapons imports may be balanced by an increase in imports of intermediate and investment goods necessary for the production of arms. Comparing columns 1 and 2, it is clear that as the former went down, the latter went up, though by lower proportions.

However, the optimistic picture of the 1960s seems to have been reversed in recent years. Prospects of aid from the West remain nonexistent. The perceived threat from Pakistan is building up in the light of massive rearmament financed partly by US military assistance to Pakistan. Soviet arms tend to be less sophisticated than those in the arsenal of the 'enemy'. Thus recent years have seen a large import burden for the Indian economy as the country has tried to purchase the best technology from abroad. The implicit irony of this situation for a major Third World arms producer is elaborated more fully in the next chapter.

On a more general but subtle level it has been suggested that countries which tend to have specific defence problems or spend more on the military or have military governments[11] manage to attract more foreign aid, both economic and military. Since aid is a net addition to the economy's resources and adds to total investment funds, the military, albeit *indirectly*, helps in economic development and growth. *If* the basic premise is true, that aid and defence spending may be positively related, then the open economy LDC does benefit from military expenditure. Benoit (1978) himself mentioned this point when he claimed that 'bilateral economic aid of military allies might enable some LDCs to expand their defence expenditures while simultaneously increasing their rate of investment and their growth rate.'

The basic point is whether foreign aid can be used at will, without noting its specific form, to help economic growth. For example, if part of the military aid can also be used for development purposes, then growth may increase. If this defence-related resource transfer is in the form of cash or general credit, then it may be transferred from one use to another relatively simply. On the other hand if it is for a specific military capital equipment then it may be difficult to convert the aid into developmental resources. However, even in the latter case, less money need be spent domestically for security and more could be diverted to growth.

Let us consider the two major forms of aid that are in effect transferable from one use to another, in the way discussed above – bilateral government-to-government economic aid and military aid. The nature of foreign resource inflows into a developing country is crucial. Essentially, the fungibility of such inflows will determine whether they can be used for specific use or distributed at will depending on the receiving government's preference. The fungibility coefficient varying between 0 and 1 is the fraction of total external resources that can be spent *as if* it were a grant of unconditional fungible cash. Thus if this coefficient is zero, then clearly all aid is strictly conditional or tied to specific projects determined by the giver. On the other hand if the coefficient is unity, it is completely unconditional and may be used for whatever purpose suits the receiver. McGuire (1982, 1983) has formalised this concept and shown how one can econometrically determine this parameter from a system of demand equations. It is clear that the more fungible is the foreign resource, the more it could be utilised to increase either milex or investment; thus an increase in aid could raise either the defence burden or growth, independent of each other.

It is intuitively plausible that, of all the categories of resource inflows from abroad, bilateral economic aid is the most fungible, particularly when it comes to the reallocation between civilian and defence purposes. On the other hand military aid is usually strictly tied to increasing the stocks of hardware that a country receives from the donor. McGuire (1982) uses a sophisticated method to calculate that, for Israel, only 4-18 per cent of military aid is potentially convertible into other forms of expenditure, while 90-100 per cent of economic aid is capable of such conversion. Similarly, multilateral aid and private investment will be difficult to translate into military spending unless, as a bizarre possibility, they are specifically allocated by the donor for such purposes.

The argument regarding militarisation and aid is, however, not conclusive, since it is difficult to find explicit correlations between economic aid in particular and military expenditure. It is true that certain countries like Israel, Egypt, Turkey, Greece, Vietnam and Cuba have benefited from superpowers' aid and alliance military transfers. But we cannot draw a general conclusion that this will be true for most other countries. Further, the value of aid itself is nowadays questioned, and it is difficult to believe that foreign capital inflows will compensate for the resource costs that LDCs have increasingly to bear given the nature of the arms trade in very recent years.[12] It is to these costs that we now turn.

For the open economy, the effect of military expenditure is best understood from the point of view of the balance of payments. Smith and Smith (1983)[13] provide a brief but clear exposition of the subject, analysing OECD countries only. Milex affects *overall* trade balances as well as those specifically related to military flows. Defence spending increases aggregate demand. If the domestic supply is relatively inelastic, to accommodate this increased demand exports might have to be diverted for internal use and/or imports stepped up. Thus the balance of trade will become adverse, and will exacerbate the existing deficits that most LDCs suffer from. In the absence of substantial aid, this must put pressure on the exchange rate which, though generally fixed for LDCs, will still be overvalued.

Specific trade patterns attributed to the military are of course more important. Following Smith and Smith (1983), we should carefully distinguish between trade in visibles (goods, armaments) and invisibles (services, spending by foreign military personnel, foreign military aid in the form of financial transfers). Except for a few exceptions such as Brazil, LDCs usually will have to import the more sophisticated of their armaments needs.[14] LDC exports of arms are low, thus the visible account will always show a deficit. For invisibles the situation is not clear. If military aid is high or the *net* borrowing (funds borrowed minus interest payments) on the defence account is positive, then the invisible account will show a surplus. For LDCs it is expected that visibles will show a deficit and invisibles show a surplus. However, as noted earlier, the aid component is declining and the debt payment element is increasing, so LDCs' invisibles might also start showing deficits. Thus the military trade balance is expected to be in overall deficit for LDCs, unless there are special reasons like war and superpower involvement.

Israel, though exceptional in many ways, is a good example of the different forms of transfers that can potentially take place in the balance of trade accounts due to military expenditure. In Table 6.6 we give some figures for 1980.[15]

Table 6.6 *Military trade accounts for Israel, 1980 ($ million)*

(1)	Arms exports	$ 750 million
(2)	Arms imports	−$ 825 million
(3)	Military aid from US (grants and loans)	$ 1,986 million
(4)	Debt payments to US	−$ 585 million

Source: ACDA, Rivlin (1983).

A deficit item (with a minus sign) is a *payment* by the domestic economy, while a surplus item is a receipt from the overseas sector. Following Rivlin (1983), we assume that rows 3 and 4 are approximately equal to the total defence aid and defence-related debt paid by Israel. Thus, overall, there is a surplus, taking visibles (rows 1 + 2) and invisibles (rows 3 + 4), of the order of $1,326 million. However, Israel is a very special case with substantial aid from the US (it is the largest recipient), and cannot under any circumstances be taken to be a representative economy when calculating foreign burdens.

A deficit in the trade balance can from a different perspective be looked upon as an addition to a nation's resources; this will be temporary, though, since the borrowing needed to finance the deficit has to be paid back in the future. However, this concept implies that the resources are used to build up productive assets which in the future will give a return sufficient to pay back the debt. Defence-related deficits are 'unproductive' in the sense that they do not lead to asset accumulation. On the other hand, by adding to 'security', they do have an indirect productivity (at least in protecting other, more productive assets) which should not be forgotten.

The foregoing discussion, then, alerts us to two basic points. Milex in open economies leads to higher imports and consequential deficits in trade and payments balance. Financing the deficit, in the absence of full compensation by foreign aid, increases foreign debt; and its servicing (interest payments, etc.) requires us to consider the military-related debt burden. Secondly, the diversion of scarce foreign exchange to the military has a direct opportunity cost in terms of investment imports forgone. This is a direct foreign sector counterpart of the allocation cost discussed earlier in the book.

To analyse the debt burden one needs relatively precise data regarding military sales to LDCs financed by credit and concessional grants. Such data is almost impossible to find and one has to rely on estimates, some of which may have been built on rather heroic assumptions. The literature in this field is rarely empirical, and one can appreciate the problems of the researcher. However, an excellent recent paper by Brzoska (1983) tries to tackle squarely the foreign debt problem emanating from military imports during the 1970s. The estimates made by Brzoska are startling. The 'opportunity cost' of debt is measured at about 20-30 per cent. This implies that in the absence of all arms imports, the debt inflow would be approximately 20-30 per cent less than the actual amount incurred during this period. In a similar vein, *military*-related interest paid to overseas seller (lender) countries amounted to about 26 per cent of all interest paid; total indebtedness due to defence imports was about 20 per cent of the total accumulated debt for all imports; and if one looks at the disbursement of new financial capital, about 20 per cent of that was used to finance armaments imports. Finally, 'Debt service for arms imports, according to our estimate, is larger than the cost of new arms to the importing country' (Brzoska, 1983).

Consider the specific case of Argentina, which ran up a huge international debt commitment under the recent military regime, i.e. from 1976 onwards. Table 6.7 gives some figures for the foreign debt of the country as well as its arms imports. The last column gives annual arms imports as a proportion of the change in public debt, the latter being an index of new borrowing over the year. This gives us a rough approximation of how much of *new* indebtedness was used to finance the importation of weapons. The figures for 1978 and 1979 are quite dramatic. About one-quarter to one-third of debt increases could be accounted for by the military sector.

Table 6.7 *Foreign debt of Argentina (US $ billion)*

(1) Year	(2) Total	(3) Private debt	(4) Public debt	(5) Change in public debt	(6) Arms imports in $ million	(7) Col 6/5
1975	7.37	3.35	4.02		30	
1976	8.28	3.09	5.19	1.17	50	4.3%
1977	9.67	3.63	6.04	0.85	40	4.7%
1978	12.50	4.14	8.36	1.38	360	26.0%
1979	19.03	9.07	9.96	1.60	480	30.0%
1980	27.16	12.70	14.46	4.50		
1981	35.67	15.65	20.02	5.56		
1982	43.63	14.36	26.34	6.32		

Source: Debt data from *The Times* Monday 24 September 1984, article by Douglas Tweedale. Arms imports from *Nordic Journal of Latin American Studies*, vol. XII, nos 1-2, 1983.

Arms were not the only culprits for Argentina's indebtedness. It is true that millions were borrowed and spent on economic projects which were not successful. Joint hydroelectric projects with Paraguay are expected to be a fiasco even though a lot of money has been spent. The construction of the Yacyreta Dam on the Paraguay border has not even been started yet. A motorway was built in Buenos Aires at a cost of $300 million even though the 'true' cost was $100 million, the rest being illegal transactions. But, according to *The Times*, the two major spending channels could have been arms purchases and the controversial nuclear energy programme, for which no reliable figures are available.

What is surprising is that outside the realm of defence studies, there has been relatively little interest in analysing these very large figures that follow from the defence debt burden, except probably in the special case of the UK and Argentina. In spite of the upsurge of interest in the sovereign debt problem, and the attention shown to the sort of questions that start off with 'Why do LDCs get into debt?', empirical studies on a major component of international indebtedness attributable to the military seem almost nonexistent.

The other crucial aspect of armament imports is that they compete directly with imports of other types of products, particularly intermediate investment goods which may have a high productivity in increasing growth. Thus the import allocation effect of military expenditure is quite important. By buying foreign arms, LDCs are potentially reducing their 'capacity to import' investment goods which may be crucial for development. This does not mean, of course, that if military imports were stopped, all resources released would automatically be reallocated to the most productive channels available. It is possible that some foreign exchange from imported weapons could be diverted to consumption goods which may not have any growth potential. However, the basic point regarding misallocation of resources for imported products remains.

One formal method of calculating the potential cost of imported armaments transfer can be briefly discussed here. Consider an economy where total import (R) is divided into imports of consumption goods (R_c), investment (intermediate inputs) goods (R_i) and defence product (R_m). Thus

$$R = R_c + R_i + R_m \tag{6.1}$$

Assuming proportional import functions for each category, we have

$$R_c = aY \tag{6.2}$$

$$R_i = bI \tag{6.3}$$

$$R_m = eM \tag{6.4}$$

where Y is GDP, I is total investment and M is military expenditure, $(a,b,c>0)$. Equation 6.2 tells us that consumption goods imports are a (proportional) function of national income. Similarly, imports of investment goods depend on *total* investment in the economy, thus b is akin to an input-output coefficient. Finally, from equation 6.4, a part of total defence spending is being spent on weapons bought overseas, the proportion being e. Substituting equations 6.2, 6.3 and 6.4 in 6.1 we get

$$R = aY + bI + eM \tag{6.5}$$

Dividing both sides by Y, we have

$$r = a + bi + em \tag{6.6}$$

where lowercase letters r, i, m denote the share of R, I, M in GDP. It is possible to empirically estimate the coefficient (a, b, e) from data for any country over time, or, alternatively, for a set of countries given the time period. Using our own control sample, the *estimated* value of these parameters came out as

$$a = 0.34,\ b = 0.88,\ e = 0.46 \tag{6.7}$$

Now consider a situation where all military imports R_m are diverted to the import of commodities needed for investment. A rise in intermediate imports (purchased overseas) will obviously raise the level of investment output by a factor of $1/b$. This in turn will increase output through the incremental output capital ratio. An increase in investment will ultimately *raise* the growth rate (g) to the order of Δg where a simple calculation shows that

$$\Delta g = (em/bv) \tag{6.8}$$

(Δ signifies the change in g). (See Deger and Sen, 1983b.)

Equation 6.8 gives the effect on the growth of the economy

when *all* military imports are diverted to investment or intermediate goods imports. This is clearly a hypothetical situation unlikely to be realised in practice. However, the analysis does point out the sort of magnitudes involved in costing for defence spending and arms transfers, and thus serves as a useful indicator.

It has been pointed out that the above model implicitly assumes that the diversion of imports away from the military will only benefit the investment sector, and that in particular the import of consumption goods will remain the same. This assumption may not hold and some leakages will occur. On the other hand the model also presumes that import diversion will not affect the overall military burden ($m = M/Y$) but will keep it at the same level. This is unrealistic, and we may expect that the hypothesised curtailment on the foreign inputs side will mean that some complementary resources on the domestic front will be released for civilian use. The latter may increase growth rates. As a first approximation we assume that the two effects will cancel themselves out. Thus the final growth effect will be given by equation 6.8 only, provided of course all military imports can be eliminated.

Using the information from our control sample, the growth effect comes out as

$$\Delta g = 0.76 \text{ per cent} \tag{6.9}$$

In other words, 0.76 per cent is the amount by which growth is being depressed by the presence of military imports for our cross-section of countries. Alternatively, if all military imports were stopped, then growth would rise by about three-quarters of 1 per cent. The *average* growth rate for our sample during the postulated time period was about 6 per cent, which is quite high for LDCs. We could then say that if all military imports were stopped, there would be a rise (approximately) in growth rate to 6.76 per cent on average, that is an increase of 12.5 per cent from its previous value – no mean achievement.

The foregoing analysis is a rather complicated way of calculating import costs, and again can only serve as an approximate indicator. More concrete evidence is hard to come by, since it is not easy to get the detailed breakdown for import data for defence purposes, as we have already discussed in Chapter 2. Some information is, however, provided in the excellent survey by Wulf (1983a), and it is worthwhile to look at a few of the numbers. Table 6.8 gives the value of arms imports as a proportion of the imports of engineering products; the latter comes closest to the variable R_i mentioned above. Data for the fifteen largest LDC arms producers are given in the table. Two concepts are apparent. Arms production does not necessarily mean fewer imports – witness Israel and India, major producers *and* importers. Secondly, imports of weapons are a sizeable part of intermediate goods imports, crucial for domestic investment and industrialisation. For countries like India, Pakistan and Turkey, where imported capital goods have important productivity linkages with industrialisation strategy and growth, arms imports are very costly; respectively 27 per cent, 18 per cent, and 13 per cent of engineering imports were potentially diverted to arms.

We have been principally concerned with weapons and technology imports related to defence spending in open economy LDCs. One major aspect of the subject relates to domestic arms production. This is a major topic on its own and is discussed in the next chapter.

Table 6.8 *Arms imports as a share of imports of engineering products, for major arms producers, 1980 (percentages)*

Israel	52%
India	27%
Brazil	3%
Yugoslavia	4%
South Africa	3%
Argentina	6%
South Korea	11%
Philippines	2%
Turkey	13%
Indonesia	11%
Egypt	13%
North Korea	22%
Pakistan	18%
Singapore	1%

Source: Wulf (1983b).

6.4 Conclusion

This chapter has analysed the recent trends in the arms trade, as well as the resource costs involved, for LDCs consequent on the increasing commercialisation of international armaments transfers. Looking at the evidence for the last decade or so, it seems that commercial transactions rather than 'aid' proper have dominated military imports for poor countries, and this can only have caused even more of a burden than normally associated with military spending. The domestic burden of defence, in the form of domestic resource allocation, is exacerbated by the foreign exchange costs and the concomitant problems of external balance.

However, things may change and it is always hazardous to predict the nature of the weapons trade. Recently President Reagan accepted a report from the Commission on Security and Economic Assistance, headed by Frank Carlucci, the former Deputy Secretary of Defence. This commission was set up by the President to analyse US foreign aid and the relation between the economic and military components of the aid programme. The major policy statement is reflected in the following: 'The keystone to our recommendation is the conclusion that economic and military assistance must be closely integrated.'

The commission favoured bilateral aid, as well as a country-specific aid strategy, rather than project-based aid and welfare programmes in general. It recommended the creation of a new agency to administer *both* economic and military aid as well as to have an integrated policy most conducive to US defence needs globally. Overall therefore there was a strong call for the integration of economic and security-related assistance.

The report had major implications for the concept of aid in general. From our specific point of view the most important fact is that the commission suggests a reduction in the costs of military assistance, more grants and concessions in aid, as well as lowering the cost of aid servicing. If the preliminary reports coming from the commission's work are correct and the President accepts the recommendations, then we may get to see a major overhaul of the arms aid programme which may also change the qualitative character of the international trade in armaments.

However, as of now, there seems to be little prospect of a reversal in the trends of arms sales established over the last decade and more. LDCs are paying high foreign exchange costs for their defence burden and will continue to do so, short of major structural changes. So long as economic depression in the developed countries remains, the socialist bloc countries require convertible currencies for their own importation of Western technology, arms industries continue to be more 'baroque' in overspecialisation, and Third World countries are eager to buy the latest vintage weapons for military adventures, I suspect that things will not alter much. The Iran-Iraq war is a classic example; sadly it is not the only one.

7 Arms production and the newly industrialising countries

7.1 Arms manufacture

A new and interesting development in the defence-related activities of LDCs, particularly the newly industrialising countries (NICs), is the growing importance attached to domestic arms production. Wulf (1983a) lists about fifteen countries with a reasonable volume of armaments manufactures within the economy, while another seventeen produce some (albeit minor) armaments. For countries like India, Israel and Brazil the fabrication of armaments is a major component of industrialisation programmes, and the latter two countries have also entered significantly into export markets. Even though the total volume of such production is still a tiny percentage of world output, it is rising and has important implications for the domestic economy of these countries. A careful analysis of the different facets of this phenomenon is therefore necessary. Table 7.1 gives information on the volume of arms output for specific regions.

In this chapter we wish to make an in-depth study of arms production in newly industrialising countries. We first consider the motives for initiating domestic manufacture of arms. We then analyse links between weapons production and the industrialisation strategy followed by the relevant countries. Specifically we distinguish between countries following inward-looking import substitution policies and those involved in outward-looking export promotion strategies. Within this framework it will be seen that there is a close connection between developmental policy and armaments manufacture. This leads on to a discussion of the linkages between the industrial base of the economy and the defence production sectors. In particular those industries that constitute the Potential Capacity for Defence (PCD) (in the words of Kennedy, 1974) and have close inter-industrial linkages

Table 7.1 *Armaments production (in $ billion 1970 prices)*

	1970	1980	1990 (projected)
Asia	1.24	2.6	6.09
Africa	0.48	0.74	0.90
Latin America	0.375	0.450	0.546
Oil countries	0.188	1.78	2.68
South Africa	0.204	0.607	0.797
Total LDCs	2.48	6.17	11.02
Centrally planned Asia inc. China	5.85	7.35	10.78
USSR	31.71	52.59	72.47
Eastern Europe	6.41	9.41	14.84
North America	28.09	29.59	50.55
Europe	10.94	16.73	25.75

Source: Calculated from Leontief and Duchin (1983).

with arms need to be analysed with care. These are the industries that are potentially capable of contributing to and benefiting from arms manufacture. As we shall observe, both backward and forward linkages can be established. The PCD group of industries form the basic industrial framework which constitutes the necessary conditions for the establishment and expansion of domestic arms production. On the other hand inter-industrial demand and technological spin-off from defence industries may be helpful in boosting the output of the PCD group. This is one of the major reasons given in support of defence production within the economy, and if the spin-off effects are significant, could be a major positive point in favour of the domestic manufacture of weapons.

The final section will concentrate on the resource and allocation costs of military industrialisation. In particular, the initial foreign exchange requirements for such activities can be quite substantial. In fact imports may even continue, long after what is warranted by import-substituting strategies, due to the technological characteristics of modern weapons systems and rapid obsolescence. Some overall conclusions will then be drawn on the causes, rationale, impact, benefit and cost of armaments production in the NICs.

7.2 Reasons for establishing arms industries

Myriad motives lie behind the decision taken by various countries to establish domestic production of arms. The first and most often cited reason is political in nature. As Pierre (1982) notes, 'almost all of the countries that have embarked upon creating an arms-manufacturing industry have basically done this for political and security reasons. They wish to become more independent by becoming self-sufficient.' Clearly, by its very nature, arms production is expected to be motivated by political, security and military factors.

Threat perceptions are important in perpetuating arms races in the Third World (Deger and Sen, 1984a). These threats – occasionally real, more often potential – can also induce a country with access to relevant technology to produce arms within the economy. Independence from major suppliers and superpowers, who may have an undue influence on the recipient country[1] during a time of tension and hostilities, is a powerful inducement for the domestic manufacture of at least basic weapons. The Indian ordnance factory system which was languishing in the late 1950s[2] was dramatically revitalised during the Sino-Indian war and from the mid-1960s became highly organised in the manufacture of relatively sophisticated weapons. Israel and Egypt have advanced similar reasons for their armaments industrialisation. In more recent years Pakistan and South Korea have mentioned potential threats from powerful neighbours as an inducement for domestic manufacture.

Coupled with perceived threats, it has been claimed that some countries have established arms production as a result of their implicit desire for regional dominance (Wulf, 1983a). India in Southern Asia, Brazil in Latin America, and Egypt in the Arab world are often accused (usually by their smaller neighbours) of attempting to attain regional hegemony by using the domestic supply of weapons. Since the major suppliers have been known to cut off resupply during a war (witness the embargoes imposed on Greece-Turkey, India-Pakistan, Iran-Iraq), a country going for regional arms superiority will find it more useful to have domestic sources of supply at hand. In a different form, this motive may resurface in the form of 'prestige' attached to arms manufacture at home and the concomitant power that a dictatorial military government may have.

Finally, certain countries, such as South Africa, Taiwan and occasionally Israel, find themselves ostracised by sizeable sections of the international community. These countries have often invested large sums of resources for the local manufacture of weapons rather than relying on undependable imports.

As should be clear, politico-security considerations do play an important role in determining whether nations attempt the domestic production of weapons, if technologically feasible. The fifteen largest arms producers among LDCs – Israel, India, Brazil, Yugoslavia, South Africa, Argentina, Taiwan, South Korea, the Philippines, Turkey, Indonesia, Egypt, North Korea, Pakistan and Singapore – can all be slotted into one of the groups mentioned above. However, these political motives can be overemphasised, and there is always the danger that other types of causes, which may play a very big role in arms production, may get overlooked. We turn to these now.

Important economic considerations are often cited as providing the major motivation behind armaments production, particularly in NICs. These can be grouped under three categories. First, there may be technological spin-offs from defence industrialisation. These include induced R&D, increased productivity of the labour force, skill formation through learning by doing and familiarisation with advanced technology. Second, LDCs often suffer from excess capacity, thus military industries may have backward linkages and create effective demand for inputs produced by horizontally integrated civilian industrial systems. Third, as the international trade in arms increases and weapons tend to be sold rather than be given as grants or aid, the foreign exchange costs are becoming prohibitive. Import-substituting domestic weapons manufacture may reduce imports and gain scarce foreign exchange. The next stage of arms *exports* has also become relevant for countries like Brazil, Israel, and South Korea, and recently Singapore (see SIPRI, 1983). Thus foreign exchange, earned directly through exports or indirectly through imports saved, can be a major economic motive for local production.

Even though quite a few NICs produce arms, the technology is usually imported and the supplier states (DCs) are also involved in the production process (see Carranza, 1983, for a case study of Argentina, and for Peru see del Pando, 1983). The role of such suppliers in technology transfer and helping to set up plants is rather important and often controversial. Wulf (1983a) believes that developed countries, for political reasons, will continue to export arms production *technology* and thus help developing nations to set up their own weapons manufactures. This is partly due to geo-political interests and the desire to feed the recent military-industrial aspirations of client or friendly regimes. But recipients have their own political power. Since the market is essentially oligopolistic, recipients have a choice of countries from which they can buy the technology inputs for home production of arms. Thus they can bargain quite intensively, and the seller may finally have to agree to their demands in order not to lose substantial economic benefits, trading profits or political control. Thus in principle, given resource constraints, it is not too difficult for NICs to set up their own factories producing weapons. However, Pierre (1982) takes the opposite view. Given the prevalence of armed conflict in Third World countries and the attempt by superpowers to curb the problem of moral hazard, it is possible that suppliers will be careful not to allow indiscriminate importation of defence technology by client countries. It is believed that co-production and foreign licensing agreements by defence firms in the larger exporting countries (e.g. the US, the UK, France, West Germany) will be very carefully scrutinised and often stopped by the exporter governments: 'the major suppliers have begun examining requests more critically and are becoming less supportive of the ambitions of third world nations to develop their own weapons capabilities' (Pierre, 1982). Essentially the debate is inconclusive because case studies can be used to substantiate either viewpoint. Overall, we tend to agree that the major constraints on expanding arms production lie on the demand side (from NICs) rather than on the supply side (from DCs). The US embargoes on military exports to India (after the Indo-Pakistan wars) have not prevented India from building up a substantial armaments industry with the help of the USSR. Recent contracts with the West also show how India can change sides relatively quickly, and the control of the Soviet

Union is definitely not a stranglehold. Therefore the major issues in arms production for LDCs are the opportunity costs of resources involved, the various types of spin-off that may occur, and finally the potential capacity of the civilian industrial sector to sustain a military-industrial complex. These are the central problems; the behaviour of supplier countries in providing technology, know-how, licensing arrangements, and so forth is important but not crucial.

7.3 Strategies for industrialisation and arms production

Whether by design or accident, the links between strategies for domestic industrialisation followed by NICs and the type of armaments production are rather close. It will therefore be useful to recapitulate briefly some of the salient features of developmental strategies related to industrial growth.

Within the broadest possible framework, there have been two major types of trade and industrialisation strategies followed by LDCs – inward-looking and outward-looking. The former stresses domestic production rather than importation and emphasises the need for an indigenous technology appropriate for the range of factors available within the country as well as suitable for the types of products likely to be demanded in domestic markets. A major factor not often stressed in the literature is the incentive to learn and adapt technology to local needs and opportunities. As Streeton (1973) emphasises: 'Inward-looking policies, bring out the educational effects of learning to do things for oneself, especially learning to manufacture instead of importing: a kind of learning by doing without' (p. 3).

There is no supposition *per se* that inward-looking policies must emphasise import substitution and domestic production of secondary or manufactured goods. However, in practice, most LDCs have concentrated on manufacture and industrialisation.[3] Thus import-substituting industrialisation (ISI) has become the *sine qua non* of inward-looking policies and it is in this sense that we shall be analysing it.

The basic idea behind ISI is that structural change or economic growth is hindered in an open economy by too much dependence on foreign trade activities. Thus reduction of imports and additional local production will motivate structural change, create investment incentives and activate growth. As Bruton (1970) remarks describing ISI:

> Developing countries have not achieved sustained growth because of their structure or their lack of a prime mover. The IS strategy to change this structure and to provide a primum mobile is to replace imports by domestic production of *certain* commodities. Thus IS in the narrow sense is limited to specific activities and is measured by increases in the ratio of domestic production to total domestic absorption. In a broader sense, import substituting within individual sectors is a means to the more far-reaching objectives just stated.

Since ISI cannot encompass the whole economy initially, it has to move through various stages. A gradualist policy is imperative, and it is important to analyse the nature of the products chosen for import substitution at various stages of the strategy. It is usual to start off with consumer goods at the outset, restrict imports by high tariffs or other protectionist policies, create investment opportunities for domestic entrepreneurs, raise the level of absorptive capacity, use foreign exchange released from import restrictions on consumer goods to buy the capital goods from abroad required as intermediate inputs, and presumably set off a virtuous cycle of industrialisation. The first stage ends when domestic markets cannot absorb any more of the consumer products initially chosen for ISI. The choice then, in the second phase, is for the horizontal widening of the spectrum of products but within the same types of industries. 'Thus, protection is provided on as wide a range of *consumer* goods as possible' (Bruton, 1970). This is the easier option but creates problems later on, since activities tend to remain small-scale and inefficiency increases because economies of scale are not realised. Once those possibilities are exhausted, the economy must move on to the third phase and opt for intermediate and capital goods production, and ISI enters its advanced stage.

Armaments production in countries following ISI is best done in the second and third stages of industrialisation. Out of the six largest armaments producers in the Third World (Israel, India, Brazil, Yugoslavia, South Africa, Argentina) at least three countries have substantial industrial bases achieved by import substitution. These are India, South Africa and Yugoslavia. Argentina also created a relatively sophisticated arms industry during its own ISI phase under the leadership of Peron (see Carranza, 1983).

The basic philosophical motivation for producing arms – whether for security or economic reasons – is similar to that which inspires inward-looking policies in general. Excessive dependence on overseas suppliers, inappropriate technology or output, lack of learning by doing, domination by multinationals or foreign governments, are all valid reasons for having arms industries at home within the broad framework of industrialisation. Streeten's (1973) observation for ISI trade strategies holds equally well for arms manufacture: 'If you restrict trade, if you keep out the multinational enterprise . . . you will evolve your own style of development and you will be stronger, more independent, *master of your own fate*' (italics mine). It should be pointed out that arms production in LDCs is usually carried out – with a few remarkable exceptions – without direct investment from foreign multinational companies. The main reason for this is probably the fact that arms production is considered to be a part of national policy sensitive to the needs of domestic security, and foreign investment is not considered desirable. But things may be changing, as the Brazilian example will show later in the chapter. However, in general, the desire for independence from foreign supplier governments remains paramount.

At least one respect in which import substituting arms production may differ somewhat from overall ISI is in the need to evolve a relatively indigenous level of technology suitable for the needs of the economy and the availability of factors within the country. Thus, in principle at least, domestic production in favour of imported goods must involve choosing, adopting and learning 'appropriate technology':

> The point about appropriate technology is that it involves lower costs of capital equipment per worker, without raising the cost of capital per unit of output, more in line with available saving per head. It thus makes it possible to provide productive equipment for the whole work-force, whereas use of developed country technology in much poorer countries means that only a minority of workers can be provided with

> equipment and that much equipment remains under-utilised. The equipment appropriate for poor countries should be capital saving and intended for small-scale production, not the labour saving large-scale equipment and plant appropriate to the factor availability and income levels of rich countries. (Streeten, 1973)

So much for the theory. In practice, things may turn out differently. It has been often observed that import competing industries have been more capital-intensive than industries producing exportables. Thus import substitution may have led to an *increase* in the capital intensity of production. Comparing over cross-sections between 1968 and 1973, the average incremental capital-output ratio for South Korea and Brazil (countries which were going for export promotion rather than import substitution) was of the order of 2.2 and 1.4. On the other hand countries like India, Egypt, and Turkey, pursuing ISI, have incremental capital-output ratios of 4.8, 3.4 and 2.9 respectively. Thus labour surplus countries, instead of using existing factor endowments to plan their industrialisation, often used inappropriate techniques causing 'distortions' within the economy. The reason for this is clear enough. Even though the production of import-competing goods is done domestically, the technology is often imported[4] from countries whose factor endowments are radically different. The pursuit of advanced techniques and sophisticated product mix (the 'high tech' effect) sometimes gives results contrary to the spirit of inward-looking policies.

This contradiction is glaringly evident in the production of armaments in NICs which opted for ISI policies. The manufacture of weapons is an extremely sophisticated business with a very high rate of obsolescence, prohibitive R&D expenditure and a highly capital-intensive mode of production. Further the demand for the final product comes from the defence establishment, who may be caught up in an arms race with a neighbour buying the latest vintage weaponry from international markets. Under these circumstances it becomes difficult for the country concerned to produce arms using appropriate technology, which in reality may mean less advanced hardware. India is a classic example. After two decades of indigenous production and close co-operation with the Soviet Union to produce armaments domestically within the umbrella of import substitution, Indian defence planners have gone full circle and recently imported Jaguar jets (British), Mirage fighters (French) and submarines (West Germany). Argentina did the same too. As Wulf (1983a) states: 'Technology advances in industrialised countries are so fast that developing countries, even with such sophisticated research and industrial capacities like India, are not able to keep pace.' Recently Israel has been having great economic problems, especially with the balance of payments, which are related to huge imports of intermediate goods for armaments production.

One must of course distinguish between the product itself and the process required to manufacture the product (process technology). It is possible to have a high-tech product using a low-tech process. Then the resource costs are low for an LDC, and the technology compatible with import substituting industrialisation and the philosophy of inward-looking strategies. However, for the production of arms this is not generally true. For reasons mentioned in the previous paragraph, if the need is for an advanced product the process itself will be usually sophisticated.

Advanced import substitution strategy in civilian sectors such as the manufacture of engineering goods or machine tools, even though capital intensive, at least has the saving grace that it replaces overseas imports. The machines may not be the 'first best' in terms of international technology but are reasonably competent to meet domestic demands. Further the demand itself for such intermediates is geared to the technical quality of the product, so that extremely sophisticated machinery is not strictly necessary. A vintage that may be obsolete in a developed country will do quite well in a developing economy because the efficiency norms are less stringent. Once again, the case for arms production may be different. Quite often, the 'demand' for arms is determined by exogenous factors such as weapons acquisition from DCs by a belligerent neighbour. Under the circumstances, the best available technology in weapons is considered a *sine qua non* for security, and domestic production may not match up to the high standards set. Then in spite of ISI for the military-industrial complex, the relevant country will have to import a substantial quantity of arms. It is not surprising that ACDA (1983) data shows that in 1980, the two largest Third World arms producers, Israel and India, were also the two largest arms importers. We believe, therefore, that though import substitution strategies in armaments may be laudable from the point of view of economic and security-based independence, they are constrained in their applicability due to the nature of the product, the rapidly changing level of technology and the type of 'demand' that is being created in strife-torn developing countries.

An example may help to clarify matters. Consider a country which imports electrical motor pumps whose function is to pump water upwards in residential buildings. Suppose these pumps are currently imported from the US and are designed for buildings fifty floors high. The average height of buildings in our LDC is, say, five floors high. When this country goes for import substitution, it will start producing pumps which are suitable for domestic needs, and though not as technically efficient as the US pumps, they will be 'appropriate' for domestic demand. Here we have the case of necessity being the mother of invention. Now consider an alternative scenario where our country is importing sophisticated tanks from the US. If it goes for ISI in military products, it may decide to manufacture tanks domestically but the quality will be much inferior. Suppose its antagonistic neighbouring country imports the latest technology tank from abroad and begins a war. Since the demand for tanks is determined by the ability to fight wars effectively, our prototype country is at a disadvantage and will be forced to import again, thus defeating the rationale of ISI strategies. Here we have a case of (imported) invention being the mother of necessity. The current upsurge of arms imports to India in response to Pakistan's weapons purchase and aid from the US is a good example of this.

There are obviously counter-cases to this argument. Tanks imported from the US require highly skilled engineers to maintain them and advanced support equipment to keep them functioning. Without these facilities, which are not widely available in LDCs, the weapons are unreliable. If in combat they break down and cannot be used, while the simpler, appropriate technology tanks of the opponents keep running, the picture is rather different. An example can be provided from the Indo-Pakistan war of 1965, in which a major engagement was fought at the tank battle of Sialkot, reputed to be the 'largest tank battle at that time since the end of World War II' (*World Armies*, 1983). Pakistan had the technologically far superior US-made Patton tanks, which were better than the relatively obsolete Indian Centurion tanks. Yet in actual combat the latter did extremely well; the Patton failed to live up to expectations, probably because of its complicated mechanism which was difficult to handle by the crew. Currently the Indian army uses about 1,100 Vijayanta tanks which are all indigenously produced, and is quite confident in this area at least of holding its own. Another example is that of the GIs in Vietnam who allegedly threw away their high-technology but unreliable M16s and used the simple, rugged Kalashnikov captured from dead Vietcong soldiers. Overall, however, the temptation to buy 'off the shelf' when an adversary does so remains, since *perceived* security needs are the crucial component of the final demands of arms industries.

Outward-looking policies leading to export promotion have also resulted in arms production and exports by certain NICs, principally Brazil and Israel, and to a lesser extent South Korea, Taiwan and Singapore. Thus LDCs have themselves entered the export market for arms, though they have obtained only a small share by international standards. Again this export drive is closely linked to domestic strategy. Brazil is the classic example: it vigorously promotes defence exports promotion and has a rising indigenous military industry based partly on booming exports. An interesting though relatively new and isolated feature is the entry of multinational corporations (MNC) in the field. One of the major reasons, of course, why MNCs may wish to join Third World arms production is to evade arms exports restrictions in their DC 'home' countries. The recent decisions by Aermacchi and Aeritalia of Italy and Embraer of Brazil to pool resources to produce the AM-X strike fighters (SIPRI, 1982) may simply be an early signal of many more such developments. The major motive is economic, and politico-ideological considerations take a back seat in arms exports by these countries. SIPRI (1982) quotes a Brazilian official commenting on arms sales: 'we are looking to the Third World, and we'll sell to the right and the left and centre.'

Just as in other sectors, Brazil's 'export miracle' in defence industries is truly remarkable by LDC standards. Starting only in the mid-1970s, Brazil now sells almost 50 per cent of total Third

World arms exports; this may be small by world standards, but it is rapidly expanding. The SIPRI register for arms trade (SIPRI, 1983) reports that Canada, the UK and France imported from Brazil, the only developing country to sell arms to such major industrial giants. Within LDCs, the register showed seventeen countries, out of a total list of eighty-four, importing arms from Brazil during the previous years.

The state is in direct control of part of the arms industry. The navy has its own shipyard at Guanabara Bay for construction and repair of naval vessels. It also undertakes commercial contracts if there is temporary excess capacity. The army runs eight ordnance factories which produce small arms and ammunition. Overall supervision is in the hands of Imbel, a nationalised company which was set up in 1975 and is run by the Defence Ministry. Imbel also helps in arranging collaborative ventures with foreign arms manufacturers and is a major agency for negotiating arms exports.

In the private sector are large companies like Engesa, Embraer and Avibras. Engesa manufactures and exports armoured cars, and its Cascavel armoured vehicles have now been sold to thirty-two countries, mostly in the Middle East and Africa. It also produces the amphibious Urutu as well as the tank destroyer Sucuri – all according to international specifications and highly competitive in world markets. Embraer is a very large aircraft manufacturer producing among other things jet trainers, transport planes, counter-insurgency aircrafts and helicopters. Brazil is now contracted to supply Xingu trainer jets to France, a country with a very sophisticated arms manufacturing base. The Embraer Company designed its own twin-turboprop transport aircraft (called Banderirante), which is already established in both military and civilian markets. This firm is the only non-US company to be ranked among the top ten in the world in the 'general aviation class'. Avibras specialises in missiles and rockets, and recent reports claim that it is trying to produce its own indigenous designs for surface-to-air and air-to-air missiles. Avibras sells air-to-ground missiles to Iraq, Libya, and possibly other countries.

Within developing countries, Brazil's success in exporting arms is quite phenomenal. The reasons are simple. The arms are not the most sophisticated in the world. However, LDCs do not need maximum sophistication. Brazilian weapons are produced with Third World conditions in mind: they are of good quality, but rugged, and need less maintenance, as well as being operative in harsher environmental conditions. The arms are much cheaper compared to those from industrial countries since wage costs are low, and delivery dates are scrupulously maintained.

Many of the arms are made from US or European designs but they are *adapted* to developing countries' needs – for example, for limited-war or counter-insurgency purposes. State patronage, cheap labour, multinational technology, adaptable specifications, quick delivery and ideological indifference – all have contributed to the astonishing increase in Brazilian arms production and exports.

However, very recent reports suggest that Brazil is probably reaching the end of its expansionary phase. The arms industry is probably at a threshold with further advances constrained by the availability of imported Western technology and concomitant joint venture production using cheap Brazilian labour and other resources. Brazil abrogated its military pact with the US in 1977 during the Carter regime's insistence on human rights programmes, on which the country has a poor record. But the go-it-alone cycle seems to be ending and there are strong indications that Brazil needs access to US defence technology. In return she must accept controls on weapons sales, particularly to countries like Libya. A recent *Financial Times* report[5] claims that the US has persuaded Brazil to accept some restrictions on LDC arms sales.

Export-oriented trade and industrialisation strategies essentially integrate a small open economy with both international markets and international production processes and division of labour. Wulf (1983a) details the different temporal phases by which the integration takes place, with special reference to arms production. Usually, five stages can be identified. These are (a) assembly work; (b) production of components; (c) production of arms under the control of companies in developing countries; (d) direct investment by foreign companies; and (e) manufacture in free-production zones. Defence related exports are still confined mainly to the first three phases, with a few cases in the fourth and none in the final stage.[6]

The total impact of NIC arms exports on international

suppliers is still very small; only 2.4 per cent of the global trade in conventional weapons is accounted for by Third World producers. However, for specific countries like Brazil, arms exports are obviously quite important. Further these exportables are meshed in with the general orientation of industrialisation policies geared to world markets. As Wulf (1983a) succinctly puts it:

> The characteristic feature of Brazil's economic sector has been an open-door policy leading to large-scale investment by trans national corporations and to an export-oriented industrial pattern. The entire international automobile industry is represented in Brazil . . . It is therefore not surprising to observe a fast growing arms industry that is based on collaboration of the transportation and the machinery industries. Brazil's arms industry strategy is obviously, with some time lag, fairly well synchronised to the general export-oriented industrialisation pattern.

The links between domestic production of armaments and the overall industrial structure are twofold. First a relatively well-developed industrial base may be a necessary (though not sufficient) precondition for an economy to embark on the manufacture of arms. Second, after the arms industries have been set up, they will have backward linkages, thus creating inter-industrial demand and a concomitant spin-off for the underlying industrial base. We deal with each in turn.

It is apparent that the military-industrial complex in LDCs would have crucial technical linkages with certain specific industries rather than the whole industrial structure. In particular certain forms of heavy industry producing capital and intermediate goods are important for supplying the inputs on the basis of which domestic weapons production can be established. Kennedy (1974) and Wulf (1983b) emphasise the significance of these sectors, which are (i) iron and steel, (ii) nonferrous metals, (iii) metal products, (iv) nonelectrical machinery, (v) electrical machinery, (vi) shipbuilding and repairing, (vii) motor vehicles. The framework is termed the Potential Defence Capacity (PDC) by Kennedy (1974), and the Potential Arms Production Base (PAPB) by Wulf (1983b). The question for analysis is, then, for specific (arms producing) countries, whether the prior existence of PAPB or PDC industries or sectors, and their *importance* within the overall economy, are interrelated with the volume of arms manufacture. Henceforth we shall use the terms PDC and PAPB interchangeably.

Constructing a suitable index for the potential base for arms production is difficult. Such an index will not only have to take care of the capacity of the relevant industries, but also to incorporate information regarding the manpower potential of the economy. By their very nature, these industries (as well as those producing arms specifically) are highly skill-intensive and technical labour is essential for their successful operation. Even if the economy has sufficient physical resources in terms of domestic investment and foreign exchange, lack of human capital resources may be an overriding constraint. It should be clear that the availability of this human capital base potentially useful to weapons production is closely related to the absorptive capacity of the economy which was discussed in earlier chapters. Thus arms manufacture, by requiring and using these skills, may be potentially harmful to the rest of the economy, unless of course the beneficial spin-off effects (to be discussed later) are sufficiently large.

Wulf (1983a) suggests five criteria for ranking countries according to PAPB. These are (a) the share of manufacturing as a percentage of GDP; (b) the volume of production of the relevant PDC industries as a percentage of manufacturing output; (c) total output in the PDC sectors; (d) the number of scientists and technical personnel engaged in R&D; and finally (e) the labour force employed in the PAPB group of industries. The first three categories constitute the industrial base for domestic arms production, and the last two constitute the human capital base.

Subject to data availability, Wulf (1983a) gives a comprehensive volume of information on these variables for a large number of LDCs including almost all the major arms producers in Third World countries. Table 7.2 reproduces part of the available data. The first column is derived from his overall PAPB ranking, but no explicit indications are given regarding the method of deriving these final rank orders. We believe that a more formal method of *aggregating* over the rank ordering of each individual criterion is probably desirable.

First we need to rank the countries according to each category

Table 7.2 *Potential arms production base relevant for PDC*

(1)	(2)	(3)	(4)	(5)	(6)	(7)
1	India	16	32	5,025	97[xy]	1,688
2	Brazil	25	36	17,025	8	1,194
3	Yugoslavia	31	40	4,800	32	578
4	South Africa	23	38[y]	3,925	—	396[y]
5	Mexico	28	—	—	6[xy]	167
6	Argentina	37	—	—	19	112
7	Taiwan	37	38	3,375	—	263
8	S. Korea	25	21	2,500	19	322
9	Turkey	20	21	2,050	9[xy]	218
10	Greece	19	23	1,375	4	114
11	Iran	13	35	3,500	6[y]	90
12	Israel	30	33	1,300	3[x]	97
13	Portugal	36	20	1,275	4	130
14	Egypt	24	20[y]	875	11[y]	98[y]
15	Chile	20	45	1,325	6[y]	76
16	Venezuela	15	22	1,300	4[y]	79
17	Philippines	25	15	900	—	80
18	Colombia	19	17	625	1[x]	88
19	Thailand	20	21[y]	900	6[x]	—
20	Singapore	25	32	600	1	91
21	Indonesia	9	12	525	19	61
22	Pakistan	16	12[y]	325	9	78[y]
23	Peru	19	25	425	—	49[y]
24	Malaysia	18	15[y]	425	—	72[y]
25	Nigeria	9	17	465	3[y]	23
26	S. Arabia	5	—	—	—	—
27	Zimbabwe	21	30	225	—	47

Source: Wulf (1983a).
Col. 1 Rank of countries.
Col. 2 Name of countries.
Col. 3 Manufacturing as % of GDP.
Col. 4 Relevant industries as % of manufacturing.
Col. 5 Output of relevant industries in US $ million.
Col. 6 Scientists, engineers, technicans in R&D (thousands).
Col. 7 Employees/persons engaged in the relevant industries (thousands).
x = only scientists and engineers.
y = no recent data after 1974 available.

of information, then aggregate. Tables 7.3 (first three columns) and 7.4 (first two columns) rank these criteria (using the information from Table 7.2) in ascending order of magnitude. As is evident, the ranking is made among countries for which we have information on *all* the criteria in each table; thus Mexico or Argentina is left out of the rankings in Table 7.3 since we do not have data for the share of PDC industries in manufacturing nor for its total output. This is done because our major interest is in construction of an aggregate rank, using all the criteria available for each country.

Table 7.3 *Rank order for industrial base relevant for PDC*

Countries	(1) Manufacturing / GDP	(2) PDC industries / manufacturing	(3) Output of PDC indust.	(4) Borda scores	(5) Rank by Borda scores
Israel	4	7	11	22	5
India	19	8	2	29	8
Brazil	5	5	1	11	3
Yugoslavia	3	2	3	8	1
S. Africa	10	3	4	17	4
Taiwan	1	3	6	10	2
S. Korea	5	14	7	26	7
Philippines	5	21	14	40	14
Turkey	12	14	8	34	12
Indonesia	23	23	19	65	23
Egypt	9	17	16	42	16
Pakistan	19	23	23	65	23
Singapore	5	8	18	31	9
Iran	22	6	5	33	11
Colombia	15	19	17	51	20
Portugal	2	17	13	32	10
Greece	15	12	9	36	13
Peru	15	11	22	48	19
Thailand	12	14	14	40	14
Venezuela	21	13	11	45	17
Nigeria	23	19	20	62	22
Malaysia	18	21	21	60	21
Chile	12	1	10	23	6
Zimbabwe	11	10	24	45	17

Table 7.4 *Rank order for human capital*

Countries	(1) No. of scientists	(2) Total employees	(3) Borda scores	(4) Rank on basis of Borda scores
Israel	16	11	27	14
India	1	1	2	2
Brazil	9	2	11	4
Yugoslavia	2	3	5	2
Argentina	3	9	12	5
S. Korea	3	4	7	3
Turkey	7	5	12	5
Indonesia	3	18	21	10
Egypt	6	10	16	7
Pakistan	7	16	23	12
Singapore	18	12	30	17
Iran	10	13	23	12
Colombia	18	14	32	18
Portugal	13	7	20	9
Greece	13	8	21	10
Venezuela	13	15	28	16
Nigeria	16	19	35	19
Mexico	10	6	16	7
Chile	10	17	27	14

Aggregation among the different indices still poses a major problem. The most satisfactory method of comparison is given by the concept of 'Lorenz dominance' (Sen, 1981). Country *X* Lorenz dominates *Y* if the former has at least the same rank as the latter for each criterion and a strictly dominant (lower) rank for at least one criterion. As Sen (1981) claims: 'When Lorenz dominance holds, many interpretable conclusions can be drawn . . . on the other hand, this is a demanding criterion, and very often neither country Lorenz dominates the other in a pairwise comparison.' As is clear from Table 7.3, columns 1-3, and Table 7.4, columns 1 and 2, it is difficult to get a Lorenz ranking which can order the countries according to their potential for arms production.

Sen (1981) has suggested that

> some less demanding method of ranking has to be chosen . . .

> if completeness is sought. A simple method of choosing this – surprisingly little used in empirical comparisons – is to follow Borda's (1781) method of rank-order scoring, giving points equal to the rank value of each country in each criterion of comparative ranking. This produces a complete ordering based on all the criteria taken together in terms of lowness of the sum of ranks (Borda scores).

This interesting method has the advantages of simplicity and completeness as well as allowing us to make comparative analysis.

Table 7.3, column 4, gives the Borda scores for the industrial base of the economy most relevant for arms production. Column 5 then is the rank order which combines the three criteria appropriate for the basic industrial structure. Similarly, Table 7.4, column 3, gives the Borda scores for the manpower base necessary for weapons manufactures, and column 4 of the same table is the corresponding rank for human capital. Unfortunately, data availability restricts us in making a complete classification of all the countries in the sample. Using the Borda scores for both industrial structure and human capital availability, Table 7.5, column 2, gives the final aggregative rank ordering (by adding the Borda scores in Tables 7.3 and 7.4) for PDC or PAPB for seventeen countries for which data on *all five* criteria were available. Column 1 of the same table indicates the ranks of actual production *for these seventeen countries only*.

A large variety of interesting conclusions can be drawn on a comparative basis for those countries which have some form of domestic armaments production. For reasons of space we concentrate on the final rank order given in Table 7.5, though similar analyses are possible for the subgroups related to industrial and human capital bases separately. For the top six countries (Israel, India, Brazil, Yugoslavia, South Korea and Turkey), there seems to be a close connection between the ranks given by actual arms production and the potential capacity of defence manufacturers. Thus the industrial base needed for military production in terms of relevant industries, human capital stock and absorptive capacity is probably quite important for relatively large weapons manufacturers. (Israel is a possible exception since it is a 'siege' economy.) Lower down the list the

Table 7.5 *Ranks of actual and potential capacity for defence industries*

Countries	(1) Actual arms production	(2) Potential for arms production
1 Israel	1	6
2 India	2	3
3 Brazil	3	2
4 Yugoslavia	4	1
5 S. Korea	5	4
6 Turkey	6	5
7 Indonesia	7	15
8 Egypt	8	11
9 Pakistan	9	16
10 Singapore	10	12
11 Iran	11	9
12 Colombia	12	14
13 Portugal	13	8
14 Greece	14	10
15 Venezuela	15	13
16 Nigeria	16	17
17 Chile	17	7

Source: Col. 1 adapted from Wulf (1983b), Col. 2 my own calculation from Tables 7.1, 7.2 and 7.3.

position is not very clear. For example, Indonesia is eighth in the list for actual arms output while fifteenth for potential production. Similarly Pakistan's relative importance in the production list is not matched by potentiality. On the other hand in the case of Chile (or Greece, or Portugal), the position is reversed. However, the deviant cases usually have exogenous factors which may affect their willingness to produce defence goods domestically. Independent of potential capacity, external threat (for Pakistan, Egypt, Israel), oil revenue (for Indonesia), membership of a security alliance (for Greece in NATO), may well have contributed to the discrepancy between the two rankings reported in Table 7.5. Overall, we can conclude that having a pre-existing industrial base and specific human capital endowments may be quite helpful in setting up and maintaining an arms-industrial complex. On the other hand countries with special security problems may be locked into weapons manufacture which they can barely afford. The absorptive capacity constraints for the civilian sectors are thus more binding, and the ultimate effect on the economy would be relatively more harmful. Countries with a larger rank order (weaker capacity) for potential capacity for defence, relative to actual arms production (see Table 7.5), may have a disproportionately high burden of defence industrialisation since the manufacturing and human capital base is inadequate to support the military-industrial superstructure.

Having considered the role of PDC sectors in the creation of defence industrialisation, let us now turn to the spin-off effects that arms production may have through backward linkages with the industrial base of the economy. Once again the type of spin-off that we are considering should be most evident for the PDC sectors mentioned earlier, precisely because of the technical linkages that exist between them and defence production.

At this stage it will be instructive to consider more exactly the nature of spin-off that military spending may have in the specific context of the NICs. The beneficial effects of defence can be split up into two components for analytical purposes, though there are interrelationships among them. First, if there is underutilised capacity and underemployment of capital, then the military-industrial complex may be used to create effective demand. The inter-industrial demand linkages of this complex with productive sectors of the economy will clearly stimulate civilian industrial output. Second, through new skill formation, creation of management and organisational expertise, R&D and so forth, technological progress can be introduced into the economy. This will shift the production function outwards and reduce unit costs, once again helping industrial production. It is plausible that due to technical progress initiated by the defence sectors, spin-off might more reasonably influence unit-costs and specifically reduce the average cost of production. The effect of this would be to shift the supply curve of output in these industries to the right. Thus the equilibrium level of output will increase from its previous level, given normal sloping demand and supply curves.

It is to be expected that for an NIC intent on having a relatively self-sufficient defence industry of its own, an increase in total military expenditure (M) would tend to increase the volume of domestic arms production over time since a part of defence spending will be utilised for weapons manufacture. This in turn, through the channels mentioned in the previous paragraph, is expected to have a positive effect on the output of the specific PDC industries. Further, military spending *per se* will have a large capital expenditure component which will create, independently, demand from civilian industries particularly in the PDC categories. Overall therefore we should expect an increase in total defence expenditure to have a positive effect on the volume index of output in the industries mentioned above (mostly in the metal and engineering groups). This would support and validate the spin-off argument for defence expenditure and production.

Heuristic discussions in this area are confident that positive spin-off exists and is significant (see Benoit, 1973, 1978; Kennedy, 1974; Ball, 1983). Specific Indian industries like electronics have reputedly been helped by defence orders. The meteoric rise of the South Korean textile industry is attributed to military demand (see Westphal, 1978). In Argentina, the General Directorate of Military Factories (Dirección General de Fabricaciones Militares) from the early 1940s not only laid the foundation of defence industrialisation but also helped the overall policy of input-substituting industrialisation. Many defence factories produced goods for the civilian sectors, and the 'interaction between military and civilian heavy/light industries is a crucial factor in the process of industrial development in Argentina' (Carranza, 1983). Neuman (1978) reports the interrelationships between defence and civilian industrialisation for the Iranian economy. The Military Industries Organisation has, as a number of subsidiaries, industrial establishments which produce a range of products from ammunition to electronics. In addition to creating inter-industrial demands, its output also meets civilian needs such as the supply of batteries or radios. But more important is the fact that due to high set-up and other fixed costs, the rate of return on investment can be quite low in the initial stages of production. Thus many of these civilian-related industries would not have been established without the direct intervention of the military, since the private sector was not interested, due to low profits, and the public sector had little motivation and no coherent plan. It was left to the military to start some of these industries.

We can look a bit more closely at R&D and technical progress. It has been claimed that military-related R&D can be beneficial to the civilian sector. One of the LDCs to be mentioned in this context is India. From the 1960s onwards, India spent large sums of money on military R&D, as part of defence industrialisation within an inward-looking ISI strategy. Since self-sufficiency was the final objective, technological progress had to be generated endogenously, and R&D was considered the major vehicle of such technical progress. SIPRI (1981) provides data for eighteen developed countries and India to show comparative performance in defence-related research and innovation. In spite of its low *per capita* income and backward structural characteristics, India does extremely well in the field. For example, during 1976-79, the last period for which all data was available, the percentage share of military R&D in total national expenditure on R&D in India was higher than in all other OECD countries except France, the UK, and the US. In absolute terms, for 1979, India had a higher defence-industrial R&D than Greece. Whatever the index, there can be little doubt that military R&D has made significant quantitative advances in India.

Table 7.6 gives some comparative figures for military R&D. Japan and the UK have often been cited as classic polar cases; the former has spent very little on defence and yet done substantially better than the UK in industrial production and manufacturing growth. Greece is included since it still contains elements of underdevelopment and is also considered to be a newly industrialising country. The annual average expenditure on

Table 7.6 *Military R&D (1976-79)*

	India	Japan	UK	Greece
Percentage share in total government R&D	18.8	2.3	51.6	3.7
Percentage share in national expenditure on R&D	15.1	0.6	29.3	3.6
Percentage share in GDP	0.074	0.012	0.604	0.006
Annual average military R&D expenditure (constant price, US $million 1980)	102	111	3,043.5	2.57
GDP *per capita* 1981	256	10,085	9,112	4,418

Source: SIPRI (1984) and World Bank, *World Tables* (1983).

military R&D is almost the same in India and Japan, and substantially higher than that of Greece. The relative figures in the first three rows all show the importance of this form of technological progress in the Indian economy. The contrast is heightened when viewed in terms of *per capita* national product, where India lags far behind the other three. Given the figures, there can be little doubt that military R&D is important in India. If the spin-off hypothesis is to be substantiated, India should receive the benefits of the substantial investment in defence inventions and research.

We would like to analyse the issues in a more formal structure, but without some form of quantification the arguments lack suitable empirical foundations. Deger and Sen (1983a) attempt such a quantification and it is interesting to summarise the conclusions. An empirical test for the existence of spin-off is given by estimating the following equation for any country:

$$x_i = a_{0i} + a_{1i}M + a_{2i}V + u_i$$

(M is defence spending, V is any exogenous variable, x_i is the output of *each* of the potential defence capacity industries and u_i is an error term). If a_{1i} is positive and significant, then an increase in M (proxy for defence industrialisation) increases x_i and has a beneficial spin-off effect on PDC industries.

It is clear that, given the diversified industrial structure of LDCs and NICs, cross-sectional studies are not adequate here. It is preferable to do a time series analysis for a single country and study the possible effects. The problem of country studies is that there is always the implied criticism of bias in the choice of country. Deger and Sen (1983a) chose India as the vehicle of their analysis. This is because, in India, economic spin-off from the military is intuitively expected to have a *positive* effect. Since the 1950s, India has consistently gone for a policy of self-sufficient industrialisation, import controls and the expansion of manufacturing activity. Simultaneously, in spite of accepting military aid occasionally, it has tried relentlessly to produce armaments within the country and to build up near self-sufficiency in all but the most sophisticated military hardware. Given this parallel growth in civilian and military industrialisation, it is natural to expect that if spin-off does have a positive effect, it will be clearly reflected in the Indian case. In other words, if empirical analysis shows the existence of beneficial spin-off effects, we should not be surprised. On the other hand if this is not found for India, then there exists a counter-intuitive result and it will have to be accepted that the beneficial consequences of spin-off may have been vastly overrated. Empirical estimation reported in Deger and Sen (1983a) fails to reveal significant evidence of spin-off. The country and industries chosen have the best chance of receiving the fruits of spin-off. Yet with all these factors loaded in favour of a beneficial effect, we find that the coefficients are insignificant and not much different from zero (in some cases they are actually negative). Thus in the apparently most favourable case, the effect of economic spin-off is negligible. Obviously, in other cases it could well be even less. We may conclude that the emphasis of spin-off in the defence literature is misplaced since its actual consequences are barely observable. A descriptive case study has been done for Turkey by Ayres (1983), who obtains a similar result to India.

Some spin-off from arms industrialisation undoubtedly exists. Simon Kuznets (1980) may be quoted in this context: 'The effective search for new knowledge and for its exploitation in the production of goods for peace type uses, served in good part also war purposes – because of the technological affinity between the two. Reciprocally, some of the search for new knowledge and for its exploitation specifically for war purposes was of use for peace type production.' The debate relates to the actual quantifiable effect.

In a careful study of the macroeconomic costs of military expenditure during 1960-70 in India, Terhal (1981) analyses some of the specific spin-offs that arms production may have had on the rest of the economy. For example, some 40 per cent of output of defence-industrial establishments was made up of civilian goods. Further, military-related R&D contributed to 20 per cent of total R&D in India in the early 1970s. Finally, 'With respect to the common fund of basic scientific knowledge the contribution of military oriented research may have been more important. It is needless to emphasise the potential civilian benefits of this common fund of knowledge' (Terhal, 1981). There can be little doubt that many of the most sophisticated research and industrial projects would not have been carried out without the stimulus from defence needs. This is particularly true for 'dual purpose technology' where basic research is conducted for military purposes but which has substantial civilian productivity. The foundations for advanced research in India, in the areas of nuclear energy, space satellites and electronics, were laid in the 1960s principally as a response to strategic requirements. The recent progress made by Indian scientists in these fields would not have been possible without the stimulus from defence. Yet the overall conclusions that Terhal (1981) draws after a massive survey of the data is pessimistic: 'with respect to the civilian spin-off of applied military research . . . we tend to feel that these benefits were not very important'.

There are some basic reasons why the economic and industrial spill-overs may not be that significant. Firstly, the technology adopted by the defence sectors may be far too advanced for the rest of the economy, thus the latter would not be enthusiastic in applying the new methods. Secondly, strategic considerations would mean that the technology and research would be kept secret and would not be allowed to disseminate to civilian production. Thirdly, military projects are sometimes necessary for pure security reasons only and thus may not be able to generate high profits in commercial production. Thus they may not be sufficiently cost-effective in a competitive market environment and so may be relatively useless for private entrepreneurs.

The Indian case is a pointer that one must treat the concept of spin-off from military industrialisation with some caution. Further research with other major producers such as Brazil is necessary to make a proper comparative evaluation.

7.4 Resource and import costs

It is possible that arms industrialisation imposes quite heavy resource costs on the newly developed potential base for arms manufacture, and absorptive capacity constraints are accentuated when an NIC decides to go in for large-scale production of weapons.

A major potential loss to the economy is skilled manpower. As Terhal's (1981) important study on India categorically states:

> The effects of many thousands of highly skilled scientific and technical personnel were directed from potential civilian to military innovation. In view of the important input which civilian research and development means for increasing productivity and efficiency this has certainly tended to cause a serious drawback for potential economic growth. Within the Indian build-up of scientific research and development, the military segment has got preferential treatment. The direct civilian opportunity costs of this priority are difficult to estimate, but not negligible.

If the military sector, in the pursuit of arms manufacturing, has a sizeable spin-off in the form of training, the creation of new skills and R&D, then of course the opportunity costs are mitigated. But as we have seen, such beneficial effects have not been very important to India.

More generally, there are three types of opportunity costs that domestic defence industrialisation entails. It will need financing and capital, which may reduce civilian capital accumulation. However, if there is excess capacity and underutilisation of capital, the costs will be low and there may even be benefits from demand creation. Defence sectors need on average more skilled labour than the civilian economy, and this reduces absorptive capacity. Once again training in military factories creates skills to compensate partially for the costs. Finally, intermediate imports for defence industrialisation reduce foreign exchange reserves for other productive uses. But if armaments industries can export goods, then some of the losses are recouped.

The more conventional costs in terms of capital and labour take on a new twist in the context of military industrialisation. As discussed earlier, the relative sophistication of modern arms and the method by which new 'demand' is created induce rapid technical change and obsolescence. We must therefore consider the implications of defence-oriented technical progress in the context of the available supply of factors of production.

There are two aspects of technical progress that need explanation. First, most technical innovation is induced: it does not fall 'like manna from heaven'; rather it requires R&D and investment, which are in turn influenced by the state of development of the country concerned. Second, technical progress often limits the degree of substitution between inputs like labour and capital needed to produce the final product. An extreme example is the putty clay model (see Dixit, 1976, for a formal exposition) where there is perfect substitution between factor inputs before investment (following from technical change), but none after.

Let us consider the issues within a theoretical model. There exists a military technology where the output of arms (D) is produced by two factors: capital (K) and labour (L). Suppose prior to technical change there is a high possibility of substitution between K and L, so that D can be produced by a widely different range of capital-labour ratios. The usual shaped isoquant AB in Figure 7.1 represents current technology.

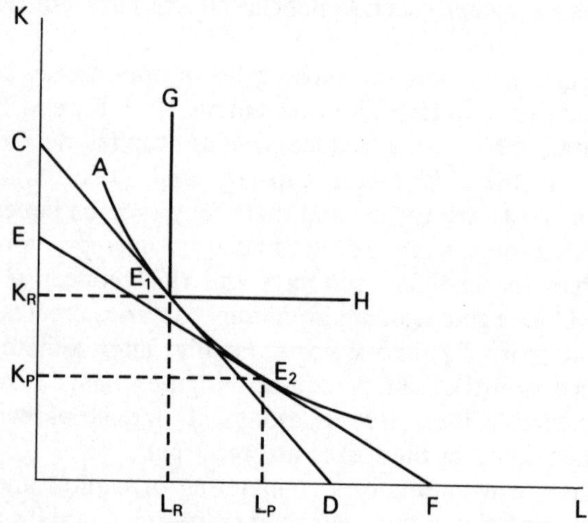

Figure 7.1 The transfer of military technology

Suppose this technology is freely available. A developed (rich) country with higher capital endowments will choose to produce output at E_1 with the slope of CD giving the wage-rental ratio. The factors in use will be K_R and L_R. An underdeveloped (poor) country with abundant labour and lower wage-rental ratio will produce at E_2 using more labour (L_P) and less capital (K_P).

Given the sophistication and costs of military research, most technical progress in defence production takes place in developed countries. So when technical change is induced in DCs, they will work to move out the production frontier around the point at which they are currently located, developing a very specialised technology appropriate to their *own* wage-rental ratio. In the putty clay model, in the limit, there will be an L-shaped isoquant where there is no possibility of substitution between the two factors. Since the innovation comes from the economy where wage-rental is high, it is expected that the vertex of the isoquant (the most efficient point) will lie at E_2, thus the technology will be useful for the country having low labour but high capital stocks. The total effect of *DC*-induced innovation and the shrinking of the substitution possibility will give a new isoquant of the type GE_1H. Clearly, this *new* technology is inappropriate for LDCs, unlike the old one. To use techniques most efficiently, the LDC might have to shed labour and create unemployment, or alternatively, at L_P, increase capital stock substantially to reach the relevant optimum point of the isoquants. It is obvious that inappropriate technology is the bane of LDCs, and this is particularly true in military-oriented fields, where technical progress is faster, usually induced in DCs with more investment and R&D infrastructure, often needs to be imported without control or adaptation, and involves massive resource costs, particularly the inputs which are in short supply.

The theoretical discussion above pinpoints a salient feature of military-oriented technology transfer and the choice of feasible techniques by LDCs. From a purely strategic efficiency point of view it may be optimal for LDCs to choose the most efficient technology. However, increasing proportions being spent on new vintages will, by increasing obsolescence, make the resource cost prohibitive. The macroeconomic cost of inappropriate technology will have to be considered too. Labour-surplus developing countries might be saddled by highly capital-intensive methods of production leading to a choice of techniques incompatible with endowments and factor-price ratios. Thus even though technology transfer might have some general beneficial effects, the costs will be extremely high.

The foregoing analysis has concentrated on domestic resources utilisation and costs. However, implicit in the discussion remains the fact that most defence technology is imported even for economies which have adopted ISI strategies. The major expenditures will have to be borne with foreign exchange, and it is this external constraint that has overriding importance. We turn to this issue now.

Even though arms industrialisation in NICs is often initiated to reduce import and foreign exchange costs, in practice it has sometimes turned out to be quite different. Table 7.7 gives ranks for arms production and imports for major LDC weapons manufacturers. Among the fifteen largest arms producers in the Third World, Israel and India rank as the top two both in weapons production and in arms imports. On the other hand among these fifteen countries, Brazil, Yugoslavia and South Africa rank third, fourth and fifth in arms production while being tenth, eleventh and thirteenth in arms imports. Clearly, for the latter three, domestic production has alleviated in some measure the huge burden of imported armaments.

Imports may of course be at a high level for some countries *independent* of domestic production, due to specific security concerns. Again, an arms race in terms of weapons stocks purchased in international markets and thus technologically superior may induce 'unnecessary' imports as a requisite sacrifice

Table 7.7 *Arms production and imports in the late 1970s: ranks*

Countries	(1) Production	(2) Imports
Israel	1	1
India	2	2
Brazil	3	10
Yugoslavia	4	11
South Africa	5	13
Argentina	6	6
Taiwan	7	5
S. Korea	8	3
Philippines	9	14
Turkey	10	6
Indonesia	11	9
Egypt	12	4
N. Korea	13	12
Pakistan	14	6
Singapore	15	15

Source: Wulf (1983b), ACDA and own calculations.

to the concept of deterrence. Note that in the group of fifteen, the five leading arms importers – Israel, India, South Korea, Egypt and Taiwan – all claim to have some special or specific regional security problems.

The reasons why a newly initiated domestic military-industrial complex would *increase* rather than decrease the import burden of an economy needs to be analysed. Since military industrialisation is at the forefront of modern technology, and even LDCs need to produce reasonably superior vintages to maintain their security balance, much of the technology, blueprints, intermediate products and components will have to be imported. The total foreign exchange costs of this input package may be quite substantial. The overall macroeconomic opportunity cost in terms of growth effects in an open economy has been dealt with elsewhere (see Chapter 6). Here we stress the direct cost, in terms of imports and foreign exchange.

Consider the case of indigenous defence production in India. We have already seen in the previous chapter that the massive defence industrialisation drive pursued by the Indian government, particularly after the Chinese war of 1962, did help in reducing the import costs of the military, especially in the initial years. India, of course, had a heritage of military production even from colonial days. At the time of independence (1947), there were more than fifteen well-established ordnance factories producing small arms, ammunition, field artillery, etc. Some of them, such as the unit in Ishapore, were quite large and sophisticated for contemporary needs. Production lagged in the 1950s, but picked up rapidly thereafter. By the early 1970s, twelve or so new ordnance factories had been established. Further, a new class of state economic enterprise called public sector undertakings was set up to produce more sophisticated products such as aircraft, warships and tanks. The Avadi heavy vehicles factory produces the much acclaimed Vijayanta tank, which has proved its battle worthiness quite often. Given the rapid rise in India's defence *needs* from about 1960 (three major wars in a decade, perceived hostility with two large neighbours, etc.), the establishment of these industries must have saved a great amount of foreign exchange which would otherwise have been necessary for imported armaments.

Table 7.8 indicates the importance of defence production.

Table 7.8 *Expenditure on defence production and foreign exchange requirements of military spending: India, 1951-72 (percentage share of total defence budgets)*

	(1)	(2)
1951	11.5	12.3
1952	14.0	13.4
1953	13.2	12.1
1954	12.1	16.3
1955	11.8	24.3
1956	9.6	29.1
1957	9.4	24.5
1958	11.7	30.5
1959	12.9	35.7
1960	13.2	35.1
1961	15.3	27.1
1962	17.2	13.4
1963	15.8	13.4
1964	13.2	10.1
1965	14.0	8.7
1966	14.3	14.3
1967	16.9	11.0
1968	16.0	12.5
1969	15.1	12.8
1970	16.3	12.2
1971	16.5	12.6
1972	18.2	14.3

Source: Col. 1 gives the ratio of spending on military industry to total defence expenditure. This is calculated from Ball (1983). Col. 2 is the foreign exchange component of defence spending as a percentage of total military budget. See Table 6.5.

Column 1 shows the expenditure on military industry as a proportion of the total defence budget. The share rises over time; noting that the total budget increased by over 150 per cent in real terms during this time period, we can be confident that defence production was given high priority by the planners. Column 2 shows the foreign exchange costs of the military as a percentage of total defence spending. Again the 1960s show a dramatic reduction. As mentioned in the previous chapter, part of this reduction was due to foreign aid; but defence industrialisation must have contributed a lot.

However, these figures do not reveal whether the Indian military-related import cost went down at an absolute level due to domestic production. Once again Terhal (1981) is instructive here regarding the imports needed for the Indian arms industrialisation programme in the 1960s:

> During the '60s India changed its strategy to reduce the foreign exchange burden of the military sector. She tried hard to substitute ready made hardware imports by indigenous production. The effect on the balance of payments was to shift the bulk of the foreign exchange allocation to the defence industries.

Table 7.9, which uses selected estimated data from Terhal (1981), clearly shows the effect of domestic fabrication of arms on the level of imports.

Table 7.9 *Value of arms imports for India, selected years (US $ million 1972)*

	Direct defence imports	Imports for defence industries	Others	Total
1950-51	50	9	27	86
Percentage	58.1	10.5	31.4	100
1955-56	102	32	22	156
Percentage	65.4	20.5	14.1	100
1960-61	200	46	24	270
Percentage	74.1	17.0	8.9	100
1972-73	101	115	52	268
Percentage	37.7	42.9	19.4	100

Source: Calculated from Terhal (1982).

The 1960s witnessed the rapid growth of domestic production of arms in India, with the trend accelerating in the early 1970s. Table 7.9 shows that the total foreign exchange burden did fall slightly between 1960-61 and 1972-73. However, imports for defence industries increased by almost two and a half times, while direct defence imports halved. Import substitution had some benefits in reducing direct defence imports, and the related foreign exchange cost, debt servicing, repayments burden, and so forth. However, the imports needed for domestic manufacture almost compensated for the reduction in costs.

The recent splurge in defence imports bears witness to the fact that, at least in part, it has been difficult to keep down foreign exchange costs in spite of successful military industrialisation. Modernising industries, paying for foreign R&D, buying new technology and importing intermediate goods for new investment, will mean that domestic defence production will still have substantial foreign exchange costs.

Thus, overall, domestic manufacture of weapons may not be the hoped-for panacea for rising import prices, at least in the short run. As Wulf (1983b) says:

> The capability of developing countries to import what is needed for development and industrialisation is often drastically reduced by the importation of military technologies. Engaging in domestic arms production is no solution to this problem as can be demonstrated. Dependence on imports of weapons and licenses has not been reduced in most cases.

However, it is expected that in the long run increasing self-sufficiency in armaments should have some beneficial effects in terms of foreign exchange and import savings. Once again much will depend on the need or demand for the latest technology weapons. As we have repeatedly stressed, from a single country's point of view the demand for arms is crucially dependent on autonomous factors (such as its regional rivals' arms purchases); thus it is difficult to forecast the nature and value of arms imports even after a reasonably independent arms technology has been established domestically.

8 Economic growth and military expenditure

8.1 The basic issues

Directly or indirectly, the previous chapters of this book have analysed the relationships between military expenditure and growth. Savings, investment, human capital, foreign resources are all important for growth and development, and we have taken each in turn, analysing the implication of additional defence spending on those variables. The time has now come to look explicitly and more specifically at growth and to provide an overview of the link between the growth process and military expenditure in LDCs.

The most startling economic and econometric evidence in favour of defence expenditure stimulating growth is of course the work of Emile Benoit. A succinct summary of his larger analytical study is given in his paper written for *Economic Development and Cultural Change* (1978). It is important to critically evaluate this paper since a large number of further studies are based implicitly on Benoit's work. This is done in Section 8.2.

Economic growth can be viewed as an interaction of factors that operate from the demand as well as the supply side of aggregate output and its sectoral composition. If the growth of demand is sufficient, then labour-abundant LDCs need physical and human capital to increase growth from the supply side. The policy-makers need to decide on the optimum rate of saving; the method by which this saving is to be translated into investment; the allocation of investable resources into its sectoral components (agriculture/manufacture, consumer/producer goods, etc.); the availability of co-operative factors such as skilled labour; and finally the appropriate choice of techniques.

These are essentially problems of planning, and it is important to integrate strategic (military) planning for security with economic (developmental) planning for growth. However, most LDCs are also dominated by market sectors in the form of private enterprise, thus the proper incentive mechanisms by which planners (governments) induce private agents to act could be critical. In planning for defence spending, the response of the private sector to government policy in the form of tax, transfer, money creation and so forth may be quite important. The supply side issues are elaborated in Section 8.3.

Aggregate growth models of the Harrod-Domar or (more specifically for semi-planned economies) the Domar-Feldman type were often used as the basis for developmental planning and growth strategies from the 1950s onwards.[1] The structure was of course much more elaborate but the basic methodological points remained the same. Emphasis on the *supply* side, the importance of capital formation, the vital role of industrialisation and the economy's capacity to generate resources were the hallmarks of this approach. Quite often the plans were inward-looking with the domestic saving propensity playing a major role in the growth process. At best foreign aid – resources as 'manna from heaven' – were thought to augment the economy's resource pool and thus help growth. The alternative point of view, that *demand* may be the constraining factor to growth, has slowly gained acceptance, and today stands on solid intellectual ground (Kaldor, 1975). The importance of domestic or overseas demand for the growth of manufacturing and investment goods production cannot be ignored, and it is this version of balanced sectoral growth that also needs to be analysed in the context of defence spending and industrialisation. Section 8.4 deals with demand factors.

The details of the statistical evidence for the military growth relation is discussed more fully in the Appendix. However, the empirical analysis throws up the possibility that the simple military burden/growth rate relations may not be unidirectional, and they may have substantial nonlinearities inherent in them (Boulding, 1974). The presence of such nonlinearities implies that as countries grow they pass through different stages of development, and it is possible that the military may help growth at one stage and hinder it at another. The precise nature of these stages is a matter of some speculation, and more research will be needed to sort out the details. But some tentative conclusions are reported in Section 8.5.

8.2 The findings of Emile Benoit

Using a large sample of forty-four countries as well as some studies on specific countries, Benoit tries to establish that defence expenditure overall stimulates rather than retards growth in LDCs. The best thing to do is to let him speak for himself:

> It has usually been supposed by economists that defence expenditure reduces the resources available for investment and so slows down growth . . . However, in a large study of less developed countries, an opposite pattern seemed to appear, and this finding was so unexpected and challenging that it seemed worthwhile exploring in detail . . . Contrary to my expectations, countries with a heavy defence burden had the most rapid rate of growth, and those with the lowest defence burden tended to show the lowest growth rates. (Benoit, 1978)

A large and relatively comprehensive volume of evidence is presented (particularly in his book) regarding the *causality* of the interrelationship between growth and defence. It is of course plausible that high growth induces high defence expenditure, since resource costs are relatively low and financial constraints may be more relaxed. However, he shows that the causation runs from defence to growth, and for all practical purposes defence spending may be taken as relatively autonomous of domestic growth prospects. As we showed earlier, the public good aspect of military budgets or the availability of higher government revenues may mean more milex for specific economies. But two points seem to be well established. First, the major cause for military expansion is the perceived or actual threat and security considerations faced by any country. Second, high growth *per se* need not cause the defence burden to rise. 'And in multiple regression analysis economic growth did not emerge as a significant determinant of the defence burden' (Benoit, 1978).

Given that a high defence burden may promote growth, the specific channels through which this operates are important. One fundamental point is stressed at the beginning. If a part of the gross domestic product is not spent on defence, then it does not necessarily flow into investment. Rather, conspicuous consumption or the social wage may rise, so the opportunity cost for defence may not be as high for LDCs. Even so-called 'productive investment' may not be that productive after all, since inefficient management and execution of projects will make alternative allocation schemes less efficient than usual. This is a familiar tirade emphasising some of the organisational weaknesses of LDC government and socio-economic structure. A more subtle reasoning showing absorptive capacity problems for developing economies has already been discussed in an earlier chapter. However, this argument *per se* does not establish the fact that defence is productive, only that the alternatives are not necessarily so.

Benoit goes on to actually establish the fact that military spending and organisation may have an indirect productivity which could be potentially very strong. The following quote succinctly summarises much of the argument:

> Defence programs of most countries make tangible contributions to the civilian economies by (1) feeding, clothing, and housing a number of people who would otherwise have to be fed, housed, and clothed by the civilian economy – and sometimes doing so, especially in LDCs, in ways that involve sharply raising their nutritional and other consumption standards and expectations; (2) providing education and medical care as well as vocational and technical training (e.g. in the operation and repair of cars, planes and radios; in hygiene and medical care; in construction methods) that may have high civilian utility; (3) engaging in a variety of public works – roads, dams, river improvements, airports, communication networks, etc. – that may in part serve civilian uses; and (4) engaging in scientific and technical specialities such as hydrographic studies, mapping, aerial surveys, dredging, meteorology, soil conservation, and forestry projects as well as certain quasi-civilian activities such as coast guard, lighthouse operation, customs work, border guard, and disaster relief which would otherwise have to be performed by civilian personnel. Military forces also engage in certain R&D and production activities which diffuse skills to the civilian economy and engage in or finance self-help projects producing certain manufactured items for combined civilian and military use (e.g., batteries and tyres) which might not be economically produced solely for civilian demand. (Benoit, 1978)

In addition, modernisation, various other forms of spin-off, inflation and finally the psychological links between defence and growth, are contributory factors emphasised to show why defence may bolster growth. Overall, Benoit stresses the importance of civic-action programmes which the military are able to do efficiently and which have substantial indirect benefits. In a little-noted section of his paper written in 1978 he stresses that, as a matter of policy, the military should become more interested in such civilian-oriented activities and in a sense blur the civil-military distinction, alternatively emphasising their productivity-augmenting role.

There are of course substantial adverse effects that a defence build-up may cause to the growth prospects of an economy. The military establishment may take over resources which would otherwise be employed in more productive civilian investment. This is a simple reallocation effect of the guns/tractor variety and is the one most often quoted as the ill-effects of defence. Further, the defence sector (like the government sector in general) exhibits no measured productivity increase and therefore a shift in resources will show up in lower growth rates. Finally, there will be 'income shifts' in the sense that an increase in defence spending will reduce the civilian domestic product, *cet. par*. The total effect of all these changes is also calculated by Benoit. He estimates that a 1 per cent increase in shares of defence in GDP would reduce civilian growth by 0.25 per cent. But the negative impact is more than balanced by the stimulation provided by the military sector. Overall, therefore, the positive effects dominate and growth is helped by defence.

Note once again precisely what Benoit actually means in the defence-growth relation. He is trying to estimate two broad categories of effects: one which will allocate resources away from relatively more productive occupations – the allocation effect; the second which will give a boost to growth – the spin-off effect. Both of these are *direct*: more defence spending means less money for investment; on the other hand there are beneficial spin-offs for the civilian economy if the military is strengthened. The defence sector is one component of the national economy. Allocating resources to it deprives the other sectors of funds which could possibly have been used more productively. Yet it also has an economic spin-off which is output-augmenting, so defence may also help productivity. The argument, put simply, is as follows: on the one hand it gives, and on the other hand it takes away; what then is the total effect? This is the sophisticated version of the butter and guns argument, with the addition of the concept of spin-off.

However, what we have stressed in the book is not only this more observable relationship, but a much more crucial factor which is not always easily identifiable, but which may have an overriding influence in the way that military expenditure may affect growth. This is the *mobilisation of resources effect*. As defence spending increases, it affects and changes the resource structure of the economy. It influences taxation, forced saving, changes in absorptive capacity, human capital formation, inflation and various other channels which contribute directly and indirectly to mobilising, augmenting or reducing the resources of the economy. The quest therefore is to find the net effect in this area. Our general discussions in previous chapters have tended to show that overall the effect of military expenditure will be negative; it will depress or reduce the potential increase in resources and erode away the savings base of the economy. Hence our fundamental difference and extension from much of the literature in the field. Attention by Benoit, and others criticising his work, has generally focused on allocation based on a *given* production possibility frontier in the short run. This book, however, claims that even in the short run the very act of allocation will tend to shift the output possibilities open to the economy. Overall, therefore, we have to consider all three effects together – allocation, spin-off and mobilisation.

It is easy to say, as some critics do, that a pound allocated to defence takes away a pound from another sector which may have greater productivity. In this sense it is almost simple arithmetic. But, of course, the case against defence is not so clear-cut. If there are positive spin-offs, and the alternatives to defence spending have no apparent productivity, then military expenditure may, after all, be growth-augmenting. This is what the defenders say. But the fundamental point is whether these possible positive effects are 'over and above' the benefits that one could get from the civilian sector using equivalent resources. One must also remember that the foregoing cost benefit analysis must include the strategic and security based returns that the defence sector provides, for that, after all, is its main function. Thus, it is not the total contribution (including the provision of security) that defence makes to the economy which is relevant. What is important is the additional effect, over and above those possible in the civilian sectors. Judged by these criteria, it can be shown that military expenditure does not increase growth and very often depresses it.

Consider a hypothetical example. £x of national resources can be allocated in three alternative ways: it can be used to produce arms, build tractors or for conspicuous consumption. The choice between the first and third options is relatively easy: the former is a better use since it provides security to the nation and may have other benefits. The choice between the first and second is not that simple. It can be argued that production of arms, in addition to security, also generates spin-off – inter-industrial linkages, training, R&D and so forth. Thus it is growth-augmenting. But this is not enough. If the mobilisation argument is included, then the externalities attached to the given allocation for arms will have to be evaluated. For various reasons discussed earlier, £x allocated to the defence sector may mean that the economy may have lost (or gained) £y elsewhere. Thus the *true* cost of defence is £$(x + y)$ or alternatively £$(x - y)$.

Now let us turn to the production of tractors. It will be equally growth-enhancing in its indirect effects, and in addition it has direct productivity, since it will increase agricultural output. The defender of investment in arms must show that their positive effects are over and above what the alternatives can do. Clearly, if the marginal return from security is overriding and almost infinite, no amount of socio-economic costing will do. Unfortunately, in most Third World countries, the questions are not posed in this way, therefore we are not *sure* about the overwhelming importance of strategic needs or the economic opportunity cost attached to them.

The precise statistical results derived by Benoit from his cross-section sample have come in for a lot of criticism (Deger and Smith, 1983; Lim, 1983).[2] A more fundamental point is whether statistical analysis is at all adequate for such studies trying to identify the effect of defence on growth. Neuman (1978) criticises such analysis from a methodological point of view. After listing a large number of problems that the use of statistical methods may face in the area, she argues cogently for specific country studies, based on field research, stressing the cultural and historical dimensions of the issues at stake:

> Apparently, secondary manipulation of macrostatistical indicators, by academic and policy making centres thousands of miles from the areas being studied, misses the essence of what is actually going on in the countries under study. There may be no substitute for field research on this issue, at least until we have discovered which are the relevant variables and have collected sufficient information about them.

She goes on to analyse the specific case of the Iranian military under the rule of the Shah and shows the positive modernising influence that militarism has had in that country. Though the point of view taken may be correct in some respects, it does not inspire too much confidence to note that a few months after the publication of the paper, Iran went over to a rule by theocracy and became *less* 'modern', at least from the standpoint taken by modernisers.

Any analysis based on the common characteristics of a large number of diverse countries should be handled with some care by the analyst. There are specific econometric methods (such as the use of dummy variables, application of error-in-variables techniques) which are available to ensure that invalid generalisations are not made. Further, cross-section analysis is used to give an *overall* picture and needs to be supplemented by case studies and specific country analysis. But all this does not invalidate the basic point that macroeconomic models supplemented by statistical technique can give us a good idea of the issues involved. As Smith and Smith's (1979) critique of Neuman points out forcefully:

> Neuman's discussion does not distinguish between conceptual limitations which make macrostatistical analysis impossible (or invalid) in *principle* and those problems in current models and data which make it difficult *in practice* . . . Practical problems will always remain and it is the task of the researcher to identify them with better techniques. But the same applies to *any* methods that one uses. Neuman did not adequately identify the latent resistance to, and failure of, modernisation

[in her work on Iran], during the late 70's [Neuman, 1978] and is a case in point that in-depth country studies may also reveal glaring weaknesses.

Benoit – as befits a pioneer in the field – does both. The cross-section econometric analysis is supplemented by actual experiences from India, South Korea, Mexico, Israel, Egypt and Argentina. Overall, his findings from the total sample of forty-four countries is substantiated by the examples drawn from individual countries. There are exceptions, of course. Mexico stands out from his data period 1950-65, as a low defence burden-high growth country relative to others. Similarly, India has a moderately high defence-income ratio and a low rate of growth. But on balance defence seems to have a positive effect on growth.

If the causation is correct that the defence burden leads ('causes') more (or less) growth rather than the opposite, then Benoit's empirical results *within his framework* seem to be robust. Single equation estimates of the form

$$g = a_0 + a_1 m + a_2 Z$$

(g is growth rate, m is military burden, Z is a vector of other exogenous variables) do tend to give positive and often significant coefficients for a_1 capturing the positive effect of the military burden on growth. This is particularly true if LDC samples are subdivided and attention focused on high income or less resource-constrained countries (see Deger and Smith, 1983). But this is precisely because Benoit is taking only the two direct effects of milex on growth, that of positive spin-off and negative resource allocation. As we have repeatedly stressed, when the indirect effects via resource mobilisation are taken into account, the sum total of effects turns adverse. To understand this more formally, we now turn to a description of the growth process.

8.3 Supply factors in growth

Conceptually it is preferable to separate out the factors emanating from the supply and demand sides when analysing growth and development, though in reality they are often intertwined. We deal with each in turn, emphasising the role of military expenditure at each step.

On the supply side, as neo-classical growth models predict, the aggregate quantity of resources available for accumulation is essential for development. These may be produced means of production (capital stock), natural resources (oil, land), technology (improved methods of using the same inputs to produce more or better output) or human capital (education, health, etc., which improves productivity). The choices involved are threefold. The nation has to decide first the 'required' surplus or saving that can contribute to asset (resource) accumulation after current income has been partly used up for current consumption expenditure. Requirements vary from country to country, depending on societies' intertemporal substitution. For a country which wishes to have more consumption today, achieving target capital accumulation and high growth will take longer. On the other hand, growth will be faster if current consumption is sacrificed in the interests of saving and capital formation. The saving-income ratio of a country is a good approximation of this first-level choice.

Given the volume of saving, investment allocation among different sectors becomes important. In the simplest aggregative model, these could be consumption and capital goods sectors. Again the choice depends on societies' preference between present sacrifice and future gains. Emphasising capital goods (as in India in the late 1950s and Turkey in the late 1960s) might have as its rewards a higher long-term growth rate since capital goods are a direct input into the productive process. However, this has its immediate or medium-term cost in the form of shortages, inflation and structural imbalances. This second-level choice leads on to the third, where the most appropriate techniques (say between labour-intensive and capital-intensive or between traditional and modern methods) are to be selected within the context of a labour surplus, capital scarce LDC. Again the choices are not simple, since they depend on the long-term and short-term objectives of society. For an economy intent on maximising its surplus, it may be worthwhile to invest in capital-intensive processes in spite of the fact that labour is cheap.[3] These two concepts – determination of investment allocation and choice of techniques – are reflected at the *aggregate* level by the incremental capital-output ratio (ICOR), which if high might mean that the country has opted for investment goods production using capital-intensive techniques.[4] This may mean a medium-term sacrifice in the rate of increase of output,[5] but it will also imply a long-term gain by having higher capital stock and thus a higher output in the future. Much will of course depend on the efficiency with which capital is used – remember the discussion on absorptive capacity.

Open economy considerations can easily be integrated into the foregoing framework. Foreign capital, in the form of aid, transfers or overseas investment, adds to the total stock of capital just as domestic saving does. Thus the saving propensity can be augmented by foreign capital. The allocation and choice of techniques problems are also intricately linked with the overseas sector and trade strategy. A country may wish to import relatively cheaper capital goods rather than producing them at home; thus it will allocate more capital to consumption goods for exports. Outward-looking or inward-looking policies for growth are essential counterparts of the concept of planning for capital formation discussed thus far.

How does the role of military expenditure fit into this picture? The military helps to mobilise more saving, through taxation, (possibly) inflation and other means. On the other hand, by reducing the availability of public goods, it pushes up consumption expenditure and reduces private saving. It will also reduce government saving. Overall, at the level of the first-choice problem, the military is expected to have a negative effect. This was analysed in Chapter 4. Introducing military expenditure into the aggregate equilibrium relations of the economy means that saving will now need to finance both investment and defence. For investment allocation – the classic choice between machines and guns – the military unambiguously has a negative impact. The choice of techniques specifically related to arms industrialisation will also be influenced by defence expenditure. It may increase the productivity of capital in civilian industries by adding to effective demand; it may lead to more capital-intensive modes of production in tune with the military-industrial complex, and it may produce through R&D a greater measure of technical progress.

Again, the framework discussed above can easily integrate the role of the overseas sector in an open economy. If countries with high milex can also get large quantities of foreign resources (as in Taiwan, Israel or South Korea), then defence spending becomes less of a burden. If the majority of sophisticated arms are imported at subsidised prices from abroad, then the allocation burden is also reduced and a more economic plan can be formulated without spending more for security. The choice of techniques may also be affected since the defence sector will not now emphasise domestic production of arms. As Benoit (1978) stated:

> For this reason, military-assistance programmes that provide military equipment free or at greatly reduced cost may reduce the adverse growth effect of defence on the recipients . . . by making their own defence programmes less capital intensive and more labour intensive – a type of specialisation conducive to development.

There are, then, *two* sets of concepts in thinking of the military with respect to growth. The first consists of the three effects discussed in the previous section: allocation, spin-off and mobilisation. The second relates to the choice problem analysed in this section: total saving, investment allocation and choice of techniques. We need to relate them. To do so formally, consider the equilibrium relation for aggregate output

$$Y = C + I + M + X - R \tag{8.1}$$

(where the only form of government spending is for simplicity taken to be on the military M). Define saving S as

$$S = Y - C - T \tag{8.2}$$

we get

$$S = I + M - T + X - R \tag{8.3}$$

Assume following an adaptation of the Harrod-Domar model of growth that household saving is a proportional function of disposable income, while investment is given by the accelerator relation (Hahn and Matthews, 1969). Thus

$$S = s(Y - T) \tag{8.4}$$

$$I = v\dot{Y} \tag{8.5}$$

(where s and v are the propensity to save and ICOR respectively, while $\dot{Y} = dY/dt$ is the time derivative of output).

Substituting equations 8.4 and 8.5 in 8.3, and simplifying, we get

$$v\dot{Y} = sY + (1 - s)T - M + B \tag{8.6}$$

(where $B = R - X$, the deficit in the balance of trade, or foreign capital inflow).

Equation 8.6 has on its left-hand side total investment which is financed by saving by domestic households, government taxes, and the net deficit in the balance of trade which implies foreign capital *inflows* or saving from the overseas sector. Military expenditure reduces real resources available for investment.

Dividing equation 8.6 by Y we get

$$g = (1/v)\ (s + (1 - s)t - m + b) \tag{8.7}$$

(where $g = \dot{Y}/Y$ is the growth rate, $s = S/Y$ the saving-income ratio, $t = T/Y$ the tax effect, $m = M/Y$ the defence burden, and $b = B/Y$ net foreign resources as a proportion of GDP; note s, $1 - s$, t and b are all generally less than unity).

The direct coefficient on m in equation 8.7 is minus unity, (divided, of course, by the capital-output ratio); this reflects the allocation effect whereby the defence burden reduces growth. However, if there are intangible or unmeasurable spin-offs, such as modernisation, it is useful to have a coefficient different from unity, so that we rewrite 8.7 as

$$g = (1/v)\ (s + (1 - s)\ t - (1 - f)m + b) \tag{8.8}$$

If positive spin-off dominates the negative allocation effect, then f is greater than 1, $-(1-f)$ is positive, and a rise in m may even cause g to rise.

Note now in the light of our analysis that the parameters v, s, t

and b are not constants, but functions of the military burden (m). Thus we get

$$g = (1/v(m))\ (s(m) + (1 - s(m))\ t(m) - (1-f)m + b(m)) \quad (8.9)$$

Equation 8.9 can be interpreted in terms of our previous discussion. Clearly the dependence of the saving-income ratio (s) and tax effort (t) on the military burden (m) is related to the mobilisation effect, as well as the first-choice problem of planning for capital formation. The coefficient $(1 - f)$ is the sum total of allocation and spin-off as well as being related to the second-choice problem of investment planning. The relation between ICOR and milex ($v(m)$) can be traced back to the issue of choice of techniques. Finally, $b(m)$ summarises the open economy effects of defence spending.

By differentiating g with respect to m in equation 8.9 we can now discover whether an increase in the defence burden raises or depresses the growth rate. We get

$$dg/dm = (A/v)(A'/A - v'/v) \quad (8.10)$$

where a prime (') denotes the first derivative and

$$A = s(m) + (1 - s(m))t(m) - (1 - f)m + b(m) > 0 \quad (8.11)$$

$$A' = (1 - t)s' + (1 - s)t' - (1 - f) + b' \quad (8.12)$$

We would expect from the analysis in previous chapters that an increase in m would reduce the saving-income ratio (s), increase the tax income ratio (t) and increase the trade deficit (b). Thus

$$s' < 0,\ t' > 0,\ b' > 0 \quad (8.13)$$

As is clear, it is not possible unambiguously to sign dg/dm from equation 8.10 using the information given in 8.11, 8.12 and 8.13. Even if we assume that changes in the defence burden would not significantly affect v, particularly for a country not having a large defence industry, thus $v' = 0$, but still the growth effect of milex could go either way since $A' = dA/dm$ can be positive or negative. Note that since Benoit did not consider the possibility that s' could be negative, he in effect[6] had instead of equations 8.10 and 8.12, the following:

$$dg/dm = A'/v \tag{8.10)'}$$

$$A' = (1 - s)t' - (1 - f) + b' \tag{8.12)'}$$

(assuming $v' = 0$).

It is clear that since t' and b' are positive, and $(1 - f)$ at best positive and at worst negative but small, there is a strong supposition that $A' > 0$, thus giving a positive effect of the military on growth.

The three choice problems analysed thus far are essentially those of planning. If the country concerned is a command economy, then the solution in principle is easy. However, most planned LDCs[7] operate within a mixed economy, where a flourishing market-oriented system co-exists within the broad framework of a plan. Thus an indicative plan is more important than an imperative one. A whole system of incentive mechanisms has to be generated so that the choices thought feasible and optimal by the planners are also accepted as such by the agents in the economy. Only then will the actual values of the variables turn out to be the same as the optimal ones determined by the government. The importance of incentive compatible plans, where the planners (government) and the rest of the economy move in co-ordination towards similar goals, is important and should be recognised, though a formal study of the issues goes beyond the scope of this book.

What is important in the context of defence spending within market-oriented plans and concomitant incentives is that military expenditure affects other components of the economic plan and in turn is affected by them. For example, if a rise in the defence burden has to be financed by taxation and additional money supply, then the allocation between these two sources of revenue will have implications for the overall structure of the plan. Thus the interactions of the defence sector with the rest of the economy, particularly its growth prospects, should be carefully considered by LDC governments. In effect, there is an essential need for integrating a defence plan (for security) with an economic plan (for growth). Further, a proper incentive mechanism by which a specific defence burden is consistent with the optimising behaviour of the rest of the economy needs to be formulated. As Benoit claims (1978):

> Because of the importance of the composition as well as the size of defence programs, there would appear to be considerable scope for a closer integration of defence planning and economic planning, which in most developing countries have so far very little to do with each other. The introduction of standards of economic efficiency and cost-benefit analysis into defence planning might render substantial benefits, often with positive improvements in security as well.

8.4 Aggregate demand and growth

The emphasis thus far has been on the supply side. Prior saving is necessary before rapid growth can be achieved. Saving contributes to the supply of resources. This saving can be converted into investment, with the assumption that there is always sufficient demand for investment goods. The sectoral allocation of the total volume of investment (equal to saving), as well as appropriate choice of techniques, completes the specification from the supply side. Thus saving is both necessary and sufficient for economic growth. This is the classical viewpoint.[8]

The opposite point of view, where aggregate or intersectoral demand may be the effective constraint for output expansion, emanates from Keynes, and has been increasingly vocal in developing countries in recent years. Kaldor (1976, 1979) emphasises the interrelationship between demand creation in agriculture and manufacturing, which complement each other in equilibrium growth. Prior saving might be necessary but is not sufficient for growth and development. Rather, demand for these resources will determine whether investment (and growth) will actually take place or not. Further, demand may itself create new saving so that the classical causation is reversed and demand (for resources) creates its own supply.

Consider an example in a two-sector model of a developing country. If the manufacturing sector demands more agricultural goods (either as factor inputs or wage goods) then the relative price of the latter will go up. Assuming a positively sloping supply curve, output will rise, thus creating more income and therefore more saving in agriculture. This will contribute positively to the saving in the whole economy.

There is a long structuralist tradition (particularly in Latin America) which strongly stresses the role of intersectoral demand and the fact that growth can be retarded by the 'structural' backwardness of the lagging sector. For example, the overemphasis of manufactures and the neglect of agriculture might mean that the domestic market for the former does not expand fast enough, and output therefore fails to respond to supply stimulus. This is clearly the sophisticated version of the old balanced growth argument, but its specific emphasis on structural characteristics of balanced demand creation is new. A number of important papers embodying the formal characteristics of this school have recently been published, and interested readers can get a good survey in Taylor (1980).

For our purposes, a summary of the basic concept is sufficient. Equilibrium agricultural prices depend on supply and demand for goods, thus prices adjust to clear the market for agricultural products. Therefore excess supply (demand) pushes down (up) the price in agriculture. Manufacturing prices on the other hand are cost-based, so that input costs, the wage rate and the mark-up determine the price level here. Excess demand or supply causes quantity adjustments, and it is only in the long run, with persistent disequilibrium, that prices do change. The growth rate in manufacturing is a positive function of its price level, thus higher prices cause an expansion in this sector. For simplicity assume that the growth rate in agriculture is constant. We may use Figure 8.1 to give a visual representation of the process involved. (P_m, P_a, g_m, g_a are respectively the price and growth rate of manufacture and agriculture output. The terms of trade or relative price is $p = P_m/P_a$.)

If the initial price is p_1 then the growth in manufacturing is high compared to the growth in agriculture. The former creates demand for agricultural products, but since g_a is low the supply responses of agriculture are inadequate. The price of agriculture P_a goes up and p comes down. Equilibrium is restored at E_1 with $p = p^*$ and $g_a = g_a^* = g_m$, i.e. balanced growth.

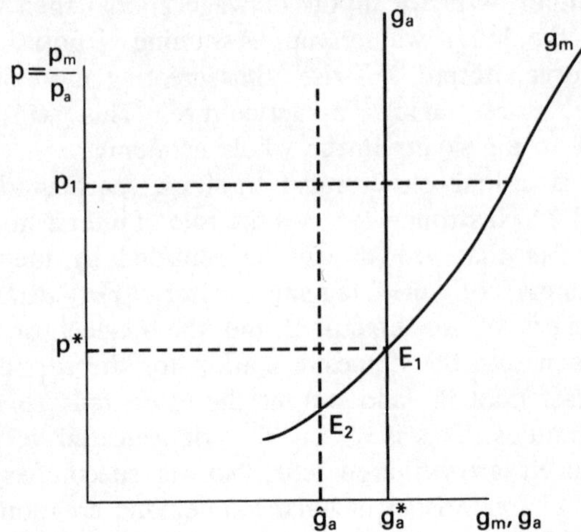

Figure 8.1 The interrelationship between growth in manufacture and growth in agriculture

If now the productivity in agriculture declines or growth is reduced to $\hat{g}_a < g_a^*$, then the vertical line in Figure 8.1 shifts to the left (given by the dotted line) and the new equilibrium is at E_2. Lack of agricultural supply at the old equilibrium E_1 pushes up P_a, reduces the terms of trade which become adverse for manufacture, and finally growth in manufacture suffers. The main motivation here is demand, since the fall in g_a reduces agriculture's demand from industry and this in turn reduces industrial growth rates. Markets do not expand fast enough to make growth sufficiently high.

Low productivity, low investment and low growth in agriculture are often the central problem of underdevelopment if one looks at the growth process from a Keynesian-structuralist point of view. A virtuous cycle can be set up by investing in the primary sector and increasing its own and the economy's equilibrium growth rate. However, we have already seen that private investors or rural landlords are rarely interested in investment and concomitant technological progress in the agricultural sector. Chakravarty (1984) presents this argument lucidly:

> the crux of the problem of underdevelopment often lies in the low productivity of labour in agriculture, specifically food related agriculture. This tends to produce a secular deterioration in the terms of trade as argued by Lewis, a very restricted domestic market for industrial products which are often characterised by increasing returns to scale and also a severe demographic imbalance. Investment in agriculture and agriculture-related industries can help to break the vicious circle and promote fast growth with a better distribution of incomes.

How does military expenditure fit into this picture? As we have repeatedly mentioned, defence spending is primarily done by governments, thus an increasing milex puts a strain on government budgets. On the other hand, given the agrarian backwardness of most LDCs, investment in agriculture is not a major priority of the private sector. Growth-enhancing technological change needs to be initiated first and foremost by the government, through direct investment, infrastructural improvement, extension services, dissemination of information, and finally R&D. When defence spending reduces this type of expenditure, as it may well do, then the effects are more far-reaching than for many other categories of public spending. The direct stimulus provided by the military for manufacture's demand or the residual spin-off from defence investment may not compensate for the lower agricultural investment consequent on higher defence spending.

8.5 Nonlinearities

The previous sections have emphasised that there are a number of ways in which military expenditure can influence growth: through a change in the total volume of resources available for investment; through a reallocation of investable funds; and through residual spin-off. In turn, both supply and demand factors contributing to growth are affected by the defence burden. The sum total of channels form a rather complex phenomenon and the final effect may be difficult to estimate.

The problems are compounded if it is realised that countries at different stages of development may react quite differently to military expenditure. Thus a study with a wide-ranging sample of LDCs may have elements of both positive and negative relationships (or maybe none at all), since the countries may not have common structural characteristics. Statistical analysis using dummy variables (as in the Appendix) can take care of some of the problems, but more analytical discussions based on the economics of underdevelopment should be attempted. Note that single country studies are not immune from this critique, because results derived from one country during the sample period may be totally inadequate for another. By its very nature, cross-section analysis looking at a wide spectrum of economies at various stages of development gives us an indication of long-term behaviour, and therefore may be more useful for deriving general conclusions.

The basic issue is quite simple. We are asking the question whether an increase in the military burden raises or lowers the economy's growth rate. We are therefore seeking a monotonic relationship between growth and the defence burden. The simplest case is the *linear* one. Thus we would like to claim that countries with a high defence burden have a low (or high) rate of growth. But what if the relations are not unidirectional or nonmonotonic and nonlinear? Suppose low and high growth countries behave in similar ways, i.e. *for example* (only), defence expenditure stimulates growth. On the other hand, countries with medium growth prospects show the *opposite* relationship so that military spending depresses growth. Such nonlinearities in the cross-sectional functions investigated may be quite important. Boulding (1974) in his important review of Benoit's book categorically states: 'All the relationships explored are linear, yet it is clear from quite casual inspection that significant nonlinear relationships may be involved.'

Essentially nonlinearities in the milex-growth relation imply that, within a wide-ranging sample, some countries will have positive and others negative relationships (and maybe some none at all). It is expected (and hoped!) that there will be a pattern to these slopes and the positive and negative effects can be identified with certain common characteristics of the countries concerned and the relevant 'stage' of development.

Following Boulding (1974), the basic characteristics can be

observed simply by setting up a quartile table. Using our sample of fifty countries for 1965-73 averages, the countries are placed into four quartiles, low, medium low, medium high, and high, for the two variables under study – military burden and growth rate. A large number of other exogenous variables distort the picture, and Table 8.1 can only give us a very preliminary view. There are outliers like Sri Lanka, Gabon and Saudi Arabia. But consider each column corresponding to the four categories of military burden. Choose that element of the matrix (the box in the

Table 8.1 *Nonmonotonic relation between growth and military burden*

	Low milex	Medium low milex	Medium high milex	High milex
Low growth		Positive II		Negative IV
	Sri Lanka Honduras	Chile (H) Ghana (M) Uganda (L) Ethiopia (L)	India Sudan Chad	Burma (L) Jordan (M) Vietnam Egypt (M)
Medium low growth	Argentina El Salvador Tanzania	S. Africa Venezuela	Morocco Peru	Pakistan
Medium high growth	Negative I			
	Colombia (M) Costa Rica (M) Guatemala (M) Kenya (L) Mexico (H) Philippines (M) Tunisia (M)	Ecuador Thailand Algeria	Indonesia Malaysia Spain Turkey	Iraq Syria
High growth			Positive III	
	Gabon	Brazil Dep. Rep Libya	Greece (H) Nigeria (L) S. Korea (M) Guinea (L)	Iran Israel S. Arabia

diagram) which has the highest number of entries. These are respectively those numbered I, II, III, IV. Now note that two sets of countries stand out quite clearly.

In the first set (boxes I and IV) we have countries with a low military burden and medium high growth (seven in number) as well as those with a high military burden and low growth (five in number). In the second set we can put countries with a moderately low burden but also low growth (four) as well as those with a medium high burden and high growth (five). If the causality runs from military burden to growth as has been argued throughout, then the first set of countries are showing a negative relation between defence and growth, as we have often claimed in this book. On the other hand, if the second set of countries are considered only, then we may find a positive causation between military spending and growth – as claimed by Benoit.

The basic problem, then, is to categorise the cross-section of countries into suitable groups, so that they have common characteristics in terms of stages of development, and then analyse the milex-growth interrelationship. Frederiksen and Looney (1983) divide countries into resource abundant and resource constrained groups. They claim that the adverse effects of military spending are more pronounced in the latter group; one would therefore expect a negative relation between defence burden and growth. On the other hand, they say, 'the reverse is true for countries that have a relative abundance of financial resources. These countries can more easily afford the growth oriented capital expenditure programme concomitant with maintaining or even increasing, defence programmes'. Resource abundance is identified by high growth in foreign exchange earnings, a low debt-service ratio, a low incremental capital-output ratio, a high ratio of the current account deficit (foreign saving) to national output, and a high multiplier. They found using the same regression as Benoit[9] that there was a positive relation between defence and growth for resource rich countries, while for resource poor economies the opposite was true. Thus the empirical findings were consistent with their hypothesis.

In a comprehensive study of the sensitivity of the defence-growth relation, Deger and Smith (1983) subclassify countries with respect to *per capita* income. Economies are identified as low, middle and high income countries and a simple growth-military equation, *without any other variables included in the specification*, is tested. The details of our results are found in the paper, but overall we found that high income countries had a positive relation, middle income countries had a negative relation, and for lower income countries no discernible connection could be found. This was of course the simplest testable hypothesis; the more complicated model analysing a simultaneous equation system gave *negative* coefficients for all three groups.[10] However, the basic point still remains. If the direct effect of military expenditure on growth is estimated (embodying resource allocation and spin-off), then the effect may not be unidirectional and there is a possibility of reversal.

As we have said before, formal research in this area is still in its infancy. But we can discuss some tentative hypotheses from a recent unpublished paper by Sen (1984). Consider Table 8.1 once again, in particular the countries in boxes I, II, III, IV. The brackets beside their names contain H, M, L standing for high, middle and low *per capita* incomes. Using *World Tables* data we have categorised these countries into three income groups. Among the nine countries exhibiting a possible positive relative (boxes II and III), seven are in high and low income categories, while only two are in the middle. Among the negative effect countries (boxes I and IV), the position is reversed: five have H and L while six have M.[11] A plausible hypothesis from studying these facts would therefore be that high and low income countries can derive and absorb the benefits of military expenditure, while middle income countries tend to suffer more than they gain.

Formally we are claiming that

$$g = a + bm \tag{8.1}$$

and that

$$b = b(y) \tag{8.2}$$

so that when y is small b is positive; as y rises b becomes negative; but finally with high y, b becomes positive once again. The nonlinearity can be shown in a diagram (Figure 8.2). For a low income country at y_1, b_1 is greater than zero, similarly at y_3. However, in between middle income countries have negative b.

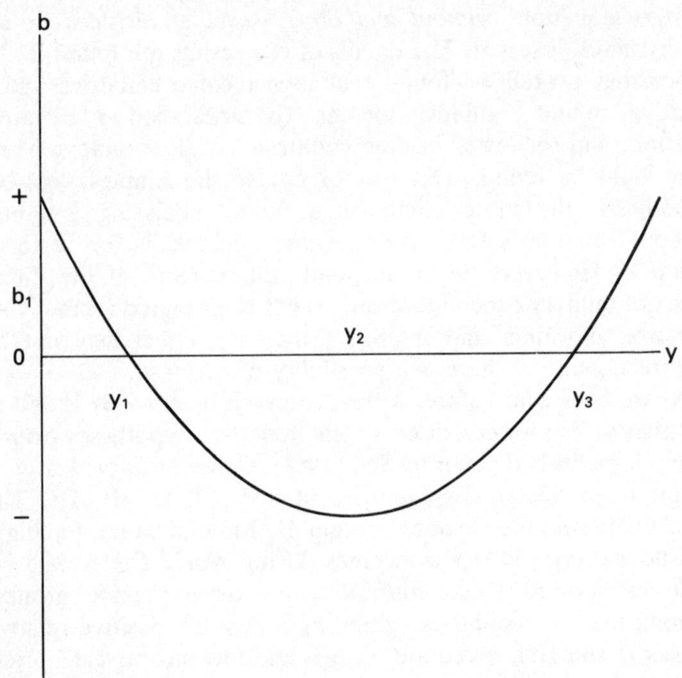

Figure 8.2 Nonlinearities in the defence burden and growth relation

The explanation behind this nonlinearity is important. *All* countries, whatever their *per capita* income, lose out from allocation effects with military spending reducing the amount of resources available for productive expenditure. But the military also has spin-offs. It is possible that high and low income economies receive more of the beneficial effects of defence related spin-off than do the countries in the middle. Low income countries at an early stage of development may gain from the whole plethora of concepts termed most generally 'modernisation'. If the country is not specifically at war, the civic action programmes of the military may help in development. If the country is at war, as was Nigeria during this period, then the military might contribute to the modernisation of the state. The Nigerian civil war, as pointed out by Kennedy (1974), might have helped to build the nation rather than divide it, due to the exemplary behaviour of the central army after victory. High income countries on the other hand gain from technological spin-off and effective demand creation (Greece, South Korea) particularly if they are starting their own arms building capacity. On the other hand middle income countries are sufficiently advanced in development not to get much leverage from modernisation, and yet the economy is not advanced enough to benefit from the military-industrial complex. Thus the allocation effects dominate the weak spin-off, and increases in military burden tend to depress growth. This is clearly an area for further empirical research.

Overall then we can conclude that the military-growth relationship is complex, and a simple guns versus machines concept will not do. To understand the process properly, we must take into account the nature of growth-oriented development *per se*, the importance of supply and demand factors, the planning and incentive mechanism for capital formation (which the military may compete with or augment), and the various nonlinearities associated with the channels that flow from the military to growth. Empirical cross-section studies can provide some idea of the issues involved, in particular the long-term coefficients and their signs. Time series studies for specific countries on the other hand may give more short-term results. Overall, the issues are complicated and the researcher should tread the minefield of evidence with caution.

9 Economic development and the military

9.1 Growth and development

Our analysis of the economic effects of military expenditure in less developed countries has generally concerned itself with the direct channels by which defence can harm or help economic growth and development. We have generally concentrated on the short-term resource allocation and long-term growth effects of milex. The time has now come to broaden the framework. We wish to analyse the indirect, and often intangible, effects that are present in the defence-development relationship. Further, we would like to consider the broader concept of socio-economic development in the context of defence spending.

As mentioned earlier, growth is often necessary for development – a means to an end. It is also, occasionally, sufficient. But there are a significant number of cases where growth *per se* has not led to the much wider requirements of socio-economic development and the concomitant entitlements of the mass of people living in a developing country. We have been generally aware of the possible hiatus between growth and development, as the discussion in Chapter 1 indicates. But it should be borne in mind that there are links too. For example, we have demonstrated that there may exist a negative and significant trade-off between military spending and government's expenditure on education. The latter may act as a proxy for human capital; thus increased militarisation may lead to lower human capital and absorptive capacity. Therefore investment and growth will suffer. However, a reduction in educational opportunities, resulting from additional defence spending, is also related to reduced entitlements. When educational activities lose public funds, the poorer sections of the society find it difficult to claim the 'right' to be educated. Thus (educational) capabilities decline and development suffers. The same economic phenomenon can thus have positive influences on both growth and development.

It is possible, however, that policies which aid growth may have harmful effects on development, particularly in the short and medium term. An unequal distribution of income may increase saving in the economy, thus helping the growth rate to rise. On the other hand, this may mean that poorer sections of the community will suffer disproportionately. The military may provide domestic security within which production can prosper and profits grow. But this may be achieved by a suppression of workers' economic rights and entitlements. The former will increase growth; the latter can lower development.

Overall, therefore, we have to be careful in delineating the links between growth and development, particularly in the context of defence. Growth can both help and harm development. Policies which will prove useful for one may also be helpful to the other; however, there will be exceptions where this will not hold. A general model is much more difficult to construct when one is analysing such a broad and amorphous concept as socio-economic development. Descriptive case studies will play a major part in the analytical structure of this chapter.

Less developed countries, in spite of their structural heterogeneity, also tend to be developmentally similar. Otherwise, of course, there would be little sense in the very subject of development economics. Thus one can talk of broad categories of developing countries and construct theoretical models embodying underlying characteristics. This methodology is particularly helpful for objective (and quantifiable) criteria like growth, investment or aid. However, when we move on to a broader field of inquiry, the very diffusion of concepts leads to developmentally unique features appearing. Differences become as important as similarities. We have to recognise this feature as we analyse the wider implications of the military for economic development.

To keep the subject within manageable proportions,[1] we concentrate on three issues which seem to be the most important in the area. The first is the concept of modernisation, which many political economists have considered to be a major positive contribution that the military can make towards economic development. The second issue deals with the role of the military in resolving domestic conflicts which arise out of the dynamics of economic and social change. In the process the military can contribute to growth-inducing structural change, but simultaneously, through repressive measures, reduce the rights of society. This leads us on to the third feature, dealing with rights and entitlements, some of which are only tangentially economic but are still vital if the developing society is to mature into fully-fledged economic development. The next three sections deal with these issues.

9.2 Modernisation

The early writers who emphasised the modernisation arguments had a great deal of influence not only in initiating this important debate on the role of the military, but also in influencing US defence aid to military establishments in the Third World. Pye (1962a, b) analysed these concepts in two papers, one of which set down the political theories for his arguments and the other applied them to the case of Burmese politics. He argued that when colonial rulers tried to establish modern institutions in their subject countries, they generally failed to do so – except in the case of military organisations. The military became the most 'modern' institution, an industrial type entity, providing 'responsible nationalism', pride in its organisational structure, adaptability to rapid technological change, and an opportunity to move upwards in the social hierarchy. Further, army life provided more security for the villagers compared with the deprivation that most other migrants to urban ghettoes would face. The military could foster better international relations, accept foreign aid and be aware of the necessity to open the economy to external influences.

Janowitz (1964) claims that the army in LDCs is principally recruited from the middle classes and thus has an aptitude for breaking the rigidities of social structure imposed by the traditional elitist rich. Halpern (1963) also asserts the role of the new middle class in moulding military establishments and putting them in the vanguard of a progressive society. In particular, 'within the army, modern technology was eagerly welcomed and its usefulness and power appreciated. By contrast, the political system showed greater inertia, inefficiency, scepticism and greed in utilising the product of modern science.'

The problem with such heuristic arguments is that equally plausible ones can be made against the contention that the military is truly a modern institution in LDCs. Nordlinger (1970) is forceful in denying the modernising attitudes of military organisations. They do not like 'any divergences from the status quo that contain the potential for unwieldy change'; they are static institutions, have little or no adaptability to local economic conditions and their value structure is rigid and hierarchical. Eleazu (1973) takes the same view in the context of ex-colonial countries in West Africa.

Many case studies have been provided both for and against the concept of modernisation emanating from the military. Turkey is often mentioned as a country where the military establishments, inspired by the secular and modern ideas of Kemal Ataturk (the founder of the Turkish Republic), have been a beacon light of stability when the civilian regimes were taking the country onto its chaotic path. However, as Sezer (1981) so lucidly points out, such a modernising role ascribed to the military is mainly applicable to the initial stages of Turkey's political development. Ataturk himself reduced the role of the military in the economic life of the nation and kept it independent of mainstream movements. 'The experience of military rule in 1960-61 and military intervention in 1971 seemed to suggest that it could not govern an increasingly modern complex society' (Sezer, 1981). It should be noted, however, that the Turkish military has inevitably believed that the country should be governed by an elected democracy; thus it has always returned to its strategic functions after a temporary intervention, leaving the ruling of the country to civilians.

A similar picture can be drawn for India, whose army was once thought to be an exemplary symbol of colonial success. In post-independence India, the army has stood aloof from civilian politics and has been generally free to develop its own institutional structure. It is widely believed that the military is disciplined, efficient, modern and tuned to the latest technology. Armed with these premises a notable Indian journalist recently investigated the inner mechanisms of the military, and was shocked to find that much of the anecdotal progressiveness of the defence establishments was largely mythical. Not unnaturally, he found that the military organisation did not stand independent of (and being idealised by) the rest of society. Rather it reflected the moods and passions of the wider cross-section of classes and castes from which it is drawn: 'I do not believe for one moment that the defence services are insulated from the general national environment which is not very healthy' (Thapar, 1981). The judgment seems to be unduly harsh and may not be accepted *in toto*; but some of its implications could be relevant.

Another interesting area of analysis for the modernising argument has been the Middle East, where leaders like Nasser of Egypt and organised groups like the Ba'athists of Iraq have used military establishments to change the socio-economic structure of traditional peasant societies. Earlier writers like Halpern (1962) have been extremely favourable to military rule, hailing it as the most important modernising force in the Middle East. Arab writers like Murad (1966, quoted in Khuri, 1981) think that the military forms 'the technical college of society'. After the emergence of many of these countries from colonial or comprador authority, the military rulers seemed to be at the forefront of the most progressive sections of society. But according to Khuri (1981), this reasoning is circular. The military is dependent on, and integrated with, the society around it. A relatively more dynamic and progressive society has influenced its military hierarchy to move with the times. On the other hand a conservative and reactionary society has produced a military system which is extremely backward in its attitudes. As he stated: 'Instead of asking how does the military modernise society, we should ask how does society modernise the military?' (Khuri, 1981).

Overall, summarising the evidence from a large number of Middle Eastern states from a historical point of view as well as from current structures, Khuri finds little evidence of modernisation coming from the military. He categorises the problems of the defence sectors as 'the lack of distinction between civil and military subcultures, the continuation of peasant, community-based ties and values within military organisation, the emergence of the military elite as a bureaucratic group, the class distinctions between officers and peasant masses, the limited capacity of the military to generate technical skills in society'. Clearly the influence of the military on the rest of society is minimal.

To sum up, therefore, it is very difficult to assert one way or the other whether the military is a modernising force in LDCs. The role of this institution in leading the country along a more 'modern' path is difficult to judge and will vary from country to country.

We therefore discuss briefly the nature of modernisation in the army and its possible impact on civilian society in four countries. Since our discussion in earlier chapters mentioned Brazil and South Korea often, we analyse them once again in the light of the modernising hypothesis. The other two countries are India and Indonesia; the former has little militarisation but, as mentioned earlier, is often discussed in the literature; the latter has a deep involvement of the military at every level of society and provides fruitful material for analysis.

(a) Brazil

Brazil has been ruled by a military oligarchy from about 1964, and the same period has also seen a rapid rise in growth rates fuelled by an export-oriented domestic industrialisation strategy. One of the interesting features of the Brazilian elite is the influence of the Escola Superior de Guerva (ESG), the Superior War College. Founded in 1949, it is a cross between the Sorbonne and the Ecole Militaire, and has been the training ground of the highest professionals in the land – both military and civilian. It is essentially a postgraduate institution for the most important echelons of military command as well as prominent civilians in commerce, industry, banking and the civil service. The close interconnections between the military and technocratic elites are established here, and a select group destined to lead the country are trained in security and economic policy. The curriculum emphasises not only military matters but also a wide range of subjects including economics, political science and sociology. Essentially, the military high command is expected to learn about the socio-economic conditions of Brazil and thus be able to rule the country effectively and control the economy efficiently. There can be little doubt that, for this very small band of elitist individuals, the ESG has contributed to the broad concept of 'modernisation'.

However, it is essentially due to the extreme narrowness of the base from which the elite operates that the power does not percolate downwards. The ruling junta may be efficient, but its very efficiency has led to more exploitation, ruthless subjugation of vast masses of the people, greater inequality and massive deprivation of the working classes. 'While the senior officers of the armed forces are loosely aligned into harder- and softer-line factions, over the issues of authoritarian rule versus the maintenance of the constitutional facade, of straightforward repression of dissent versus relative tolerance . . . they are alike hemmed in by the realisation that they cannot pursue their economic/political goal of making Brazil a great power quickly, and at the same time enjoy the sort of popular support that would make genuinely representative institutions possible' (Dyer and English, in *World Armies*, 1983).[2] In practice the overriding consideration has been growth and power; thus development is exceedingly narrow-based, feeding on human deprivation. The reader is asked to decide whether this is a 'modern' structure or not.

There is also the question whether this system provides an effective military force, able to perform well in combat with external enemies. It may be argued that the elitist and hierarchical structure is useful for military operations since commands are transmitted efficiently and executed smoothly. On the other hand, it is possible that flexibility is a useful advantage in combat. It is difficult to test these competing hypotheses with examples taken from the Brazilian case, since actual wars have been almost nonexistent in recent years. There have been rivalry and tensions with Argentina and other southern neighbours like Uruguay. But there have been no wars or even skirmishes, so it is difficult to tell whether the postulated structure of the army leads to more efficiency or not.

(b) South Korea

The role of military expenditure, investment and security in the economic and social development of South Korea is extremely interesting. On the one hand the economy is geared to an outward-looking export-oriented strategy. Competitive markets, exploitation of cheap labour, comparative advantage in goods with buoyant world demand, large foreign investments, involvement of multinationals producing for international markets, have all contributed to the Korean miracle. During 1970-77, its average annual growth rate of 9.9 per cent was exceeded by only three other countries in the world – Botswana, Saudi Arabia and Malta![3] Growth, through the trickle-down effect, has also improved Korea's socio-economic entitlements, and as Sen (1981) shows, the country has done reasonably well, in an international comparative sense, in the field of social development. On the other hand, Korea has had to maintain high military expenditure given the threat from the north, and the role of the army in the Korean political system is paramount.

For any country, particularly with regional tension and militarily strong neighbours, domestic security is important. For a country which relies heavily on foreign investment, free flows of goods and services, an open economy and multinational resources, strategic and political security, in the widest sense of the term, is absolutely vital. Since expectations play a crucial role in the volatile workings of the market mechanism, any adverse expectations of a 'threat' could have disastrous consequences for the economy. 'South Korea remains, . . . a country in which the army's ability to defend its frontiers against large-scale conventional attack is of prime importance in considering its future. No-one is more aware of this than the South Koreans themselves, who recognise that their new prosperity depends upon convincing foreign investors and traders of their ability to defend themselves' (Keegan, in *World Armies*, 1983).

The government has also been actively involved in the provision of a proper strategic economic environment in which the economy can prosper. The role of the state in encouraging investment into desirable channels, creating infrastructure, facilitating transfer of real and financial capital towards business, establishing trade restrictions for infant industries, using state-sponsored financial institutions like nationalised banks to reallocate resources in a systematic fashion, are all well documented (see Sen, 1981, and Datta-Chaudhuri, 1979). In the same vein the government has always influenced the military and in turn been influenced by it. President (General) Park ruled the country almost from the military coup of 1961 until his assassination in 1979; and although officially elected President as a civilian, he always had close army links. The military burden is above 6 per cent (exceeded in the region only by Taiwan and North Korea, for obvious reasons) and over a third of the government budget is devoted to defence.

Korea seems to be one country where the role of the military in providing a stable strategic framework within which economic activity can progress satisfactorily has helped in economic growth. However, it should always be borne in mind that the pace of social change and the improvement in the quality of life that economic growth is supposed to bring, has been rather slow in coming for South Korea. As A. Sen (1983) points out, in terms of the level of achievement and performance in fields like health, nutrition, life expectancy, education, literacy, South Korea is just about equal to Sri Lanka, yet the former had a GNP *per capita* of $1,520 per head in 1980 while the comparable figure for the latter is $270. With five times the *per capita* income, the end product of economic development, quality of life, is almost the same for South Korea as it is for much poorer Sri Lanka. It may be instructive to note that in 1980 Sri Lanka spent $3 *per capita* on the military while South Korea spent $91, over *thirty* times as much.

(c) India

In India the body politic in particular and Hindu society in general are blemished with the outdated concept of caste, which creates a hierarchical structure on the basis of birth and not ability or skills. The state is secular and the constitution grants equal rights to all, irrespective of caste or religion. Exceptions are made for *positive* discrimination, so that the 'scheduled castes'[4] get extra rights which were denied them in the past. But in principle all are the same in the eyes of society. In practice, things are different, and caste divisions still play an important role, not only in personal affairs like marriage or dowry, but also in public appointments, political patronage and socio-legal rights. If the military is in some sense more modern, we would expect it to break down these artificial barriers.

The British Indian army of course maintained and encouraged the class, caste and racial distinctions of the local population. Regimental and army groupings were formed on the basis of caste, 'the martial races' or religion. Since independence there have been feeble attempts to break down these barriers, but overall the attempts have not been highly successful. An Indian defence spokesman writes: 'Regiments composed of particular classes, through several decades, developed a certain kind of cohesion and while steps are taken to broadbase their composition, it is essential to ensure that the sentimental attachment arising out of such composition is not suddenly disturbed.'[5] Substitute 'castes' for 'classes', 'generations' for 'decades', 'integration' for 'cohesion', and 'caste loyalty' for 'sentimental attachment' in the preceding sentence, and one gets a picture of the *lack* of modernisation of the Indian army.

In spite of the repeated attempts to get 'mixed' regiments irrespective of birth, caste, race and religion, a large number of 'communal' units still remain. Examples are the following: the Mahar Regiment (scheduled caste, northern Hindus); the Dogra Regiment (composed of Dogras, high-caste northern Hindus); the Gurkha Rifles (Nepalese Gurkhas); the Jat Regiment (middle-caste Hindus from Rajasthan, Haryana); the Sikh Regiment (Sikhs, generally high caste). Obviously things are changing, but there are no strong indications here that the army is adapting faster to modernisation than civilian society.

But again, one must be careful. The army's allegiance to civil authority has been unquestioned. This is quite exemplary in a region of the world where military coups have been the rule rather than the exception. If belief in democracy is a modernising trait, as it should be, then the Indian army has done rather well. The cohesion and integrity of the armed forces during the recent Sikh crisis (there were some exceptions), and their aversion to communal issues, are also favourable signs of progressive behaviour.

(d) Indonesia

The Indonesian armed forces have played an important and dominant role in the body politic since the overthrow of Sukarno and the installation of General Suharto as head of state in the mid-1960s. However, it is interesting to note that the military burden did not rise significantly under the political dominance of the army. In 1966, the military budget was approximately 5 per cent of national income. For the latest five years for which data is available, i.e. between 1977 to 1981, the military burden has been of the order of 4.3, 4.0, 3.2, 2.1, 2.3 per cent. Yet the dominance of the military forces in all levels of society is quite overwhelming, and this has proved to have a number of beneficial effects from the point of view of socio-economic development.

The military proclaimed *Orba*, or Orde Baru the New Order, as a method of integrating the armed forces into the social fabric and of having the sort of integration between economic and strategic planning that is considered desirable. Social conflict and competitive allocations between the civilian and the defence sector are to be avoided at all costs and economic development is the basis of the successful society from which everyone (including the military) can benefit. As we have noted, this attitude has even led to a sacrifice in the military share in the national product so that civilian resources and growth can be increased. Civic action by the army has been the order of the day, and though not all the attempts made have been uniformly successful, overall there can be little doubt that the Indonesian military has made some positive contribution in the last two decades or so.

The role of the military in influencing and almost penetrating every sector of society has been termed 'Total People's Defence and Security' (Drummond, *World Armies*, 1983), with the emphasis on *People's*. The military has two functions: as a driving social force towards faster growth and greater development as well as simultaneously protecting security and defending the nation. This is known as 'Dual Functionalism' and has led the army to participate in various civilian-economic activities. It builds roads, schools and rural infrastructure. It helps in irrigation projects and land reclamation. It builds bridges in the islands for civilian communication. It is integrated into local administration and helps in policing the remoter regions. Its men and officers are trained in social studies and encouraged to participate in communal and social life.

In the top echelons of economic administration, the military plays a dominant role also. The major state oil company, Pertamina, was organised by a general, Ibnu Sutowo, and there are other instances of military officials running public utility companies and holding other administrative offices. It has been estimated that about one-third of army personnel are involved in administrative and civilian duties.

The Indonesian armed forces seem to have been involved quite actively in the 'modernisation' of a traditional society and in participating in the process of economic development. There have been problems and criticism also. The repressive measures taken by the army in the Timor independence/secessionist movement have been quite extreme. Student riots in the late 1970s focused on the alleged increase in inequality during the Orde Baru as well as the strong action taken by the military in quelling dissent. Efficiency has not been as high as reputedly claimed for military personnel in civilian jobs, the classic case being the mismanagement of the oil company by General Sutowo. The Sukarno ideal of self-sufficient development has not been adhered to, and there have been other problems such as alleged corruption in government economic activities (for example licensing) run by the armed forces. Whether society has been 'modernised' or 'militarised' by the army is difficult to tell. Again, clear-cut judgments are not easy but these problems should be borne in mind.

9.3 Growth, conflict, structural change and the military

Economic growth will depend not only on factors such as the saving propensity or the ability to invest productively, but also on structural change which allows production to operate effectively. In the early years of development, with low *per capita* income but high potential for growth (thus causing high expectations), there are inevitable conflicts associated with structural change. In a relatively static economy, the size and distribution of the national cake are relatively predetermined, often by history and custom. Growth involves a dynamic process; as output starts rising fast, distributional conflicts appear.

One way out of this dilemma, albeit temporary, is to have inflation. Early inflation theorists (see Turvey, 1951) recognised this phenomenon. When claims on real output by different competing groups (say workers and employers, sharecroppers and landlords) are inconsistent with each other, aggregate prices rise so that the money value of claims can be satisfied. Real shares either do not change substantially, or when they do it is because of non-economic factors such as political power or strength of alliances. The process can be self-defeating if aspirations substantially exceed the actual change in the national product. Inflation leads to hyper-inflation and the social fabric breaks down. The military may intervene, either to prevent chaos or to control anarchic conditions or even because they are power-hungry and believe they can do a better job than civilians, thus increasing militarisation. Turkish military coups have followed an approximately ten-year cycle, the intervention being necessary after a period of socio-economic conflicts, high inflation and a run on the domestic currency. Latin America may have followed this model of 'conflict' inflation too.

Less developed countries in other regions of the world have not faced very high inflation, except in the post oil-shock period. Thus the foregoing conflict either appeared with less force or it was dissipated by other means. It is unrealistic to believe that basic conflicts arising out of growth, structural change and expectations will be absent in various parts of the world which are undergoing rapid transformation. It is here that the military may have played an alternative role in forcibly reducing the types of problems that we have discussed.

Deger and Smith (1983) put it clearly:

> The coercive power provided by a strong military may enable the state to increase the rate of exploitation of available resources. Surplus labour may be mobilised, raw material production developed in the face of opposition, agrarian surplus transferred to industry, consumption restricted, industrial disputes suppressed, and the rate of work increased. Without the organised force provided by the military, the state might not have the power to mobilise or exploit the potential resources to the same extent.

It has been argued that the role of the military in such cases is a prime example of 'growth without development'. Though such policies would enhance the growth rate of GDP, the lot of the common masses will suffer drastically. However, this is only partly true. If the suppression of 'conflict' is temporary and the final consequences beneficial, then this may be the bitter medicine neeed for the ailing economy. The alternative may be even worse – prolonged stagnation. It is possible that certain societies perform more efficiently under a relatively centralised authoritarian framework (the shadow of oriental despotism?), and that the military might be the only force which can give the relative degree of cohesion, unity and leadership.

There is nothing to stop the military from adopting a less repressive stand, or alternatively from using its power against the more vested interests that dominate developing countries' societies. There need not be any *necessary* antipathy between the military hierarchy and the victims of oppression. 'Third World armed forces could also, in principle, play a key role in growth-generating structural changes of a more progressive kind emphasising, for example, "redistribution with growth" strategies. Since such strategies are bitterly opposed by entrenched and powerful vested interests some degree of coercion would be necessary to achieve the desired ends' (Mack, 1981). However, Mack also goes on to say that 'throughout most of the Third World, the military has historically, and with few exceptions, allied itself with the powerful vested interests and not with their victims'. There are, of course, major exceptions. Egypt (under Nasser), North Vietnam and Libya (early Gaddafi) have shown the impact of military personnel in seeking far-reaching, progressive, radical and often mass-oriented programmes of socio-economic change.

The military, as an institutional force, does have the power and authority to reduce or suppress domestic conflict, and this may, in the long run, produce structural changes which are beneficial to the growth process. On the other hand, as we shall see later, some of these measures are in direct opposition to the type of entitlements that should, in principle, characterise optimal development. It is necessary to impose a sort of structure to this process, and identify common characteristics in the behaviour of armed forces. Luckham (1978) discusses an interesting classificatory scheme to identify and characterise the role of the military in curtailing internal conflicts and, possibly, enhancing structural change which may be growth-generating. We discuss this.

Table 9.1 shows the different types of function that the defence establishments can play in various types of countries. The latter are divided into two broad categories: those concentrating on primary production (agriculture and mining), and those going for major industrialisation. Each group is further subdivided depending on the degree of integration which the specific country has with the rest of the world. Examples of countries are given in brackets. The role of the military, in suppressing internal conflict, aiding structural change or protecting the *status quo*, is given in the second column. We deal with each entry briefly.

Table 9.1 *The role of the military in domestic conflict reduction and growth-inducing structural change*

	Economic structure	Role of military
(A) Primary producing LDCs: agriculture and mining		
(1) Low integration with the international economy	Small-scale production little involvement of foreign capital (Bangladesh)	Domestic conflicts in a semi-feudal society; military holds the country together, gives it national identity
(2) High integration	Enclave production; sophisticated technology; foreign capital important; output for export (Chile)	Conflict between enclave and rest of economy; military 'protects' enclave
(B) Industrialising LDCs		
(1) ISI	Domestic investment in industrialisation; self-sufficiency (Argentina, India)	Conflict between labour and capital, industry and agriculture; military provides internal security, active against guerrillas, etc.; suppression of organised labour
(2) Export-oriented strategy	Export promotion; importance of foreign capital; outward-looking policies (Brazil)	Similar to above but with greater intensity

Bangladesh is a prime example of an economy with relatively small-scale production units, agriculture being the dominant component of GDP. It became independent in 1971, after a successful secessionist movement from Pakistan. The first president of the country, Sheikh Mujibur Rahman, was assassinated in 1975 and the military intervened in a series of coups which thrust General Ziaur Rahman to power. Until his own assassination in 1981, General Zia succeeded in establishing relative peace and security within which the economy could be governed reasonably well. Though not notably successful in administration, the military has managed to hold the country together and reduce somewhat the turbulence of the early years of independence.

In recent years, Chile has developed a large manufacturing sector (accounting for approximately one-fifth of GDP). But copper remains important and its share in exports is still around 40 per cent of the total. Private foreign investment remains high, and debt servicing can still eat up almost 20 per cent of export earnings. The military in Chile had historically been reticent in getting *directly* involved in the body politic. The apolitical stance was broken forcefully in 1973 when President Allende and his Popular Unity government were overthrown and General Pinochet came to power after a bloody coup. Allende's attempts to break up the 'enclave', nationalise foreign capital, reduce the power of the industrial oligarchy and forge an alliance with the Soviet Union and Cuba, were considered unacceptable by the military, who intervened in violent style. The harsh deflationary policies followed by Pinochet and the deprivation of the Chilean masses in recent years are a testimony to the fact that the primary economic role of the military may be to 'protect' the enclave.

Turning now to countries which are more heavily dependent on industrialisation, the differences in the role of the military between economies following ISI and EPI are ones of degree and not of kind. There will be inevitable conflicts between various sectors of society, particularly in the urban areas where the new industries are burgeoning. The military may then be instrumental in suppressing organised labour, thus increasing the share of profits in output and aiding and abetting domestic growth through industrialisation. There are major exceptions to this general rule, to which we shall give more attention later. Here we just mention that the Peronist governments in Argentina prior to 1976 could form a reasonable alliance with both the military and the trade unions. However, the coup of 1976 changed all that. Further, the Argentine military has been particularly active against guerrilla movements throughout the 1970s. The ERP (Ejercito Revolucionario del Pueblo (People's Revolutionary Army)) and many other such organisations have been especially involved in fighting the armed forces, and one of the claims of the junta that ruled from 1976 to 1983 was that they had managed to suppress many of these factions. The methods used, including the creation of counter-terrorist vigilante murder squads, have of course been dubious. The Indian army, though famous for its politically non-interventionist policies, has likewise been engaged in maintaining 'law and order' against Maoist revolutionaries in the eastern states of the country. These groups, known as the Naxalites, had some notable successes in rural and urban guerrilla warfare, but army intervention has led to their demise.

Similar instances can be given of countries which have gone for export promotion, after passing through an initial phase of ISI. Brazil is a notable example of the involvement of the military not only in maintaining external security but also in safeguarding the economic interests of the ruling economic oligarchy and their representative governments. As Ball (1983) points out:

> Brazil, Pakistan and South Korea all were governed by the military when their economic miracle occurred. This should not be at all surprising since externally oriented, capital-intensive industrialisation, failing as it does to fulfill the basic requirement of large portions of third-world populations, is most likely to 'succeed' where the demands of the majority can be kept in check.

Overall, therefore, growth and development entails structural change, and the dynamic process often gives rise to conflicting claims and expectations. In so far as the military can control, reduce or even suppress some of these conflicting situations, particularly those which are nonlegitimate, subversive or anti-national, it does serve a useful purpose. On the other hand, the dividing line of legitimacy is rather thin. It is highly probable that the military can produce its own set of domestic conflicts (witness Argentina, Pakistan, etc.), which may be harmful to national progress. Finally, in trying to reduce conflict and foster social change, the military may, instead, take away the basic rights and entitlements of the citizens of the country concerned. Even as a short-term policy, this will not be conducive to proper development.

The preceding discussion has concentrated on the role of the military in society *vis-à-vis* domestic conflicts. It is also important to realise that this role will be influenced by external threats, particularly in areas of regional conflict, for example the Middle East or the Indian subcontinent. It is reasonable to believe that there is a direct relation between the role and influence of the military on domestic society and its success in counteracting external threats. Thus a military which has been successful in protecting the country from the influence of external conflict is expected to have a higher status within society. On the other hand a failure in war will imply a corresponding diminution of domestic militarisation. The recent example of Argentina's defeat in the Falklands conflict, and the consequent withdrawal of the army from political leadership, is well known. However, the interconnections are more complex. Consider the case of Pakistan after the 1971 Bangladesh war. The armed forces suffered a humiliating defeat, particularly in the eastern wing, and withdrew from the political arena, effectively for the first time since 1958. But this withdrawal proved to be shortlived; in 1977 General Zia ul-Haq took over power and has ruled ever since. Thus external defeats in war need not imply the long-term decline of militarisation; the effects may be temporary.

The nature of society, its cultural and ideological framework, will determine the importance of the military within domestic society, relative to external conflicts. This can be vividly illustrated by considering some extreme cases in the context of the relationship between religion and the military that has characterised many developing countries in the Middle East, for example Pakistan, Israel and Iran. In all of these countries religion has played an important role, firstly, in laying the foundation of the nation-state as well as giving an identity to the people, and secondly, in influencing the cultural values of society. Religion has also played a role, albeit implicitly and indirectly, in defining the 'enemy' as a source of external conflicts. The three countries are also highly militarised, have fought wars with their neighbours, and spend a high proportion of their GDP on defence budgets. Yet the relationship between religion and the army, as institutions, rests on uneasy foundations. Religious authorities can be potentially backward-looking, particularly in terms of mores and conventions. The armed forces, as modernisers, tend to be basically secular, and more progressive in their views on customs, norms and technology. In the course of external conflicts, the armed forces, as defenders of the nation, have a major role. But given the power of the religious authorities a compromise has to be reached. How the coalition is formed will then influence the relationship of military and society.

In Pakistan the military rulers in recent years have spearheaded Islamic society in terms of formal rules and regulations, where the law of the land is expected to follow the canonical traditions of Islam. There can be no doubt that external threats from India have always strengthened the position of the army in Pakistan. After all one does not sack one's bodyguard (without a replacement) if there is an impending threat! But the anti-democratic stance of the armed forces could have led to more opposition from the masses if the religious alliance had not been formed. Thus the army rationalises its importance in two ways: (a) from the external threat, and (b) as the founder-member of the new society. In this way, military leadership has subsumed or subordinated religious leadership, the latter now helping the former in gaining more prominence. The army, of course, pays its due respects and often compromises, but overall gains more than it loses.

Much the opposite has taken place in Iran, where once again the army has to ward off external threats but also come to terms with domestic upheavals. Here the religious authorities have dominated the military by essentially changing the structure of the armed forces. They have formed militias of zealots who in a frenzied demonstration of religious fervour are willing to die for God and country. The traditional military finds itself relatively subservient to the dictates of the politico-religious leadership. In spite of external threats, the role of the old army, in domestic society, is minimal.

Israel has, within a democratic framework, tried to keep the two groups separate. It has been reasonably successful in doing so. Thus the military is clearly the protector and defender of the nation without, however, having a major say in socio-cultural and religious issues. The army is respected, well funded and looked after. But potential conflict situations are defused quickly. In a sense, if the democratic form survives in Israel, then the separation will be optimal. If it fails, as it may well do, then there is little doubt that the army and populist religious groups will have a conflict of aims and interests.

Thus we can see that, in a situation of external threat, it is not necessarily true that the influence of the military in society will increase because it is 'defending' the nation. The examples above, stressing the role of religion, are illustrative. They are designed to show how important *domestic* cultural and social factors could be in delineating the role of the military.

Another factor may also be quite important in the context of external threat and the internal role of the military. This relates to the political and ideological bias of the 'enemy'. If the country from which external threat emanates has an opposite political complexion to the home country, then the role of the military, in external conflict, tends to be exaggerated. *Ceteris paribus*, its domestic importance grows since it is now hailed as a protector of the system against an alien form of ideology. Thus, strategic threats are coupled with ideological threats; then the defence forces are given a greater position in society and thus can have a bigger role to play. In a sense, ideological conflicts with foreign countries have an *independent* effect on external relations over and above what the defence-related position might be. This independent influence can add to the importance of the military and thereby increase domestic militarisation. Again, the opposite is true also. If the two belligerent neighbours also happen to have similar international political alliances, then the effective importance of the military in external conflicts tends to be reduced; this in turn leads to a lower level of influence.

Some examples will clarify this. Even though Greece and Turkey have major security conflicts, their closeness on the political spectrum implies that the role of the military is commensurately less in domestic society, provided of course all other factors remain constant. On the other hand Cuba is an important political foe for many countries in Central America. Thus, though strategic conflicts are relatively less important, militarisation in the region remains high.

Summing up, the relationships between structural change, domestic influence of the military and the role of external threats are quite intricate. Our brief analysis has simply been intended to raise some of the issues involved. Since the major interest of the monograph is on economic effects, we have given only a selective review of socio-cultural factors and their interconnection with defence. Nevertheless, it is worth stressing again that the issues are important and need to be understood properly.

9.4 Economic entitlements and the military

Our discussion on the relation between entitlements, military expenditure and the militarisation of society will generally confine itself to socio-economic factors. The wider issues of political freedoms and human rights, though important, are beyond the scope of this book. The major concern here is to understand the relationship between milex and *economic* development in a broad framework; emphasising, in general, the concept of entitlement, and stressing, in particular, the requirements of an improved physical quality of life. A major problem is quantification and systematic comparison. There are many indices that can be used to categorise development in the sense of enhancement of entitlements and capabilities. In a way it is easier to understand than to categorise, to identify *ex post* than to predict *ex ante*, and to describe intuitively than to formalise precisely. Yet, as mentioned in Chapter 1, the subject is of obvious importance and needs to be understood as clearly as possible.

Consider first the sorts of indicators we can use to identify 'good' or 'bad' performers in the field. Sen (1981) uses life expectancy at birth, adult literacy rate and income distributional and poverty measures to judge the quality of life in developing countries. Sivard (1983) gives us information on 142 countries and thirteen variables which give in some measure an indication of development in a wider sense than the usual indicators such as growth, manufacturing share, investment ratio, etc. These are grouped under three headings, education, health, and sanitation, as well as nutrition. The first contains information on public expenditure on education *per capita*, school age population per teacher, the percentage of school age population at school, the percentage of women among university students, and literacy rates. The second tells us about the number of doctors and hospital beds per head of population, infant mortality rates, life expectancy, as well as the percentage of the total population with access to safe water. Nutritional information deals with calorie and protein supply intake *per capita*. The amount of information is potentially vast and a lot of selectivity is required before any reasonable conclusions can be given. On the other hand the criterion for inclusion, whether of countries or variables, may contain bias. The analysis is therefore to be done with caution and is not definitive. Rigorous research in the area is still in its infancy.

In Table 9.2 we give data on certain indicators of socio-economic development. *Per capita* GNP is also included as a control variable; it is often thought that the higher the income per head the easier it is for society to provide the services that may increase entitlements; this needs to be verified. All data is

Table 9.2 *Social and military indicators*

	(1) GNP per capita	(2) Literacy rate	(3) Infant mortality	(4) Life expectancy	(5) % pop. safe water	(6) Milex burden	(7) Military influence
Brazil	2,002	76	77	63	63	1.06	H
Argentina	4,361	93	45	70	60	2.2	H
Mexico	2,590	83	60	65	59	0.62	L
Peru	1,056	80	88	58	49	5.3	H
S. Korea	1,388	94	34	65	79	5.0	H
Pakistan	292	32	126	51	29	5.4	H
India	230	40	123	52	41	3.0	L
Sri Lanka	279	85	40	66	22	0.74	L
Tanzania	264	70	103	52	39	4.5	L
Nigeria	1,035	34	135	48	28	3.6	H
S. Arabia	12,484	25	114	54	64	14.3	I
Egypt	600	50	103	55	84	20.7	I
LDC	8,477	99	20	73	94	4.7	
DC	749	59	96	58	44	5.0	

Source: World Tables (1980), Sivard (1983), SIPRI (1984).

for 1980. The influence of defence can be seen from two indices, the military burden (as usual) and militarisation indexed by *H* (high), *I* (intermediate), and *L* (low). The last variable, by its very nature, is subjective.

The countries are grouped in terms of geographical regions. Looking at Latin America, Argentina, despite having high militarisation and relatively large military expenditure by regional standards, does reasonably well on socio-economic development. Its literacy rate and life expectancy values are the highest in the group and also comparable with the average for developed countries. Even though the influence of the military is high, this does not seem to have gone against development. Of course, *per capita* income must have had a positive influence.

Almost the opposite can be said of Brazil. Its *per capita* income is double that of Peru and almost the same as that of Mexico. Yet its record on the variables indicating the quality of life is almost similar to that of the much poorer Peru and is worse, on many counts, than Mexico's. Brazil does not spend much on defence but the presence of the military is overwhelming. Here is the classic example of an economy with high growth and capital formation but a society with low social development coupled with a strong military and high militarisation.

A similar analysis can be done with the countries of South and East Asia. Sri Lanka stands out in the subcontinent, with similar *per capita* income to India and Pakistan but having a brilliant record of achievement in improving the condition of life of the impoverished masses. Its reticence in the military domain seems to be more than compensated for by its performance elsewhere. Indeed, with a *per capita* income of only *one-sixth* of South Korea's its level of development in the broader sense is exactly similar. Sri Lanka has a poor record of economic growth compared with the redoubtable South Korea, but when it comes to entitlements Sri Lanka holds its head high. Lack of militarisation must have helped considerably in achieving the desired standards, particularly since resources have not been diverted into the defence sector from more desirable ends.

The other regional classifications also show interesting variations. The choice of years biases Tanzania's defence burden: historically this has been much lower than that shown. Military involvement in the political system has also been much less than in most African countries. This contrasts with Nigeria which, starting from the Civil War, has had a high degree of militarisation culminating in the coup at the end of 1983. Another contrast, but which is much more remarkable, is in the levels of socio-economic development. Looking at the data given by international agencies (see Table 9.2), the 'representative' Nigerian, in spite of earning *five* times the income of the average Tanzanian, seems to have a higher possibility of being illiterate, a larger probability of dying at birth, a lower life expectancy and a lesser chance of drinking safe water. Again increased militarisation is, maybe, having a deleterious effect on the quality of life.

It should be noted, however, that militarisation, or lack of it, for some of the countries in the above list is very much dependent upon the degree of internal conflict they have had due to political reasons. The Nigerian Civil War has left deep scars in the socio-economic structure. The behaviour of the military after the war, in reunification, has been exemplary and there can be little doubt that, in some basic sense, the armed forces have managed to hold the country together. On the other hand Sri Lanka now has its own secessionist movement among the Tamils. It is not clear what effect this will have, on economic development and on increased militarisation, particularly among the minority Tamil population. Recent reports of army excesses and repression among the Tamils tend to distort the favourable picture provided by the data.

As mentioned earlier, military influences in Arab countries have always been reasonably important because of early nationalism and also due to the many local conflicts. Yet, in contrast to South America, direct coups have been infrequent in recent years. As Ataturk showed many years back in Turkey, military leaders forming civilian administrations are often the most adept at keeping the armed forces out of the body politic. Egypt, from Nasser onwards, is a good recent example. Thus, in spite of the very high military expenditure in the two Arab countries in the sample (Egypt and South Arabia) due to war and oil, they are classified as 'intermediate' in military influence. Again there is a strong contrast. Egypt has only 5 per cent of Saudi Arabia's *per capita* income and yet outperforms the latter in every category of social development.

It is not clear whether Arab countries in general have been

more efficient in fostering social development than in promoting militarisation. Of course, the stupendous increase in wealth, emanating from oil in the region, has meant that all forms of public expenditure have increased substantially. This has led to more welfare expenditure by the state, which in turn has increased entitlements to socio-economic benefits. Further, the countries have been in a state of war or security-related emergency for many years and this has caused high defence budgets. Chirouf (1982) claims: 'It seems quite clear that the military development of Arab countries has proceeded further than economic and social development.'

There are, of course, substantial inter-country differences. The contrast between Egypt and Saudi Arabia has been noted. Algeria, in spite of being an oil exporter, is a moderate spender on defence (by regional standards) and has a low military burden. On the other hand it outperforms many of its neighbours in health, literacy and sanitation indicators. Libya and Kuwait are average in the table of defence allocations, but have a notable record in social development. By contrast, countries like the Yemen and Mauritania have low income, a high defence burden, and an unenviable performance in the wider aspects of development.[6]

Are there any common features to be gleaned from this information set? What are the lessons to be learned? A few are clear-cut; others are more doubtful. It is obvious that there is no necessary connection between *per capita* income and the availability of the wider measures of development. Income-raising and growth-inducing economic policies can help, as in South Korea; but Sri Lanka shows that if a society, or its representative government, is adamant and follows appropriate policies it can improve the 'quality of life' even though income and growth are low. There is also some evidence that the military burden is having a depressing effect on socio-economic development: contrast Sri Lanka and Pakistan. This is essentially due to government budgetary allocations. Many of the indicators used in Table 9.2 are crucially influenced by, and dependent on, public expenditure on social, welfare and developmental budgets. We have seen earlier how the trade-off between defence and other parts of the government budget operates. There can be little doubt that defence budgets can eat into expenditures that may potentially provide higher entitlements. More subtle is the effect of militarisation, as opposed to defence expenditure *per se*. Brazil has tended recently to spend less on the military than Argentina; yet the former has a much poorer record on the broad proxies for development. A similar conclusion can be drawn from comparing the two African countries in the sample; Tanzania does very well on all developmental criteria, but also has a higher defence burden. Here, I think, militarisation, particularly its specific national form, becomes relevant. If the military can be generally involved in nation-building and made to believe in equitable growth with justice, there is a good chance that entitlements will not suffer. Tanzania is a good example. Julius Nyerere formed the TPDF (Tanzanian Peoples' Defence Force) on a relatively left-wing and socialist basis after the mutiny of the traditional British-modelled army in the early years of independence. The armed forces have had a notable recent success in their traditional role of guarding national security: they threw out Idi Amin of Uganda in a victorious war in 1979 (this also explains the high defence burden – see Table 9.2). But the army is also involved in national reconstruction, rural development and rural resettlements in the communal villages called the *ujama*. On the contrary, as we saw earlier, Brazil's military establishments have been rather elitist, and this may have contributed to their isolation from entitlement-enhancing policies.

There is some evidence, therefore, that a negative trade-off exists between socio-economic development and military influence (either in the form of higher militarisation or increasing defence budgets). But the hypothesis is not supported *strongly* by the facts and therefore more analysis is necessary. In particular we need to broaden our set of indicators and proxies to provide for more information and allow a finer analysis. One of the major factors influencing the endowment of people, and thus allowing them more scope for enhancing their capabilities, is a more equitable distribution of income. Thus it is preferable to include some criterion of comparative performance in the field of income distribution. Given its importance the measure should be compared, on its own, with military influence on a cross-country basis.

Table 9.3 gives information for ten countries. These are ranked, in column 1, according to their performance in terms of their relative equalities of income distribution; thus Sri Lanka has the most egalitarian distribution in the sample while Brazil is the worst in this category. The ranking has been constructed from the data in Sen (1981); all non-European countries with data for some years in the 1970s are included here. In column 2 we have a ranking of these countries based on their performance in an *aggregate* socio-economic index (SEI). The SEI is constructed from the following information: (a) percentage of school age population at school; (b) percentage of women among university students; (c) literacy rate; (d) population per physician; (d) population per hospital bed; (e) infant mortality rate; (d) life expectancy at birth; (e) calorie and protein intake per head; (f) percentage of total population with access to safe water. The SEI therefore represents, in principle, an aggregation over entitlements to basic education, literacy, women's educational rights, health care, longevity, nutrition and basic sanitation. Column 3 gives the ranks for average military burdens for 1975-80. Since it has been claimed that both the military burden and social development may depend upon *per capita* income, the final column gives the corresponding ranks, again in descending order. A comparison of the first three columns of ranks will give us a fair idea of the relationship between defence and those aspects of development that are not exclusively connected with growth.

Table 9.3 *Rank order for income distribution, socio-economic index, military burden and per capita income*

Countries	(1) Income distribution	(2) SEI	(3) Military burden	(4) Per capita income
Sri Lanka	1	5	8	10
South Korea	2	4	2	7
Argentina	3	1	5	1
Philippines	4	9	4	9
Costa Rica	5	2	10	5
Mexico	6	7	9	3
Venezuela	7	3	6	2
Malaysia	8	6	3	6
Peru	9	10	1	8
Brazil	10	8	7	4

The polar cases are easy to identify. Observe Sri Lanka's preeminent position once again: first in distribution, relatively high in SEI (particularly if compared with its position for income). It also has one of the lowest defence burdens. A similar story can be told for Costa Rica: very low defence outlay coupled with high ranks for development, all on the basis of middling *per capita* income. Contrast the case of Peru, the worst performer in the league of social progress, with the highest military burden in the group. Similarly, Malaysia's military burden seems to be having a detrimental effect on its ability to improve the SEI, in spite of having a relatively high *per capita* income (in fact it has the highest GNP *per capita* in the Asian subgroup).

Difficulties in interpretation remain, however. Argentina is highly militarised, spends a lot on the military, and yet does very well in terms of the norms of socio-economic change. So also does South Korea: long-term hostilities with the North, high defence expenditure and burden, but an excellent record elsewhere. Even income per head is not high enough to explain its position in the social indicator stakes. The comparison with Brazil is even more interesting. Both have encouraged export promotion, after building an industrial base through ISI, indirectly but actively encouraged by the government; both have had very high growth rates; both have pursued, occasionally, repressive domestic measures to keep discontent (and real wages) low; both are relatively militarised societies; yet there is a vast difference between their achievements in the realm of socio-economic progress. This, then, is an enigma.

There are *four* concepts, not necessarily compatible with each other, which seem to interact to provide a complex relationship. These are militarisation, military burden, growth and finally socio-economic development. Instead of first providing an analytical framework, let us once again look at specific cases to see whether there is any observable regularity. If there is, then it may help to provide some general conclusions. We have already discussed the standard ones. Let us now take the 'outliers' from Table 9.3 to see whether they follow a pattern. These countries are Mexico, Argentina, and the two 'surprises', Brazil and South Korea.

Mexico has had high, and relatively noninflationary, growth, coupled with low military expenditure and a non-interventionist army. This is the classic case discussed in the earlier parts of the book where a reduction in military spending leads to an increase in economic growth. The alleged negative trade-off that we have emphasised is most clear for Mexico. The economy has done well, in the conventional sense, by having less consumption expenditure on defence and using the released resources for capital formation and growth. Further, the military cannot be blamed for lack of entitlements since their participation has been minimal in any case. It seems that there has been no 'trickle-down effect'; rather, unequal distribution may even have helped growth through increased saving. It may be noted in passing that the percentage of national income received by the poorest 20 per cent of the population has fallen from 3.4 in 1965 to 2.9 in 1977, thereby creating more inequality. Mexico, then, follows expectations: low milex may lead to high growth but that does not necessarily increase the level of economic development in the broader sense of the term.

Despite having high *per capita* income, due to historical reasons starting from a higher base, Argentina has had low growth in recent decades coupled with some heavy doses of inflation. Table 9.4 gives growth (of GDP) and inflation rate for the four countries in question. Argentina does the worst here. But Table 9.2 and 9.3 give a different picture. How can we reconcile this in the context of the military? The answer is related to the concepts raised in the previous section in the context of conflict and structural change. In the post-war period the Argentine military have had long periods of relative harmony with organised labour, though there have been major exceptions, for example in the late 1970s. This was particularly true under the Perons, when implicit alliances were formed between these two powerful groups – the trade unions and military. The occasional 'marriage' between the two meant that a high growth strategy based on reducing the real wage rate through suppression of organised labour was not successful in Argentina (compared to Brazil, for example). On the other hand it was precisely because of this implicit co-operation that entitlement rights remained high and social change was not hampered. Clearly there are exceptions to this general hypothesis, but overall it seems to be valid.

The effectiveness of the military in reducing and suppressing conflict and thus promoting growth is enhanced in a system where

Table 9.4 *Growth and inflation*

Countries	1950-1960	1960-1970	1970-1980
Mexico			
Growth	5.6	7.6	6.5
Inflation	7.4	2.6	18.2
Brazil			
Growth	6.9	5.4	7.7
Inflation	18.8	46.1	42.1
Argentina			
Growth	2.7	4.3	1.9
Inflation	28.2	22.8	135.5
Korea			
Growth	5.1	8.6	9.0
Inflation	45.7	17.5	19.7

Source: World Tables (1983).

there is more organised labour, preferably in urban manufacturing. Reduction in real wages gives a competitive edge to the economy producing for the world market. To understand this issue consider Table 9.5, where urbanisation and share of manufacturing are given for our specific countries. Note that Mexico, Argentina and Brazil are highly urbanised with manufacturing being quite important in GDP. In Mexico the military did not intervene: it is possible that there was insufficient need for intervention – 'conflict' inflation was low (see Table 9.4). The economy benefited from not having a strong and expensive military – the growth rate was high; but the society did not. In Argentina the share of manufacturing and urban population ratio were higher; thus it had the greatest possibility of 'efficient' and 'militarised' growth. However, the military co-operated with organised labour. Both took their fair share of the national product, and entitlements increased and 'quality of life' was enhanced; but the national cake was not sufficient for increasing demands made by the protagonists, so that inflation increased, growth suffered and the 'consensus' broke down. Remember we are not saying that urbanisation *per se* has any effect on the military burden (see Chapter 3); only that an urbanised society

Table 9.5 *Urbanisation and manufacturing*

	1960	1965	1970	1975	1980
Mexico					
UR	50.8	54.9	59.0	63.0	66.7
MAN/GDP	18.9	21.0	23.7	24.3	24.9
Brazil					
UR	46.1	51.0	55.9	61.8	67.6
MAN/GDP	25.9	24.5	26.7	27.1	27.7
Argentina					
UR	73.6	76.1	78.4	80.4	82.4
MAN/GDP	28.4	30.4	30.0	30.8	27.9
Korea					
UR	27.7	32.4	40.7	48.1	54.8
MAN/GDP	8.5	11.1	18.0	26.0	33.2

Source: *World Tables*.
UR = Urban population as % of total population.
MAN/GDP = manufacturing as % of GDP.

makes it easier for the military to operate if it wishes to suppress internal conflict.

The economic success of Brazil and its concomitant social failure can be compared and contrasted with Argentina on the one hand and South Korea on the other. Brazil had a similar industrial labour force to Argentina's, but the military played the role of confrontation and was relatively successful. Real wage demands were kept lower than they would otherwise have been, and conflicts suppressed, entitlements destroyed and social development retarded. Growth prospered, and inflation, though always high, never became hyper-inflationary and a threat to the system. In addition, the military budget was very low, not at all commensurate with the power of the military. The country was militarised but not spending large sums of resources on 'unproductive' (defence) consumption. Thus the growth-depressing effects were not present either. Consider now South Korea. There, until about 1970, urbanisation, manufacturing and the role of organised labour were relatively unimportant (see Table 9.5). Thus the sort of *domestic* role that we have talked about (in addition to threat and security) was not very important. Real wages were initially low in any case, thus there was little necessity for military intervention in conflict suppression. Further, external threat was so vitally important that it was not possible for the defence sector to do anything except protect the country from its true enemies. Labour-intensive, employment-oriented economic strategy, carefully nurtured by the government, not only brought growth but also ultimately a high real wage which led to socio-economic development.

The issues are complex and our framework is the first, to the best of my knowledge, to put it in some sort of structure. For some countries, low military expenditure leads to more resources being released which can be used for the improvement of the socio-economic conditions of the masses. The opposite is also true: there exists a negative trade-off. For other countries, however, the relation becomes more complex. It is possible to have higher milex and more social development, but growth will suffer. On the other hand a militarised society, even though not spending large amounts on the military, will suppress entitlements, helping growth in the process, but not achieving, as a society, the fruits of development. The optimum combination, presumably represented by South Korea, is still elusive for most Third World countries. But even here a cautionary word remains. South Korea has been helped tremendously by US military aid as well as by the 'spin-off' of the Vietnam war, leading to high procurement expenditure of the American forces. Thus the drain of resources from high milex was mitigated by aid, and growth reduction was stopped. It may not be easy for LDCs to 'do' a South Korea.

10 Conclusion

10.1 What do we know?

Military expenditure is an emotive subject. Its protagonists are 'merchants of death'; it leads to wars and great human misery; it uses global resources which could be utilised for far more humanitarian purposes. But the opposite viewpoint is equally plausible: military expenditure preserves liberty and freedom from external aggression; it is an objective indicator of 'eternal vigilance'; it provides deterrence and indirectly saves lives; it generates economic and socio-cultural benefits. This book has been an attempt to look carefully (and with as little bias as possible) at some of the economic issues related to defence spending; hopefully this will help us make a proper and total evaluation of military expenditure in less developed countries. We realise that the political and strategic aspects of the subject are important and possibly paramount. In emphasising the economic consequences we do not wish to minimise the alternative motivation. It is well known that the politics of economics does play a vital role in nations' decision-making. But it should also be remembered that military spending is extremely expensive and the resource costs may even be prohibitive, especially for some countries in the Third World. Thus the economics of (defence) strategy are also crucial in a proper cost-benefit analysis of the military. We need to know what we are spending before we can evaluate 'value for money'.

The 'opportunity cost' argument – what the gains and losses are in terms of alternatives forgone – is still, to my mind, the most elemental reason for studying the economics of militarisation. But one has to be careful not to confuse the elemental with the elementary. The economic effects of defence spending are a very complex issue indeed. Our purpose here has been to delineate the intricate mechanics of the problem, in terms of a qualitative characterisation as well as a quantitative formalisation. There exists a large literature on the politics and strategy of military spending, but a meagre one for the economic aspects. This work therefore complements existing studies in related fields.

The caution mentioned elsewhere in the book should again be stressed in the concluding sections. In spite of the limitations of the data it is possible to get an idea of the total amount of milex expended by a country, region or even the world, in a given time period. It is then quite easy to claim that that specific amount could have been used for more 'productive expenditure', for example on investment or on human capital or in the enhancement of entitlements. In a sense this is the most potent form in which the argument against militarisation is conducted; its appeal is obvious. But the concepts are much more complex than the foregoing suggestions. There is no automatic one-to-one correspondence between reduced milex and increased expenditure on productive services. The withdrawal of a unit of resources from defence does not necessarily mean that it will be used for growth-enhancing policies or to better the lives of the impoverished masses; for all we know the resouce may be squandered on conspicuous consumption or whatever. The transfer may also reduce national security. Without a systematic and formal analysis it is impossible to predict the final conclusion. Our analysis relies principally on a sophisticated version of the opportunity-cost argument, but taking into account the various interdependencies in the military-development nexus.

Before summarising the results, it may be useful to consider, once again, the nature of the developmental process that we have in mind. First we emphasise the rate of growth of domestic product. Reasons for this focus are already known. We implicitly assume that economic growth is constrained first by the supply of resources. Since most LDCs are labour-abundant, the primary constraint will be the supply of new capital stock, which in turn will depend on the amount of saving, and even more on the saving-income ratio. Thus any institution which increases (or decreases) the proportion of national output being saved will have important repercussions on the growth rate. However, saving *per se* will not be translated into productive investment unless the economy has sufficient potential to absorb that investment. Thus the absorptive capacity constraint will become crucial once the saving propensity is raised to the desired levels. An economy with high saving may not be able to utilise it and translate it into capital accumulation until and unless there is demand for such investment. This demand will only come if co-operative inputs such as *skilled* labour, infrastructure, entrepreneurship, motivation, financial institutions, foreign know-how and sundry other factors are available in the right proportions. In the absence of these, savings will be frittered away through unproductive channels (hoarding of commodities, storing gold, appearance of the black economy, holding of cash, etc.). Without the potential and environment for investment, high saving will be wasted by not enhancing the growth rate. Given the importance of absorptive capacity, planners in LDCs should try to increase it. One obvious method of doing this is to increase public expenditure on education (as well as on health, nutrition, welfare, etc.). An important, efficient and egalitarian way to increase the rate of labour-augmenting technological progress, create more social mobility, and break down inhibitions fostering backwardness, is to increase government expenditure (as a proportion of national income) on education. This is a good proxy for human capital formation – one of the chief ingredients in the menu of absorptive capacity.

Three aspects of the growth process can now be identified – saving, investment (i.e. absorption) and human capital. The military as an institution, as an organised force and as a claimant for resources, can have a negative or positive effect on each of them. It is through these broad conduits that the effect of the military burden on growth has been studied in the book.

There is a large body of anecdotal and informal literature which assures us that the military can have a positive role to play in enhancing the growth rate and fostering the developmental process. It supposedly can mobilise new saving, train people, create entrepreneurship, modernise society, help in absorptive capacity and so on. The empirical evidence that we produce (using a sample of fifty countries) demonstrates that this reasoning is flawed. If the econometric specifications are accepted, then the overall effect of military expenditure is to *reduce* growth rates. If we take all interdependent effects together, an increase in the defence burden leads to a decrease in the growth rate through a decline in the saving rate, a fall in investment per unit of capital and a reduction in human capital formation. Clearly, one should discount the favourable effects of the military and overall consider it as a force whose expansion weakens the domestic economy.

Finally, the issue of spin-off still remains. We think that here the military may score some plus-points, but even then its beneficial influence has been overrated. The military-industrial complex has been considered a 'leading sector' by some development economists. Its growth and expansion are expected to have *substantial* spin-off if the domestic industrial base can respond. However, here again we see that the claims made on behalf of the military are exaggerated. The extent of spin-off on relevant sectors is much less than one would anticipate even in favourable cases.

The nature of growth and development follows the structure set up by the theory of developmental planning and capital formation in less developed economies. There are three major issues to be tackled in the context of planning. First, how much should a nation optimally save? Second, what is the structure of investment? Third, what choice of techniques should be followed? The role of the military can then be subsumed in this very broad framework. First, does the military help to generate more saving than it reallocates away from productive uses? Second, does the military foster absorptive capacity and help create a demand for investment goods? Third, does the military, through its effect on industrialisation, influence the choice of efficient techniques and raise productivity and technological progress? All three methods could have growth-augmenting effects if the answers to the preceding questions are in the affirmative.

Our quantifiable models and empirical estimates (see also the Appendix) demonstrate that, in reality, the effects of an increased military burden are growth-depressing on all three counts mentioned in the last paragraph. In terms of saving, investment and techniques (or spin-off), military expenditure has relatively more harmful effects on the growth rate of the economy and thus on the structure of development that LDCs can construct.

Finally, from the large model reported in the Appendix, the actual values of the estimates and multipliers (taking all interactive variables together) from defence to growth suggest that the growth-depressing effects could be potentially quite large. Thus the effects are certainly nontrivial and under certain hypotheses almost prohibitive. Whatever the benefits of the security aspects of defence, its economic costs are substantial.

So much for growth. What about development in the broader sense of the term? Here the relations become more complex. First, military expenditure or the military burden is neither necessary nor sufficient for militarism. A country like Brazil has a low military burden and low defence spending *per capita*, yet it has a high degree of militarism; India on the other hand has a relatively high burden, yet the involvement of the military in the political process is minimal (witness the smooth transition of political power in the post-Nehru period, mostly through democratic elections, contrary to the dire prognosis of the experts). However, it is the extent of militarism and concomitant militarisation that actually determines whether development in its widest sense – basic needs, eradication of poverty, increase in welfare services, extension of capabilities and entitlements – will be seriously affected. The overall conclusion seems to be that militarism and development do not tend to marry well, though there may be notable exceptions.

Consider the relation betwen defence spending and income distribution, a grey area of research where little analysis has been done to date. Theoretical intuition suggests that increased milex may well lead to a more unequal distribution of income. The Palme Commission report (1982) emphasises this as follows:

> People who work in the defence establishment are likely to have relatively high incomes and 'modern' tastes. Their extra demand might be met by diverting capacity and capital formation from industries producing wage goods consumed by less skilled workers and the poor. Demand increases, but as a consequence the distribution of income gets worse.

Our major concern has been the economics of military expenditure *per se* in LDCs. The related issue of the economics of Third World wars deserves far more attention and research than we can provide here; it probably needs a separate volume by itself. It is extremely difficult to generalise in this area – much more so than in the evaluation of the effects of milex. Country-, culture-, geography- and history-specific factors are much more crucial, since in many senses a war is a unique phenomenon. Harkavy (1981) claims that 'there has been almost nothing in the way of comparative analysis of the economics of war in the Third World'. This is not strictly true, though recent evidence has been scanty. Kennedy (1974) is an earlier example of an excellent analysis of the war economies of Vietnam, Nigeria, Israel, Egypt and Pakistan. His conclusion is eclectic: 'The economic impact of war is not uniform.'

Though 'hard' data and even simple information are difficult to get, particularly in the mass of propaganda that is thrown out during wars, some anecdotal evidence exists for recent times. It is thought that Israel's relatively long war of 1973, twenty-two days, cost it the astounding equivalent of a whole year's national income. The economic problems of Argentina in terms of international debt and liquidity were mentioned earlier. For Pakistan, during the period 1969-71, which included the civil war as well as the war with India, GDP fell by 44 per cent. It has been claimed that the war has inflicted damage to the civilian economy in Iran of the order of $100 billion, equal to four years of state revenues including oil. Note that this is over and above the pure military costs, which are themselves astronomical. Thus wars can be expected to be very costly.

The conclusions drawn from an analysis of wars can also be controversial. Kennedy (1974) claims that Israel and Nigeria were not badly affected while 'Egypt and Pakistan . . . can be seen to have come out of their wars with their economic programme severely damaged'. But his causal link between war and economic problems is rather odd, since it does not emphasise the costs of defence. Rather, 'The countries with the least ability to produce an effective conventional army, and to create the administrative apparatus to sustain it in conventional battle, have not only lost in a military sense, but this organisational inability has been part of the economic mismanagement of the country.' This is of doubtful validity; Pakistan's military performance in the 1965 war is rated highly by strategic experts, and its difficulties in 1971 were very much a morale problem of an army in occupation which can happen to the most professional of forces. The economic recovery after its dismemberment has also been quite remarkable; the rate of growth in the 1970s, which includes the major war, was a healthy 5 per cent per annum.

The tacit assumption throughout, in all these economic evaluations, has been that higher military expenditure does actually increase security in developing countries. This is neither the time nor the place to have a critical discussion of this issue, since the main problems fall outside the scope of the book. But the interested reader should note that, at least for some LDCs, there may also be some connections between ultra-sophistication of strategic plans, excess military spending leading to (probably unnecessary) 'over-kill', and escalation of costs. Optimally there should be another cost-benefit analysis, parallel to the one conducted in this monograph, on the purely strategic aspects of defence budgets and whether society gets the defence it deserves and pays for.

The foregoing discussion has inevitably been concerned with the domestic economy and its strategic spending. However, we have seen how, quite often, the international environment has a crucial role to play in determining the nature and quantity of milex in LDCs. Again a proper evaluation of that is beyond our scope here. But some tentative conclusions can be drawn in the summing up. This will be particularly useful in formulating policies which may be prescribed to halt the perpetual increase in defence spending that the Third World faces today. These and related concepts form the core of the last two sections of the monograph.

10.2 The international forces

As we have discussed earlier, military expenditure is positively related to the degree of economic integration that developing countries have with the international economy. This is not surprising. As the economy becomes more open, and the importance of tradables increases, the role of foreign imports becomes crucial under any circumstances. A higher proportion of domestic defence spending is also diverted to the importation of armaments from abroad. Sophistication of (imported) military technology occasionally triggers off a local arms race with neighbours joining in under perceived threats. The result is further escalation of milex.

That there exists a positive association between defence spending and arms imports can be seen from Table 10.1, where data in constant prices, for ten years, is provided for all LDCs (including OPEC but excluding South Africa). There are some exceptional years: arms imports for 1978 are an obvious outlier; in 1980-81 milex trends move significantly out of line with trade figures. But overall, there seems to be a regularity. The causal relation between these two variables tends to work both ways. An increase in the total defence budget implies a greater amount being allocated for imported arms or, for weapons-producing countries, defence technology. On the other hand, in the absence of substantial reallocation, larger imports means increased totals.

It has been suggested that the primary responsibility for the burgeoning arms trade during the last decade lies with the developed countries of the North. There are many reasons for this. Increased profitability and greater competitiveness combined forces during this period to make the 'arms bazaar' very lucrative indeed. Structural crises, in the form of ever-escalating costs following from the over-ambitious technology of the 'baroque arsenal', forced producers to look further afield for

Table 10.1 *Index of arms imports and military expenditure in constant prices for all LDCs, 1972-81*

	Imports	Milex
1972	100.0	100.0
1973	110.7	113.1
1974	152.6	144.4
1975	220.1	169.9
1976	305.6	193.9
1977	366.9	192.3
1978	628.3	199.7
1979	469.6	205.0
1980	409.2	215.5
1981	346.5	245.6

Source: Calculated from SIPRI.

markets. National security demands that a viable defence industry be based within the specific country of the North. Witness the concern in Britain or France at President Reagan's 'Star Wars' proposals which threaten to make the domestic technology of the smaller countries of NATO obsolete. But government aggregate budgetary policy makes it difficult to increase demand at home, thus overseas markets provide a desirable method of sharing costs and boosting production. Chris Smith (1984) puts it succinctly:

> the role of the North, particularly in relation to the inherent crises which bedevil the armament industries of the West, and in a different way, the Soviet Union is of immense importance. The export of armaments is no longer the murky domain of the 'merchants of death' or a tool of foreign policy, although both are still relevant. Of far greater significance is the growing importance of arms exports for any national government mandated to retain an industrial base for war preparedness and, at the same time, avoid defence expenditure rising beyond political and fiscal acceptance.[1]

Higher aggregate domestic military expenditure in northern countries can be a spur, not only to weapons production at home, but also to a greater drive towards exports. Table 10.2 gives comparative data for six developed economies. (The Soviet figures should be treated carefully since they refer to *only* convertible currency balance of payments and *not* to total external payments.) The two superpowers have high military burdens and also have high export-dependence. In the US about 2 per cent of total exports come from major weapons (minor arms cannot be accounted for); for the Soviet Union an astonishing 12.8 per cent of all hard currency earnings is due to arms. The same pattern follows on to the smaller countries: France and the UK have high military burdens and promote defence exports while precisely the opposite can be seen for Japan.

The developed countries cannot therefore be absolved from blame when it comes to searching for root causes of increasing internationalisation leading to greater militarisation. The recycling of petro-dollars, the use of sovereign debt, the wish and ability of Third World governments to convert export revenue

Table 10.2 *Comparative foreign trade data for six developed economies, 1975*

	USA	USSR	France	UK	FRG	Japan
Arms exports ($ billion)	2.343	1.0	0.593	0.647	0.138	0.002
Total exports ($ billion)	129.2	7.838	59.99	55.04	103.99	66.37
Arms exports as a prop. of total (%)	1.81	12.8	0.98	1.2	0.13	0.003
Exports/GDP (%)	8.43	—	18.53	25.93	26.37	13.68
Military burden (%)	5.9	10.3	3.8	4.9	3.6	0.9

Source: International Financial Statistic (IMF), SIPRI, Portes (1983).

(after a commodity price boom) into weapons purchases, have all been used by the arms suppliers to boost arms sales considerably. It would be naive to suggest that demand did not play a significant role; if LDC governments had steadfastly refused to buy, then obviously the position would have been different. But arms sellers have exploited the situation to the hilt, encouraging buyers' competition (among themselves) and probably fostering incipient arms races. There should have been more awareness that arms sales have unique externalities attached to them; that their market should be regulated more stringently; that political and strategic control in co-ordinated fashion must be made effective; that insubordinate client states should be punished for their belligerence and moral hazard.

It could have been expected that increased integration of LDC economies with the world economy would lead to greater interdependence and thus would possibly reduce the chance of war and military confrontation. Witness the case of Europe. Sadly this has not happened in the Third World. Regional rivalry is increasing, balkanisation continues to create problems, and belligerence among neighbours is omnipresent.

10.3 What can be done

Given that the economic effects of military expenditure can be adverse overall, the important question remains as to what can be done. The ultimate answers go far beyond the narrow realm of economics; they are basically political and depend on the will of the masses and their representatives. We can do little more than delineate some of the options.

The international environment, by its very nature, is difficult to handle by individual LDCs or even as a collective whole. The United Nations is probably the only organisation which has some authority, albeit limited, to initiate action in controlling the arms trade, which threatens to reach dangerous proportions and is also a major economic burden. A permanent secretariat to monitor, publicise, analyse, discuss, reprimand, and even threaten sanctions would be helpful. Mass movements in the West and socialist countries, though principally concerned with nuclear disarmament within their respective countries, should give more attention to the proliferation of international weapons transfers. A reduction of arms exports will not have traumatic effects on the domestic economy in the North, as various studies have shown. With a modicum of planning, conversion, of (exported) 'swords to ploughs', can be achieved without much difficulty.

The less developed countries also have an important role to play in this respect. Mass movements must grow up and the will of the people be galvanised to impose on governments, if not disarmament, a reasonable reduction of military spending and a suitable reallocation into socially and economically meaningful channels. It is not often realised that, given proper leadership, the common people of developing countries have a great deal of collective power by virtue of the unity of massive numbers. After all, Gandhian *satyagraha* did succeed, among other factors, in unseating the might of the British empire; and Ataturk's inspired but populist measures managed, given that the times were propitious, to transform the cultural values of a society almost overnight.

The military itself should be encouraged to turn its attention to civic action-oriented programmes. Soldiers, whether conscripts or volunteers, have dues to pay to their societies. Part of this is paid by laying down their lives in time of war. But during peace, which is usually more frequent, they can and should help in economic regeneration. The life of military personnel in poor countries is generally far superior to that of their civilian brethren; it is not unfair to demand some services in return. The skills that are learnt in the army can be usefully applied in the process of economic development.

The defence establishment should eschew oversophistication in equipment and planning. A conventional armed force modelled along foreign (often ex-colonial) lines is not only very expensive but also can be ineffective in combat. Simply having the technologically most advanced weapons is no guarantee that it is functionally efficient. Further, the attitudes of a so-called 'modern' army cut off from the rest of a 'backward' nation may be counter-productive not only from the society's developmental point of view but also when it comes to the actual act of defending that society. In the long run, the 'soldier in mufti', forming a part of the 'people's army', may do better in protecting the home and hearth of his countrywomen – and will also be cheaper to use.

The suggestions outlined here, I hope, do not fall into extreme categories, so that they do not become either unattainable or useless in producing changes. The tragedy of an academic's forays into policy suggestions over which he or she has no ultimate control is they tend to become either a utopian's dream or a fatalist's nightmare. I have therefore tried, as briefly as possible, to outline some ways in which the adverse effects of militarisation can be mitigated. A more detailed exposition is unnecessary: the careful reader will have gleaned policy suggestions throughout and anything more would be repetitive.

The analysis of military expenditure in less developed countries presents a dilemma to the researcher. In a sense defence spending is necessary and may even be useful in the enhancement of security and the provision of some socio-economic benefits in a static society. Indeed, in a noncooperative world of prisoners' dilemmas it could be vital for survival. The question is when can we say that enough is enough? For ultimately, military spending is the ultimate absurdity in a poverty-ridden, growth-stunted, underdeveloped economy. The military in its quest for security may add to insecurity; in trying to modernise and galvanise society it may make it more hierarchical and moribund; in an attempt to increase the rate of growth it may reduce the level of development; in an effort to reduce import costs of foreign arms it may raise the level of the national debt by importing unnecessarily sophisticated defence technology. Less developed societies, as they give to the military, find that, unlike the widow's cruse, they have even less than they originally bargained for. The economics of defence only tell us what we gain and what we lose (from an economic point of view); the final decision rests with the superpowers, and their 'Star Wars' attitudes, as also with those who follow in their footsteps in the Third World.

Appendix
An econometric evaluation of the military-growth relationship

A.1 Econometric models

Having analysed the major theoretical issues associated with the economic effects of military expenditure in LDCs, we turn to a specific econometric problem in this Appendix. This deals with the statistical test of the milex-growth relationship, which tries to empirically answer the question whether an increase in the defence burden increases or decreases growth rates in LDCs. The interest of the topic lies in the fact that it is possible to get a *positive* statistical relation between growth and defence, with a strong supposition that high military spending causes an increase in growth rates. We intend to show that even though this may be true, the postulated positive relation is partial and not generated by valid empirical methods. When *all* the effects (both direct and indirect) are taken into account and properly estimated, then it is seen that milex depresses growth.

We also intend to discuss, in some detail, how an empirical model should be set up and analysed to throw light on the types of problems that occur in the military literature which pertains to economic concepts. Thus the next section deals with the appropriate specification of such models, and the econometric issues that an analyst must resolve. Section A.3 gives the actual results from our own econometric model and also includes an appraisal of its conclusions. Section A.4 sums up the evidence.

A.2 The empirical issues

(a) Causality

The empirical model required to test the defence-growth

relationship must first sort out the problem of causality. If in correlation analysis we observe, for example, a positive relation between defence burden and growth rate, then, in the absence of *a priori* information, it is not possible to say whether high defence 'causes' high growth or vice versa. We have to be careful to note that defence expenditure (or burden) is determined exogenously of growth rates, and then investigate whether a relatively autonomous change in defence will increase or decrease economic growth. If it is high growth that is 'causing' high defence spending, then of course it is fruitless to talk about the growth *effects* of milex.

Though causality is a central concept in economic modelling, its analysis (and even its definition) is problematic due to the non-experimental nature of our subject. In an experimental science it is easier to observe the chain of causation between any two variables by eliminating all nonrandom disturbances and repeatedly doing the same experiments from exactly similar initial conditions. As Basman (1963) states: 'If, every time the mechanism is started up from approximately the same initial condition, it tends to run through approximately the same sequence of events, then the mechanism is said to be causal' (the quote is taken from Chan *et al.*, 1982). Clearly, such a method is almost impossible to implement in the social sciences.

Most (classical) econometric model builders would use prior information, either culled from theory or derived from experience, to specify the nature of endogenous and exogenous variables in the model to be estimated. In our case, as discussed earlier, the major determinants of the military burden are the twin concepts of 'security' and 'threat'. Thus strategic considerations are predominant when nations decide on their military budgets *vis-à-vis* national product. In addition, economic variables might be important, and, as Chapter 3 shows, certain theories have been proposed to analyse the determinants of public expenditure in general and defence spending in particular. Some of the variables that are expected to affect defence, and which have been proposed often in the literature, are *per capita* income, total government revenue and expenditure, as well as some exotic ones like urbanisation and the size of the population below the age of fourteen. However, to the best of our knowledge, no empirically verifiable model has claimed that growth affects defence. Partly, the reason is empirical. The proof of the pudding must be in the eating. As we discussed earlier (see Chapter 3), when growth is regressed on the military burden, no significant coefficient emerges. Thus, a general equation, with the military burden as the dependent (endogenous) variable and growth as the independent (exogenous) variable, tends to show that the coefficient of growth is statistically insignificant.

It is much more plausible, from political theory, to postulate that a country with greater strategic problems will go for a high defence share of national output, even though its growth rate is low. Security considerations may be paramount, even with major economic problems elsewhere; witness the case of Ethiopia, with famine, poverty, negative growth rates and yet a high military burden. The introductory chapter gives a detailed account of the strategic factors affecting the military burden, and it seems clear that the growth rate is not a major determinant.

An alternative way of checking on causality is to assume implicitly that we do not have *a priori* knowledge, and must rely on the data set to provide tests for causal relations. Causality is essentially defined as an intertemporal property, thus for any two variables, x and y, we want to know whether past x 'caused' present (and future) y or vice versa. Thus, for example, is it right to postulate that a high defence burden in the current period, by producing spin-off, will outweigh its adverse effects and produce higher growth rates in the future? Time series analysis defines formal methods by which it can be tested whether one variable affects the other and the causation is unidirectional (Granger, 1969). Intuitively, if the prediction of y using past x is more accurate than without using past x, we can say that x 'causes' y. If we can also show that there is no feedback, i.e. y is not causing x, then x is the independent variable exogenously determined and y is functionally dependent on x.

A formal test using the Granger-Sims method of causality is derived by Chan, Hsiao, and Kent (1982) and applied to the Benoit (1973) data. They find that growth does not 'cause' defence in the sense that lagged growth does not predict defence expenditure any better when it is included in the estimated equation than when it is left out. Thus it cannot be asserted that growth of the economy, independently determined, will affect defence spending in the economy.

These theoretical conjectures and econometric tests discussed in the literature allow us to proceed with the estimation of the model, assuming that the military burden is autonomously determined, and then investigate the 'multiplier' effect on growth for a hypothesised change in the defence variable.

(b) The sample set and choice of variables

We have fifty countries in our sample, each observation being a time series average of data for 1965-73. It is thought that cross-section estimates indicate long-term steady state parameters, while time series coefficients reflect more short-term relations. Thus the use of time series averages within a cross-sectional sample set is useful, since both long-term and short-term effects would be reflected in the estimates. The use of 1965-73 data is not fortuitous. The main reason for choosing this time period is that distortions caused by oil price shocks had not filtered through in this period. All data except milex and *per capita* income comes from the first edition of the *World Tables*, World Bank (1976). The latest issue (third edition of *World Tables*, 1983), gives data for 1970-81 averages for most LDCs. However, these include the pre-oil and post-oil-shock periods, thus various distortive influences are present. Results using such data cannot be fully trusted. It is hoped that data for the early 1980s, when the international system has been able to absorb the traumatic supply shocks of the last decade, will be available in the future; it will then be possible to check the temporal stability of the econometric results we present below.

The countries in the control sample are the following: Argentina, Algeria, Brazil, Burma, Chad, Chile, Colombia, Costa Rica, the Dominican Republic, Egypt, Ecuador, El Salvador, Ethiopia, Gabon, Ghana, Greece, Guatemala, Guinea, Honduras, India, Indonesia, Iran, Iraq, Israel, Jordan, Kenya, Libya, Malaysia, Mexico, Morocco, Nigeria, Pakistan, Peru, the Philippines, Saudi Arabia, Singapore, Somalia, South Africa, South Korea, South Vietnam, Spain, Sri Lanka, Sudan, Syria, Tanzania, Thailand, Tunisia, Turkey, Uganda and Venezuela.

A more fundamental point is which countries should be included in the sample set. We have taken a large sample with a wide-ranging but balanced distribution according to structural characteristics, geographical areas, political systems, strategic problems and so forth. Obviously, the precise values of the estimated parameters are sensitive to the data set; however, if the relationship is stable, adding or subtracting a few more countries should not change the overall sign of the multipliers. I have tested similar models for specification sensitivity, and have found the sign and magnitudes of the overall effect of defence on growth to be fairly uniform and robust.

A more basic criticism is that, since countries differ substantially in the natural environments they face and in socio-economic structures, it is inappropriate to assume that the same empirical relationship holds for all of them. This is a familiar problem in the sensitivity of cross-sectional results, particularly for less developed countries, where structural diversity may be very large.

One way out is to choose suitable dummy variables, which can distinguish between broad categories of countries through specific characteristics. We have used two, one for oil-exporting countries with large foreign exchange reserves, the other for war economies. These seem to be the most important exogenous factors that affected military spending in LDCs. Oil revenues allow 'surplus' capital funds to be used for nondevelopmental expenditures such as defence. The choice of war countries is obvious. In practice, we could have used other dummies, but the principle remains the same.

Another method by which the heterogeneity of country characteristics can be reduced is to break up the total set into smaller subsamples. There are obviously a large number, and many types, of subgroups into which the sample can be divided. We can estimate the relation between growth and the military for specific geographical samples (Asia, Africa, Latin America). A more relevant subgrouping from an economic point of view would be to divide the countries into high, middle and low income categories. Deger and Smith (1983) use a smaller model than the one reported in this book, to show how these experiments can be conducted. The overall conclusions are similar to what we shall report presently.

Choice of variables to be put in the various empirical equations is problematic. We wish to find the effect of a changing military burden on the growth rate of LDCs, preferably in the context of the open economy. These two variables therefore choose themselves automatically. The discussion in the main part of the book, particularly Chapter 8, implies that the national saving rate is important for growth. Open economy considerations force us to look also at trade balance. Thus the four major variables of interest are military burden, growth rate of GDP, saving-income ratio and trade balance (as a proportion of GDP). However, if we wish to do a simultaneous equation estimation (as we shall, for reasons discussed below), then we need more exogenous variables simply for identification.

In principle, economic theory should dictate what variables we should include in, for example, the growth equation. In practice, theory is rarely that precise. This is particularly true for behavioural and equilibrium relations pertaining to less developed countries. The determinants of growth, saving or trade balance are numerous, and each of them could make up the subject matter of an individual book. Therefore relatively *ad hoc* specifications are necessary, though these need to have intuitive plausibility.

Once again various sensitivity tests were conducted on the basic model to see how the parameters responded to changes in variables. We do not have space to report on these experimentations, but overall it can be stated that the final effect of defence on growth usually came out to be negative for plausible models.

(c) Estimation method

Prior to Emile Benoit, very little (perhaps no) empirical work had been done to test the milex-growth relation. To recapitulate the work, he used a *single* equation model of the form

$$g = a_0 + a_1 m + a_2 Z \qquad \text{(A.1)}$$

where g is growth rate, m is military burden, Z is a vector of exogenous variables, and a_0, a_1, a_2 are constant parameters. Using ordinary least squares estimation technique, he found that a_1 is significantly positive, hence the postulated positive relationship between defence (burden) and growth (rate).

Choice of estimation method depends primarily on the (economic) theoretical model and the stochastic specification assumed. The major emphasis in the main body of the book has been on the simultaneity of concepts and variables that characterise the military-growth relationship. The econometric counterpart of this interdependence would be the simultaneity and high co-variance between the various equations. Thus we need a simultaneous equation model, estimated by full information methods such as three stage least squares or (full information) maximum likelihood. As we shall see in the next section, we estimate four equations *jointly*, one each for growth, saving, trade and military. The final effect of defence on growth then comes out to be a complex functional combination of many parameters.

Looking only at the growth equation, or estimating by ordinary least squares the functional relation, is inappropriate from our point of view. The growth equation 1 gives only one effect, the direct relation. It is only when all the direct and indirect effects are considered that one can see clearly the *total* impact of defence on growth. Benoit's original problem was to look at precisely one causal chain and ignore the feedbacks that defence may have on saving, or trade variables, and thus growth indirectly. The proper multiplier is one that takes full account of the interdependence.

A.3 The econometric model

The theoretical discussion on the milex-growth relation suggests that our econometric model should allow for the following:

(i) a direct effect of military expenditure on growth through various spin-offs which may on balance be positive;
(ii) an indirect effect via saving rates, reflecting the fact that defence spending reallocates saving away from productive investment and thus hampers growth; further, resource mobilisation may also be affected, thus the very propensity to save may change with a greater defence burden;
(iii) the explicit modelling of open economy considerations; spending on military budgets will affect the trade balance, which in turn affects saving and growth; and finally,

(iv) the endogeneity of military expenditure. This indicates a four-equation simultaneous system, which may be necessary to examine the interaction of growth, saving, trade and the military. We therefore will have one equation each for growth rate, saving rate, trade balance as a share of GDP and the defence burden.

The model to be estimated is given by the following four equations:

$$g = a_0 + a_1s + a_2m + a_3B + a_4y + a_5Ag \quad \text{(A.2)}$$

$$s = b_0 + b_1m + (b_2 + b_3y)g + b_4B + b_5i \quad \text{(A.3)}$$

$$B = c_0 + c_1m + c_2g + c_3i + c_4D1 + c_5D2 \quad \text{(A.4)}$$

$$m = d_0 + d_1y + d_2D + d_3(GR) + d_4N + d_5D1 + d_6D2 \quad \text{(A.5)}$$

Definition of variables: g = average annual growth rate of GDP; s = national saving ratio; m = military burden, share of military expenditure in GDP; y = 1970 *per capita* income at official exchange rate; *Ag* = rate of growth of agriculture; n = rate of growth of population; i = inflation or rate of change of GDP deflator, *per annum*; B = balance of trade (exports minus imports); *D*1 = dummy for capital surplus oil-exporting countries Iraq, Libya, Saudi Arabia; D = difference between *per capita* income, at official exchange rate and purchasing power parity; *D*2 = dummy for war economies: Israel, Jordan, South Vietnam, Egypt, Syria; *GR* = rate of growth of government expenditure; N = total population.

Even though *m* is the exogenous (autonomous) variable that we focus our attention on, and the other endogenous variables do not enter the last equation, we still estimate the whole system consisting of four equations, by three stage least squares. This is because the error variance of the last equation can be correlated with the others. The empirical estimates are as follows:

$$g = -4.2 + 0.58s + 0.29m - 0.15B - 0.14y + 0.19Ag$$
$$\quad (-1.56) \quad (3.37) \quad (2.5) \quad (-1.75) \quad (-1.75) \quad (1.85)$$
$$R^2 = 0.3245 \quad (A.6)$$

$$s = 12.5 - 0.56m + 0.74g + 0.038gy + 0.32B - 1.75i$$
$$\quad (6.91) \quad (-3.72) \quad (2.42) \quad (3.92) \quad (4.22) \quad (-0.56)$$
$$R^2 = 0.7876 \quad (A.7)$$

$$B = -2.33 - 2.45m + 1.22g + 0.16i + 41.5D1 + 23.6D2$$
$$\quad (-0.86) \quad (-2.88) \quad (3.08) \quad (.032) \quad (7.08) \quad (0.92)$$
$$R^2 = 0.6723 \quad (A.8)$$

$$m = 1.47 - 0.25D + 4.02D1 + 11.2D2 + 0.163GR + 0.0042N + 0.15y$$
$$\quad (1.52) \quad (2.52) \quad (3.42) \quad (10.2) \quad (3.07) \quad (1.32) \quad (2.8)$$
$$R^2 = 0.8700 \quad (A.9)$$

Equation 2 makes growth rate a function of the saving-income ratio which is standard from any basic growth theoretic model. The military burden is included as a proxy for spin-offs, since there are no independent measures for these intangible effects. The *negative* of the trade surplus's (import minus export) share in national income is an index of foreign capital inflows, and this is expected to give a stimulus to growth. The level of *per capita* income (y) is included to capture the so called 'catch-up' effects. The lower the *per capita* income, the larger the gap between domestic and international technology; thus the scope for faster growth through imported technology is enhanced. Thus a_4 is expected to be negative. The growth of agriculture (Ag) is provided to give the effect of demand factors in national growth. Following structuralist ideas, if agriculture is booming it contributes positively to growth by creating larger markets for the economy's output.

The saving rate (s) is made to depend upon the defence burden in equation 3. This is consistent with much of our previous discussion. We also assume that, following life cycle theories of consumption, saving-income ratio depends on the growth rate. However, the parameter representing this effect is not constant across countries; rather it varies positively according to *per capita* income. Thus for countries with low *per capita* income, the life cycle effect is low. This is because with people on the edge of subsistence, the rate of time preference is likely to be very high; they will not be able to save for old age, and thus the growth effect *à la* life cycle will not be high. Exports and imports will affect saving, either through income-multipliers or through trade taxes. Further, higher trade surplus (increase in B) for agricultural economies often means a predominance of rich farmers producing cash crops as exportables. Thus income distribution tends to be unequal, and this increases saving propensity, since higher income people tend to save a greater proportion of their income. Finally, inflation is included in the saving equation, since there has been a considerable amount of discussion on its role as a motivator of 'forced savings'.

The trade balance equation 4 contains the military burden as an explanatory variable. This follows from our discussion on the open economy, and we expect the coefficient c_1 to be negative. Growth should affect trade balance, but the sign is not clear *a priori*. For countries following export promoting strategies, growth should give a boost to exports and thus raise B. On the other hand, countries at the earlier stages of import-substituting industrialisation may require more imports to achieve future self-sufficiency. This will lower B. Inflation is included in the trade equation since LDCs usually have a fixed exchange rate regime. Thus high inflation rate will distort the relative price structure *vis-à-vis* the rest of the world, and may affect B. The military burden equation needs no explanation, because we have already met it in Chapter 3.

Considering m as an autonomous variable, from the first three equations we get the growth multiplier as

$$dg/dm = a_2 + a_1(b_1 + c_1b_4) + a_3c_1/1 - a_1[(d_2 + b_3y) + c_2b_4)] - a_3c_2 \qquad \text{(A.10)}$$

Evaluated at mean *per capita* income, this turns out to be

$$dg/dm = -0.36 \qquad \text{(A.11)}$$

(after substituting for the estimated parameters from 6 to 9).

Similarly the effect on saving ratio of an exogenous change in burden is

$$ds/dm = [b_1 + c_1b_4] + a_2[(b_2 + b_3y) + c_2b_4] + a_3[(b_2 + b_3y)c_1 - c_2b_1]/a_1[(b_2 + b_3y) + c_2b_4)] - a_3c_2 \qquad (A.12)$$

This is

$$ds/dm = -2.56 \qquad (A.13)$$

Finally the trade balance changes by

$$dB/dm = c_1 - a_1[(b_2 + b_3y)c_1 + b_1c_2] - a_2c_2/1 - a_1[(b_2 + b_3y) + c_2b_4] - a_3c_2 \qquad (A.14)$$

Again this can be calculated as

$$dB/dm = -5.02 \qquad (A.15)$$

As is clear from equations 11, 13 and 15, the effects of a change in military burden on growth, saving ratio and trade surplus are quite substantial. If the military burden is reduced by one percentage point, growth would increase by more than one-third of a percent – a not insignificant amount. The effect on saving is even more dramatic. A 1 per cent reduction in military share in GDP releases resources which directly or indirectly increase the saving share by a massive two and a half times. Another way of interpreting this result is even more revealing. For our sample set, the domestic investment share exceeded the saving share by 2.29 per cent, thus foreign capital of the order of 2.29 per cent (of national output) had to be attracted to finance domestic capital formation. Our econometric results indicate that LDCs would not need to rely on any foreign capital inflows (given the same amount of investment) if they could reduce their defence burden by 1 per cent only. For our sample, the mean value of *m* was 4.5 per cent. Therefore, all foreign capital requirements could be eliminated and the countries would be self-sufficient in capital if the military burden went down to 3.5 per cent. Finally, the trade effects are also massive, particularly if compared to the actual values. For our sample, the *actual* share of trade balance was −1.08. The result in equation 15 demonstrates that if the military burden went down from 4.5 per cent (actual) to 3.5 per cent (postulated), then the trade balance share could move from a deficit of −1.08 per cent to a surplus of 3.94 per cent of GDP.

A.4 Concluding remarks

The presentation here gives a flavour of the sort of econometric estimation that one can do to formally test the milex-growth relation. The results show the correctness of the basic Benoit hypothesis that military expenditure in LDCs can have positive effects. The coefficient of defence in equation 2, used to represent the spin-off from milex on growth, tends to be positive and significant. However, the relation is incomplete. It leaves out important allocative effects of the military, it ignores the fact that defence can depress the saving rate, and it does not show that investment and growth can be reduced through indirect factors which are more dominant than the growth-stimulating effects. If we look at only one causal channel and ignore the feedbacks that defence may have on other variables like saving, then the picture is incomplete. When the interdependence is fully considered, the multiplier turns out to be negative.

In general, the model demonstrates that, taking both direct and indirect effects together, an increase in the military burden reduces the growth rate for empirical estimates over a large cross-section of LDCs. The result is reasonably robust even though changes in variables, estimation methods, sample sets and so on do change the value of estimates. However, the sign of the final multiplier tends to be negative generally. Thus the direction of change is not a matter of controversy, though the amount of change may be. As Deger and Smith (1983) state: 'In principle, theory should dictate what sample the model is applicable to, the required variables to be included, how they should be measured, and the appropriate stochastic specification. In practice theory is rarely that precise. Within the context of a particular specification, one can make useful inferences from the data.' In this case the inference would be that the military burden does reduce growth rates in LDCs in spite of some positive effects.

Finally, a word of caution. Given the multitude of channels by which military expenditure might influence growth in LDCs and the heterogeneity of their socio-economic structures, econometric studies in general, and cross-sectional analysis in particular, should be handled with some care by researchers.

Notes

1 Introduction

1 See Jolly (1978).
2 All data taken from Barnaby (1978) and the Palme Commission Report (1982).
3 Here Benoit's work (1973, 1978) has been seminal. A more descriptive analysis of cross-country studies is given by Kennedy (1974) and Whynes (1979).
4 Quoted from Kennedy (1974).
5 Such as P. Bauer.
6 See Lewis (1984) for an excellent review.
7 A summary of his views can be read in the Presidential Address to the Development Studies Association, Dublin, 1982.
8 All data from SIPRI.
9 See Ostrom (1977), Hollist (1977a), Majeski and Jones (1981).
10 SIPRI, 1983. Between 1973 and 1977, total imports of arms by developing countries was of the order of 61.4 billions of constant (1977) US dollars (Pierre, 1982).
11 See Prebisch (1950), Singer (1950), Bacha (1978).
12 Burmeister and Dobell (1970), Dixit (1976).
13 Some of these countries would be considered developed today, but remember the tests were conducted for data on 1965-73.

2 The analysis of the data

1 See William Paul McGreevey (ed.), *Third World Poverty: New Strategies for Measuring Development Progress*, Lexington, Mass., and Toronto; D.C. Heath, Lexington Books, 1980.
2 Neild refers to L. Freedman, *Britain and Nuclear Weapons*, London, Papermac, 1980.
3 Brzoska's paper is an excellent review of some of the political issues involved in data reporting.
4 See UN Centre for Disarmament, *Reduction of Military Budgets: International Reporting of Military Expenditure*, New York, 1981, and Ball (1984).
5 Ball (1984), p. 7.

6 UN Centre for Disarmament, *op. cit.*, and Ball (1984).
7 *Measuring Price Changes of Milex*, US Department of Commerce, Bureau of Economic Analysis (US Government Printing Office, Washington, D.C., June 1975), and Elisabeth Skons, 'Military prices', ch. 8 in SIPRI (1983).
8 See Samuelson and Swamy (1974).
9 See Brzoska (1981), pp. 261–75.
10 World Bank, *World Tables* (1983).
11 *Ibid.*
12 See especially Ball (1984), who claims that for 'many of the developing countries, even the most accurate data available may seriously understate the security expenditure of governments'.
13 Smith and Smith (1983) state: 'The tendency is for a government to use the higher numbers abroad to convince its allies it is contributing properly to joint defence and to convey a resolute image to its adversaries. Meanwhile, the lower figures may be used at home, to convince voters that there is no waste and no overspending on the military, or to convince them that, since military spending is relatively low, it ought to be increased.'
14 Figures for the Soviet Union are even more chaotic and almost always guesstimates. Holloway (1983) claims: 'In 1980 the official Soviet defence budget figure was 17.1 billion rubles; the British government estimated Soviet defence expenditure to be between 81 and 86 billion rubles in the same year.'
15 See Ugur Mumcu (1981).

3 Military spending and public expenditure

1 See Lotz (1970).
2 When the urbanisation variable (*u*) is included in my estimates of the defence burden, the sample size is forty-four, since data for the remaining six countries was not available.
3 A more complete presentation of this equation will be found in the Appendix.
4 Data on tax rate is taken from Mosley (1980).
5 The relation is approximate since net foreign assets also enter this relation, but for simplicity we ignore this at present.
6 But see Smith and Smith (1983) for an opposite point of view in which supply constraints and crowding out is emphasised for developed economies.

4 Saving, investment and military expenditure

1 We relax this assumption later, in Chapter 8, and show that the effects are more complicated.
2 See also Thirlwall (1974).

3 Again the exception is Benoit, who stresses inflationary saving, but not the concept of time preference.
4 Tests were made with a large number of cadet variables but they did not change the main findings and so are not reported here.
5 Horvat claims that the analysis of milex is not within his preview. He goes even further: 'the society will face a choice – e.g. maximum consumption as against maximum military strength – which falls outside this paper and indeed, outside the scope of economics'.
6 Chile and Peru are traditional rivals. Some claim that it originates from the so-called war of the Pacific fought between the two countries in 1879 (see del Pando, 1983).

5 Human capital formation

1 Quoted from Benoit (1978), p. 277.
2 Quoted in Jolly (1978).

6 The military burden in the open economy

1 Pierre (1982) gives an excellent recent survey of the state of the arts but from an unashamedly political point of view.
2 Once again the interested reader is referred to Pierre (1982), who says: 'Arms sales are far more than an economic occurrence, a military relationship, or an arms control challenge – *arms sales are foreign policy writ large*.'
3 Data from SIPRI (1983).
4 From SIPRI (1982), Pierre (1982).
5 See Benoit (1978).
6 Third World arms exporters will be dealt with later.
7 See Pierre (1982).
8 Quoted from Whynes (1979), who refers to Barber and Ronning (1966).
9 See Ball (1984).
10 See Terhal (1982).
11 These are not necessarily the same thing.
12 Specific characteristics of the world arms trade were discussed in section 2.
13 Smith and Smith (1983) is an excellent short review of the military and the economy in developed capitalist countries.
14 Even Israel, the largest LDC arms producer, had a deficit of the order of $75 million in 1980 on visible trade in arms.
15 Some of these are used by Rivlin (1983) to calculate Israel's defence burden.

7 Arms production and the newly industrialising countries

1 Sen and Smith (1983) analyse this influence in terms of moral hazard within a principal-agent model of economic theory.
2 It was rumoured that ordnance factories were producing simple civilian goods – like electric kettles!
3 The Green Revolution may have changed things slightly by emphasising domestic sources of *food* supply rather than imports.
4 It may not necessarily be the latest vintage.
5 *Financial Times*, 6 February 1984, A. Whitley from Washington.
6 Wulf (1983a) gives numerous examples for each group mentioned above as well as a detailed discussion of the technological problems inherent in each stage of fabrication.

8 Economic growth and military expenditure

1 Early five-year plans for India were based on the Mahalanobis model, which was an extension of these aggregate growth models. Similarly the first Turkish five-year plan (1963-68) was a multisectoral (input-output) extension of the Harrod-Domar model.
2 This is fully discussed in the Appendix.
3 Sen (1963).
4 There is no necessary connection between investment goods and capital-intensive technology. It is possible for consumption goods to have higher capital intensity than investment goods. The difference is akin to that between high tech products and high tech process.
5 Since high ICOR implies a low incremental output-capital ratio, the same investment is producing less output proportionately.
6 Though he did not specify his model.
7 The less developed CMEA economies like Cuba provide the few counter-examples.
8 This point of view is often embodied in Say's Law, 'Supply creates its own demand'. In contradiction we may have Keynes's Law, 'Demand creates its own supply'.
9 For a review of the Benoit regression see the Appendix.
10 See the Appendix.
11 We leave out Vietnam because of data nonavailability.

9 Economic development and the military

1 This topic alone could fill a separate monograph.
2 *World Armies* (1983) is an excellent collection of essays on the military in most countries of the world. It emphasises the strategic aspects.
3 Data from *World Tables*, 1980.
4 Generally untouchables and very low-caste Hindus.

5 A.L. Veukakeshwaran, *Defence Organisation in India*, New Delhi, Government Office of Information, 1969, referred to in *World Armies* (1983).

6 See Chirouf (1982) for an excellent discussion on these issues as applied to the Arab world.

10 Conclusion

1 Chris Smith (1984) goes so far as to say that 'although the *causes* of the arms race are to be found in the North, the *effects* are manifested in the Third World'.

References

ACDA (various years), United States Arms Control and Disarmament Agency, *World Military Expenditure and Arms Transfers*, Washington, DC.

Adler, J. (1965), *Absorptive Capacity and Its Determinants*, Washington, DC, Brookings Institution.

Albrecht, U. (1984), 'Militarism and underdevelopment', paper presented at the International Colloquium on Armaments Development, Human Rights and Disarmament, Paris, UNESCO. *Conference Proceedings*, forthcoming.

Albrecht, U., Ernst, D., Lock, P., Wulf, H. (1974), 'Armaments and underdevelopment', *Bulletin of Peace Proposals*.

Albrecht, U., *et al.* (1975), 'New trends in the arms transfer process to peripheral countries, some hypotheses and research proposals', mimeo, Hamburg.

Albrecht, U., *et al.* (1976), *Armaments and Underdevelopment*, Hamburg, Rowalt.

Ayres, R. (1983), 'Arms production as a form of import-substituting industrialisation: the Turkish case', *World Development*, vol. 11, no. 9, pp. 813–23.

Bacha, E.L. (1978), 'An interpretation of unequal exchange from Prebisch-Singer to Emmanuel', *Journal of Development Economics*, vol. 5.

Ball, N. (1983), 'Defence and development: a critique of the Benoit study', *Economic Development and Cultural Change*, vol. 31, April, pp. 507–24.

Ball, N. (1984), *Third World Security Expenditure: A Statistical Compendium*, Stockholm, National Defence Research Institute.

Barber, W.F., and Ronning, C.N. (1966), *International Security and Military Power: Counter Insurgency and Civic Action in Latin America*, Ohio, Mershon National Security Program.

Barnaby, F. (1978), 'The scale of world military expenditure', in Jolly (1978).

Bauer, P.T. (1965), 'The vicious circle of poverty', *Weltwirtschaftliches Archiv*, vol. 95, no. 2, pp. 4–20.

Bauer, P.T. (1966), 'Foreign aid: an instrument for progress?', in B. Ward and P.T. Bauer (eds), *Two Views on Aid to Developing*

Countries, London, Institute of Economic Affairs.
Bauer, P.T. (1971), *Dissent on Development*, London, Weidenfeld & Nicolson.
Bauer, P.T. (1983), *Equality, the Third World and Economic Delusion*, London, Methuen.
Benoit, E. (1973), *Defence and Economic Growth in Developing Countries*, Boston, D.C. Heath, Lexington Books.
Benoit, E. (1978), 'Growth and defence in developing countries', *Economic Development and Cultural Change*, vol. 26, January, pp. 271–80.
Bergstrom, T.C., and Goodman, R.P. (1973), 'Private demand for public goods', *American Economic Review*, vol. 63, June.
Bhaduri, A. (1973), 'Agricultural backwardness under semi-feudalism', *Economic Journal*.
Blaug, M. (1970), *An Introduction to the Economics of Education*, London, Penguin Books.
Blaug, M. (1979), 'Economics of education in developing countries', *Third World Quarterly*, vol. I, no. 1.
Blitzer, C.R. (1975), 'Economy-wide models and development planning', in C.R. Blitzer (ed.), *Economy-Wide Models and Development Planning*, London, Oxford University Press.
Borda, J.C. (1781), 'Mémoire sur les Elections au Scrutin', *Mémoires de l'Académie Royale des Sciences*, Paris.
Boulding, K.E. (1974), 'Defence spending: burden or boon', *War/Peace Report*, vol. 13, no. 1, pp. 19–24.
Braverman, A., and Stiglitz, J. (1982), 'Sharecropping and the interlinking of agrarian markets', *American Economic Review*, vol. 72, pp. 695–715.
Brito, D.L. (1972), 'A dynamic model of an armament race', *International Economic Review*, vol. 13, no. 2, pp. 359–75.
Brito, D.L., and Intrilligator, M.D. (1976), 'Formal models of arms races', *Journal of Peace Science*.
Bruton, H.J. (1970), 'The import substitution strategy of economic development: a survey', in I. Livingstone (ed.), *Development Economics and Policy Readings*, London, Allen & Unwin.
Brzoska, M. (1981), 'The reporting of military expenditure', *Journal of Peace Research*, vol. XVIII, no. 3.
Brzoska, M. (1983), 'The military related external debt of Third World countries', *Journal of Peace Research*, vol. XX, no. 3, pp. 271–7.
Burmeister, E., and Dobell, A.R. (1970), *Mathematical Theories of Economic Growth*, London, Macmillan.
Cardesman, A. (1981), 'US and Soviet competition in arms exports and military assistance', *Armed Forces International Journal*.
Carranza, M.E. (1983), 'The role of military expenditure in the development process: the Argentina case 1946-1980', *Nordic Journal of Latin American Studies*, vol. 12, nos 1–2, pp. 115–66.
Chakravarty, S. (1969), *Capital and Development Planning*, Cambridge, Mass., MIT Press.

Chakravarty, S. (1984), 'Notes on disarmament', paper presented in International Colloquium on Armaments, Development, Human Rights, Disarmament, Paris, UNESCO. (*Conference Proceedings*, forthcoming.)

Chan, M.W.L., Hsiao, C., and Keng, C.W.K. (1982), 'Defence expenditure and economic growth in developing countries: a temporal cross sectional analysis', in O.D. Anderson and M.R. Perryman (eds), *Applied Time Series Analysis*, Amsterdam, North Holland Publishing Co.

Chenery, H.B., and MacEwan, A. (1966), 'Optimal patterns of growth and aid: the case of Pakistan', in I. Adelman and E. Thorbecke (eds), *The Theory and Design of Economic Development*, Baltimore, MD, Johns Hopkins University Press.

Chenery, H.B., and Strout, A. (1966), 'Foreign assistance and economic development', *American Economic Review*.

Chirouf, L. (1982), 'Theory and practice of disarmament and economic development relationship in Arab politics', paper presented at the International Colloquium on Armaments, Development, Human Rights, Disarmament, Paris, UNESCO. (*Conference Proceedings*, forthcoming.)

Choucri, N., and North, R. (1975), *Nations in Conflict: National Growth and International Violence*, San Francisco: Freeman.

Cusach, T.R. (1981), 'The economic burden of defence: a comparative study', International Institute for Comparative Social Research, discussion paper.

Datta-Chaudhuri, M.K. (1979), 'Industrialization and Foreign Trade: An Analysis Based on the Development Experience of the Republic of Korea and the Philippines', ILO Working Paper, Asian Employment Programme, Bangkok, ILO.

Deger, S. (1979), 'Military expenditure and economic development', paper presented at SSRC Economic Development Study Group Meeting, London. *Economic Development and Cultural Change* (forthcoming, 1985).

Deger, S. (1981), 'Human resources, education and military expenditure in developing countries', paper presented at the 2nd World Congress of Social Economics, Jerusalem, August 1981.

Deger, S. (1982), 'Models of arms race among neighbouring countries in less developed countries', Birkbeck College discussion paper, no. 119, May.

Deger, S. (1984), 'The developmental effect of military expenditure in LDCs', paper presented at the International Colloquium on Armaments, Development, Human Rights, Disarmament, Paris, UNESCO. (*Conference Proceedings*, forthcoming.)

Deger, S., Sen, S., and Smith, R. (1980), 'The effect of growth on saving in less developed countries', mimeo, University of Birmingham.

Deger, S., and Sen, S. (1983a), 'Technology transfer and arms production in LDCs', paper presented at the World Congress of the International Economic Association (IEA), Madrid, September,

Industry and Development, no. 15, 1985.
Deger, S., and Sen, S. (1983b), 'Military expenditure, spin-off and economic development', *Journal of Development Economics*, vol. 13, pp. 67–83.
Deger, S., and Sen, S. (1984a), 'Optimal control and differential game model of military expenditure in less developed countries', *Journal of Economic Dynamics and Control*, vol. 7, pp. 153-69.
Deger, S., and Sen, S. (1984b), 'On the publicness of defence in developing countries', mimeo, University of Birmingham.
Deger, S., and Smith, R. (1983), 'Military expenditure and growth in less developed countries', *Journal of Conflict Resolution*.
del Pando, J.A.E. (1983), 'The role of military expenditure in the development process. Peru: a case study 1950-1980', *Nordic Journal of Latin American Studies*, vol. XII, nos 1–2.
Desai, M., and Blake, D. (1981), 'Modelling the ultimate absurdity: a comment on "a quantitative study of the strategic arms race in the missile age" ', *Review of Economics and Statistics*.
Dixit, A.K. (1976), *The Theory of Equilibrium Growth*, London, Oxford University Press.
Dornbusch, R., and Fischer, S. (1978), *Macroeconomics*, New York, McGraw-Hill.
Eleazu, U.O. (1973), 'The role of the army in African politics: a reconsideration of existing theories and practices', *Journal of Developing Areas*.
Faini, R., Arnez, P., and Taylor, L. (1984), 'Defence spending, economic structure and growth: evidence among countries and over time', *Economic Development and Cultural Change*, vol. 32, April, pp. 487–98.
Fontanel, J. (1982), *Military Expenditure and Economic Growth: France, Morocco*, United Nations.
Frederiksen, P.C., and Looney, R.E. (1983), 'Defence expenditure and economic growth in developing countries', *Armed Forces and Society*, vol. 9, no. 4, pp. 633–46.
Gandhi, V.P. (1974), 'India's self-inflicted defence burden', *Economic and Political Weekly*.
Gandolfo, G. (1971), *Mathematical Methods and Models in Economic Dynamics*, Amsterdam, North Holland Publishing Co.
Government Finance Statistics Yearbook, Washington, IMF.
Granger, C.W.J. (1969), 'Investigating causal relations by econometric models and cross-spectral methods', *Econometrica*, vol. 37, pp. 424–38.
Hahn, F., and Matthews, R.C.O. (1969), 'The theory of economic growth: a survey', in *Surveys of Economic Theory*, vol. II, London, Macmillan.
Halpern, M. (1962), 'The middle eastern armies and the new middle class', in Johnson (1962).
Halpern, M. (1963), *The Politics of Social Change in the Middle East and North Africa*, Rand Corporation Research Studies, Princeton University Press.

Harkavy, R.E. (1984), 'The lessons of recent wars: a comparative perspective', *Third World Quarterly*, vol. 6, no. 4, pp. 868–91.

Hirschman, A.O. (1981), *Essays in Trespassing: Economics to Politics and Beyond*, Cambridge University Press.

Hollist, W.L. (1977a), 'An analysis of arms process in the United States and Soviet Union', *International Studies Quarterly*.

Hollist, W.L. (1977b), 'Alternative explanations of competitive arms processes, tests on four pairs of nations', *American Journal of Political Science*, vol. XXI.

Holloway, D. (1983), *The Soviet Union and the Arms Race*, New Haven, Yale University Press.

Horvat, B. (1958), 'The optimum rate of investment', *Economic Journal*, vol. 68, pp. 747–67.

Janowitz, M. (1964), *Military Institutions and Coercion in the Developing Nations*, Chicago and London, University of Chicago Press.

Johnson, J.J. (ed.) (1962), *The Role of the Military in Underdeveloped Countries*, Princeton University Press.

Jolly, R. (ed.) (1978), *Disarmament and World Development*, Institute of Development Studies, University of Sussex.

Kaldor, M. (1978), 'The military in Third World development', in Jolly (1978).

Kaldor, N. (1975), 'Economic growth and the Verdoorn law: a comment on Mr. Rawthorn's article', *Economic Journal*.

Kaldor, N. (1979), 'Equilibrium theory and growth theory', in M. Baskia (ed.), *Economics and Human Welfare: Essays in Honour of Tibor Scitovsky*, New York, Academic Press.

Keegan, J. (1983), *World Armies*, London, Macmillan.

Kennedy, G. (1974), *The Military in the Third World*, London, Duckworth.

Keynes, J.M. (1940), *How to Pay for the War*, New York, Harcourt Brace Jovanovich.

Khuri, F.I. (1981), 'Modernizing societies in the Middle East', in M. Janowitz (ed.), *Civil-Military Relations: Regional Perspectives*, Beverly Hills, Calif., Sage Publications.

Kirkpatrick, C.H., and Nixson, F.I. (1976), 'The origins of inflation in less developed countries: a selective review', in M. Parkin and G. Zis (eds), *Inflation in Open Economies*, Manchester University Press. Also in I. Livingstone (ed.), *Development Economics and Policy Readings*, London, Allen & Unwin, 1981.

Kravis, I.B., Heston, A.W., and Summer, R. (1978), 'Real GNP per capita for more than one hundred countries', *Economic Journal*, vol. 88, no. 350, June, pp. 215–42.

Kuznets, S. (1980), 'Driving forces of economic growth: what can we learn from history?', *Weltwirtschaftliches Archiv*, vol. 116.

Lambelet, J.D. (1975), 'Do arms races lead to war?', *Journal of Peace Research*.

Leontief, W., and Duchin, F. (1983), *Military Spending: Facts and Figures, Worldwide Implications and Future Outlook*, New York, Oxford University Press.

Lewis, W.A. (1954), 'Economic development with unlimited supply of labour', *Manchester School*.
Lewis, W.A. (1984), 'The state of development theory', *American Economic Review*, vol. 74, no. 1, pp. 1–10.
Lim, D. (1983), 'Another look at growth and defence in less developed countries', *Economic Development and Cultural Change*, vol. 31, no. 2, pp. 377–84.
Lotz, J.R. (1970), 'Patterns of government spending in developing countries', *Manchester School*.
Lucas, R.E. (1973), 'Some international evidence on output-inflation trade-offs', *American Economic Review*, vol. 63, no. 3, pp. 326–34.
Luckham, R. (1978), 'Militarism and international dependence in disarmament and world development', in Jolly (1978).
McGuire, M. (1977), 'A quantitative study of the strategic arms race in the missile age', *Review of Economics and Statistics*.
McGuire, M. (1982), 'Foreign assistance, Israel's resource allocation, and the arms race in the Middle East', *Journal of Conflict Resolution*, June, pp. 5–42.
McGuire, M. (1983), 'Foreign assistance, investment, and defence: a methodological study with an application to Israel 1960-79', paper presented at the 7th World Congress of the IEA, Madrid, September 1983.
Mack, A. (1981), 'Militarism or development: the possibility for survival', paper presented at the Labour Economists Conference, Canberra, Australia.
Majeski, S.J., and Jones, D.L. (1981), 'Arms race modelling', *Journal of Conflict Resolution*, vol. 25.
Marris, R. (1970), 'Can we measure the need for development assistance?', *Economic Journal*.
Mathur, P.N. (1963), 'India's defence effort', *Indian Economic Journal*.
Military Balance, London, The International Institute for Strategic Studies (IISS).
Moll, D.K., and Luebbert, G.M. (1980), 'Arms race and military expenditure models', *Journal of Conflict Resolution*, vol. 24, no. 1.
Moodie, M. (1979), 'Defence industries in the third world: problems and promises', pp. 294–312 in Neuman and Harkavy (1980).
Mosley, P. (1980), 'Aid, savings and growth revisited', *Oxford Bulletin of Economics and Statistics*.
Mumcu, U. (1981), *Silah Kacakciligi ve Teror* ('Arms Smuggling and Terrorism'), Ankara, Tekin Yayinevi.
Neild, R. (1981), *How to Make Up Your Mind about the Bomb*, London, André Deutsch.
Neuman, S.G. (1978), 'Security, military expenditure and socio-economic development: reflections on Iran', *Orbis*, vol. 22, no. 3, pp. 569-95.
Neuman, S.G., and Harkavy, R.E. (eds) (1980), *Arms Transfers in the Modern World*, New York, Praeger.
Nordlinger, E.A. (1970), 'Soldiers in mufti: the impact of military rule

upon the economic and social change in the non-western states', *American Political Science Review*, vol. 64.

Ostrom, W.C. (1977), 'Evaluating alternative foreign policy decision-making models', *Journal of Conflict Resolution*, vol. 21, no. 2.

Palme, O. (1982), *Common Security: A Programme for Disarmament. The Report of the Independent Commission on Disarmament and Security Issues*, London, Pan Books.

Peacock, A.T., and Wiseman, J. (1967), *The Growth of Public Expenditure in the United Kingdom*, London, Allen & Unwin.

Pierre, A.J. (1982), *The Global Politics of Arms Sales*, Princeton University Press.

Prebisch, R. (1950), 'The economic development of Latin America and its principal problems', United Nations Department of Economic Affairs, Lake Success, NY, reprinted in *Economic Bulletin for Latin America, 1962*.

Pye, L.W. (1962a), 'The army in Burmese politics', in Johnson (1962).

Pye, L.W. (1962b), 'Armies in the process of political modernisation', in Johnson (1962).

Richardson, L. (1960), *Arms and Insecurity: A Mathematical Study of the Causes and Origins of War*, Chicago, Quadrangle.

Rivlin, P. (1983), 'The burden of defence: the case of Israel', Appendix 7D, *World Armaments and Disarmament, SIPRI Yearbook*, London and New York, Taylor & Francis.

Russett, B. (1970), *What Price Vigilance: The Burden of National Defence*, New Haven, Conn., Yale University Press.

Samuelson, P.A., and Swami, S. (1974), 'Invariant economic index numbers and canonical duality: a survey and synthesis', *American Economic Review*, vol. 64, pp. 566-93.

Schmitter, P.C. (1971), 'Military intervention, political competitiveness and public policy in Latin America: 1950-67', in M. Janowitz and J. Jacques van Doorn (eds), *On Military Intervention*, Rotterdam University Press.

Sen, A. (1963), *Choice of Technique*, Oxford, Blackwell.

Sen, A. (1981), 'Public action and the quality of life in developing countries', *Oxford Bulletin of Economics and Statistics*, vol. 43, November, pp. 287-319.

Sen, A. (1983), 'Development: which way now?', *Economic Journal*, vol. 93, December, pp. 745-62.

Sen, S. (1982), 'Wages and employment: some analytical aspects of income distribution policies in LDCs', *International Journal of Social Economics*.

Sen, S. (1983), 'Rural indebtedness and productivity changes in the primary sector', paper presented at the Arne Ryde Symposium on the Primary Sector in Economic Development, August 1983, Sweden.

Sen, S. (1984), 'On non-linearities in the defence growth relationship', mimeo, University of Birmingham.

Sen, S., and Smith, R. (1983), 'The economics of international arms transfers', Birkbeck College Discussion Paper, no. 135, February.

Sezer, D.B. (1981), 'Turkey's security policies', *Adelphi Papers*, no. 164, IISS.

Simaan, M., and Cruz, J.B. (1975), 'Formulation of Richardson's model of arms race from a differential game viewpoint', *Review of Economic Studies*, pp. 67-77.

Singer, H. (1950), 'The distribution of gains between investing and borrowing countries', *American Economic Review*, vol. 40, no. 2.

SIPRI (various years), *Stockholm International Peace Research Institute: Yearbook of World Armaments and Disarmament*, New York, Humanities Press.

Sivard, R.L. (1977), *World Military and Social Expenditure*, New York, Institute for World Order.

Sivard, R.L. (1983), *World Military and Social Expenditure*, Washington, DC, World Priorities.

Skons, E. (1983), 'Military prices', in SIPRI (1983).

Smith, C. (1984), 'Disarmament, peace movements and the Third World', *Third World Quarterly*, vol. 6, no. 4, pp. 892-910.

Smith, D., and Kidron, M. (1983), *The War Atlas – Armed Conflict – Armed Peace*, London and Sydney, Pluto Press and Pan Books.

Smith, D., and Smith, R. (1979), 'Reflections on Neuman', *Orbis*, vol. 23, no. 2.

Smith, D., and Smith, R. (1983), *The Economics of Militarism*, London, Pluto Press.

Smith, R. (1977), 'Military expenditure and capitalism', *Cambridge Journal of Economics*, March.

Smith, R. (1978), 'Military Expenditure and capitalism: a reply', *Cambridge Journal of Economics*, September.

Smith, R. (1980), 'Military expenditure and investment in OECD countries 1954-1973', *Journal of Comparative Economics*, March.

Streeten, P. (1973), 'Trade strategies for development: some themes for the seventies', in P. Streeten (ed.), *Trade Strategies for Development*, London, Macmillan.

Tait, A.A., and Heller, P.S. (1982), *International Comparisons of Government Expenditure*, Occasional Papers of IMF, Washington, DC.

Taylor, L. (1980), 'IS-LM in the tropics', in W. Cline and S. Weintraub (eds), *Economic Stabilisation in Less Developed Countries*, Washington, DC, Brookings Institution.

Terhal, P. (1981), 'Guns or grains – macro-economic costs of Indian defence 1960-1970', *Economic and Political Weekly*, vol. 55.

Terhal, P. (1982), 'Foreign exchange costs of the Indian military, 1950-1972', *Journal of Peace Research*, vol. XIX, no. 3.

Thapar, R. (1981), 'State of the military', *Statesman Weekly*, 19 September.

Thee, M. (1977), 'Militarism and militarisation in contemporary international relations', *Bulletin of Peace Proposals*.

Thirlwall, A.P. (1974), *Inflation, Saving and Growth in Developing*

Economies, New York, Macmillan.
Turvey, R. (1951), 'Some aspects of the theory of inflation in a closed economy', *Economic Journal*, vol. 61, September, pp. 531-43.
United Nations Statistical Yearbook, New York, UNO.
Vagts, A. (1937), *A History of Militarism: Romance and Realities of a Profession*, New York.
Veras, A., and Portales, C. (1983), 'The role of military expenditure in the development process: Chile 1952-1973, and 1973-1980: two contrasting cases', *Nordic Journal of Latin American Studies*, vol. XII, nos 1-2, pp. 21-50.
Weiskopf, T. (1972), 'The impact of foreign capital inflow on domestic savings in underdeveloped countries', *Journal of International Economics*, no. 2, pp. 25-38.
Westphal, L.E. (1978), 'The republic of Korea's experience with export-led industrial development', *World Development*, vol. 6, no. 3, pp. 347-82.
Whynes, D.K. (1979), *The Economics of Third World Military Expenditure*, London, Macmillan.
World Armies (1983), London, Macmillan.
World Tables (1976), Washington, World Bank.
World Tables (1980), Washington, World Bank.
World Tables (1983), Washington, World Bank.
Wulf, Herbert (1982), 'Arms production in Third World countries, effects on industrialisation', mimeo, Institut für Friedensforschung und Sicherheits politik, University of Hamburg.
Wulf, H. (1983a), 'The structure of the defence industry', in N. Ball and M. Leitenberg (eds), *The Structure of the Defence Industry: An International Survey*, London, Croom Helm.
Wulf, H. (1983b), 'Arms industry unlimited: the economic impact of the arms sector in developing countries', paper presented at the 7th World Congress of the IEA, Madrid, September 1983.

Name index

Subject index